Introduction to AccuMark, Pattern Design, and Product Data Management

Introduction to AccuMark, Pattern Design, and Product Data Management

Julia Ridgway Sharp
Centenary College

Virginia Hencken Elsasser
Centenary College

Fairchild Publications, Inc.
New York

Director of Sales and Acquisitions: Dana Meltzer-Berkowitz
Executive Editor: Olga T. Kontzias
Acquisitions Editor: Joseph Miranda
Senior Development Editor: Jennifer Crane
Development Editor: Michelle Levy
Art Director: Adam B. Bohannon
Production Manager: Ginger Hillman
Senior Production Editor: Elizabeth Marotta
Interior Design: Mary Neal Meador
Cover Design: Adam B. Bohannon

Library of Congress Catalog Card Number: 2006932418

ISBN: 978-1-56367-437-2

GST R 133004424

Printed in India

TP04

Contents

Contents

Extended Contents

CHAPTER 4

Getting Started in Pattern Design 68

CHAPTER 6

Point and Notch Functions

116

CHAPTER 7

Line Function   137

CHAPTER 8

Piece Function, Part I   164

CHAPTER 11

WebPDM, Part I   253

Preface

Introduction to AccuMark, PDS, and PDM is the first textbook of its kind. It presents industry standard computer-aided grading, pattern making, marker making, and product data management using software produced by Gerber Technology, one of the leading producers of fashion-related software and hardware.

The software is used by more than 16,000 companies in 117 different countries. Students who are competent in the use of this software will be competitive in today's rapidly evolving global marketplace. A glance at the job advertisements in *Women's Wear Daily* shows that there is a high demand for applicants with computer-aided patternmaking and product data management (PDM) skills.

Introduction to AccuMark, PDS, and PDM is appropriate for a course that introduces students to computer-aided design and product management. It is primarily geared for upper-level students in a fashion, clothing and textiles, or related curriculum.

Although this is an introductory textbook, students will gain a basic understanding of the software. After studying and completing the exercises for each chapter, they will have created a portfolio of projects to show a prospective employer. We have assumed that all students using this text are familiar with basic apparel construction and patternmaking. However, since students may have different levels of experience with grading and garment specifications, these topics are briefly reviewed in the book.

Students are encouraged to create their own slopers, grading charts, and markers. For some of the patternmaking exercises, students may use slopers they have created, ones provided by the instructor, or ones found in the Gerber training data.

The objectives for *Introduction to AccuMark, Pattern Design, and Product Data Management* are to:

- provide step-by-step instructions for the use of industry standard marking, pattern development, and product data management software and hardware.
- encourage students to recognize the importance of technology in the apparel industry.
- prepare students for fashion careers in a global economy.
- enhance student learning by extensive use of images that complement written instructions.
- enhance creativity in pattern design.

To optimize student learning, key terms are highlighted and summarized at the end of each chapter. Furthermore, exercises and review questions within each chapter provide students with opportunities for practice using the software and reinforce learning. While we were teaching our own class on the Gerber software, we found that our students became very aggravated when they could not remember which command to use or tried to use a command incorrectly. Boxed "Hints for Success," a unique component of this book, are included to help students avoid common and frustrating mistakes and to create a positive learning experience.

Other pedagogical features include a glossary and two appendices. The glossary provides easily accessible definitions of key terms. The appendices include a grade rule table and a fraction/decimal conversion chart. Information is presented in a readable, user-friendly style, and instructions for use of the functions and commands are clearly presented with numerous illustrations.

The book contains 12 chapters. Chapters 1 through 3 cover AccuMark, grading, and digitizing. Pattern Design is presented in Chapters 4 through 9. Chapter 10 reviews marker making.

Chapters 11 and 12 present an overview of Product Data Management. It is recommended that students complete Chapters 1, 2, and 3 before moving into the chapters on pattern design and marker making. Chapters 11 and 12 can stand alone and may be presented at the beginning or the end of the course. In the writing of this book, we have carefully considered the placement of exercises to optimize students' learning and appreciation of the processes. Some exercises are imbedded in the chapters, some before the chapter summary, and some at the very end of the chapter. Those at the end of the chapter are global in nature and require the student to integrate several concepts to complete the task.

We hope this book will provide students with an enjoyable learning experience and instructors with an enjoyable teaching experience.

Acknowledgments

First and foremost, we would like to thank our husbands, Raymond Sharp and Cornelius Elsasser. Their unfailing support and enthusiasm for this project encouraged us through many rewrites and the long hours spent in the computer lab.

Second, our appreciation goes to the outstanding information technology staff at Centenary College: Anjana Desai, Mark Lampi, Matthew Kelly, and Todd Bastadas, all of whom provided invaluable technical assistance with the software and hardware. Without their help, this book would not have been possible.

We also greatly appreciate the guidance and support from the staff at Fairchild Publications. Jennifer Crane and Michelle Levy were especially patient and helpful. We are also grateful to Adam Bohannon for his skill and expertise with the visuals. Thanks also to Elizabeth Marotta, senior production editor, and the copyediting staff. Fairchild Books also found reviewers who provided valuable feedback and constructive criticism: Pui Yee Chau of Ryerson University and Lisa Donofrio-Ferrezza of FIT.

Our students are a special group whose contributions are very much appreciated. The questions and comments from many current and former students shaped not only this book but also our perspective on the teaching and learning process. We learned much from them.

Lastly, we appreciate the wonderful people we work with at Gerber Technology. Carol Cusumano and our sales representatives Jonathan Smith and John McCarroll provided much support at the beginning of the Gerber initiative at Centenary College. Jenny Shin and Christi Owens provided valuable training. The Gerber technical staff was always ready to help with our questions during many telephone conversations and emails, and John Humphries keeps our plotter running smoothly.

—Julia Ridgway Sharp and
  Virginia Hencken Elsasser

CHAPTER ONE

Getting Started in AccuMark

Objectives

After studying this chapter, you will be able to

- Create and open storage areas.
- Save, move, and transfer data.
- Understand the use of parameter tables and notch tables.

2

Introduction to AccuMark

AccuMark is used for digitizing pattern pieces and/or slopers/blocks into the computer, grading, and marker making. **Digitizing** is the process of entering the shape and details of a pattern or sloper into the computer. The process requires hardware and software. The patternmaker can determine notch types, grading rules, sizes to be produced, and other patternmaking and marker-making parameters.

The term **hardware** refers to the basic computer, including the keyboard, mouse, and printer. There are two additional Gerber hardware pieces used with AccuMark: the plotter and the digitizer.

- The **plotter** draws full-size or scaled pattern pieces and markers. Information is sent to the plotter from a computer.
- The **digitizer** is a device used to enter information into the computer. The Gerber digitizer has two components: the digitizing table and the digitizing cursor.
- The **digitizing table** holds the piece to be digitized and receives the digitizing signal from the digitizing cursor.
- The **digitizing cursor** is used to trace the pattern pieces.

In order to use Gerber hardware, Gerber software must be installed on your computer. Most software has built-in defaults. A **default** is an option that is selected automatically unless an alternative is specified by the user. It is an instruction that a computer assumes, unless the user gives it other instructions. For example, when you open Microsoft Word, text automatically appears in a specific font style and size. These settings can be changed, but the next time Word is opened, the font will return to the default unless you have changed the computer's default settings.

Gerber software uses drop-down menus, toggle buttons, and look-up fields. A **drop-down menu** is a list of related commands that appears when a function is selected. Drop-down menus are nested within one another. An arrow indicates that more menu choices can be activated when the user hovers the cursor over an item. **Toggle buttons** allow the user to select options from a list or turn commands on and off. A **look-up field** allows the user to select from a preestablished list, such as a list of pattern pieces.

Storage Areas

Storage areas are used to define work spaces on a computer. Each student (or group) should have his/her/their own storage area. A storage area is used to group related work, such as pattern pieces and a marker for a particular style. Different garment styles should have different storage areas. Data, such as information about notches, can be moved from one storage area to another and can be used for many different patterns and markers.

Creating a Storage Area

The process for creating a storage area is as follows:

1. Select Gerber LaunchPad from either your desktop or from the All Programs menu of your computer. See Figure 1.1.

Figure 1.1 Gerber LaunchPad icon

The LaunchPad will open. See Figure 1.2.

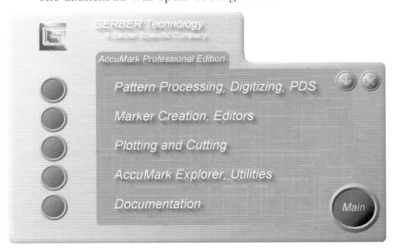

Figure 1.2 Gerber LaunchPad

4

2. Click on the button for AccuMark Explorer, Utilities. See Figure 1.3.

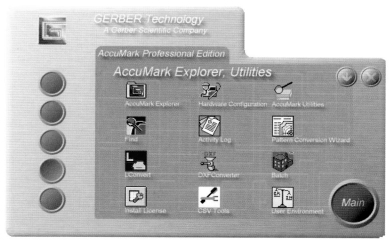

Figure 1.3 AccuMark Explorer, Utilities

3. Click on the AccuMark Explorer icon. See Figure 1.4.

Figure 1.4 AccuMark Explorer icon

This opens the AccuMark Explorer main window. See Figure 1.5.

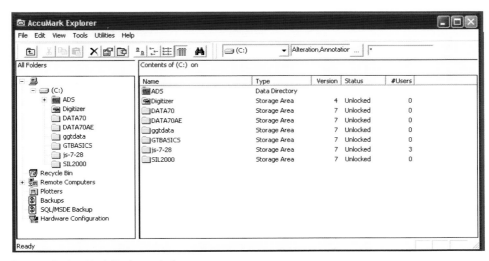

Figure 1.5 AccuMark Explorer window

This window includes a toolbar at the top and is divided into two columns. On the left-hand side of the window, there is a list of the drives available: C: indicates the hard drive, and A: indicates the floppy disk drive; other drives (CD, DVD, external hard drive, memory card) will be represented by other letters, and these may vary from computer to computer. On the right-hand side of the window, there is a list of files that are stored on the drive or in the storage area that is highlighted on the left.

4. With the C: drive highlighted, right click the mouse in an empty space in the right column of the screen. The drop-down box for creating a storage area will appear. See Figure 1.6.

Figure 1.6 Drop-down box for creating a storage area

5. Select New>Storage Area. (If data from an older version of AccuMark is to be used, select V7 Storage Area.) In the New

6

Storage Area dialog box, type the name to be used for your storage area and click on OK. A storage area name can have up to eight letters or numbers, but cannot contain spaces and symbols other than dashes and underscores. It is suggested that you label your storage area with your initials and the date (for example, js08-5-5).

6. The name of your newly created storage area should appear in the contents of the C: drive on the right-hand column of the screen. To see the content of your storage area, select your storage area's name.

Hint for Success:

When you are creating a new storage area, make sure that the right-hand column of the screen is titled "Content of (C:) on" before clicking in the empty space in the right column.

When a new storage area is established, six tables are automatically placed in the storage area. The data in these tables are the default settings for the software. These tables provide information and rules to define how slopers are digitized, modified, and plotted. These tables are: P-CUTTER, P-LAYRULE-SRCH, P-MARKER-PLOT, P-NOTCH, P-PIECE-PLOT, and P-USER-ENVIRON.

Managing Data

It is important to save your work on a regular basis to avoid possible loss of data due to computer problems. Data can be moved from one storage area to another and saved on your computer's hard drive or on a removable storage medium (e.g., a CD, an external hard drive, or a memory card). All data are managed using the AccuMark Explorer window.

Components of data management include the following:

Renaming Changing the name of a data file or folder

Deleting Removing a data file or folder from a storage area

Copying Copying data from one storage area to another area. The original data remains in the original storage area.

Dragging Copying data from one area to another by "clicking and dragging"

Saving Saving modified AccuMark tables in a designated storage area on the C: drive. Pattern pieces created in the Pattern Design system are also saved in storage areas. This data can be saved on a hard drive or a removable storage medium by exporting.

Exporting Copying data from the program files to the hard drive or to a removable storage medium. The files are saved in zip format. (Gerber files are stored in the Gerber program and are only accessible in the Gerber system on computers where AccuMark has been installed.)

Importing Copying data in a zip-file format from a removable storage medium or the hard drive to a storage area in AccuMark.

If you were working in the apparel-design industry, you would most likely save to the hard drive. However, in the academic arena, computer memories are often cleaned at the end of each day, and sometimes when a computer is turned off, the data saved on the hard drive is erased. Data created in AccuMark is automatically stored on the hard drive. It is recommended that you export your data to a removable storage medium at the end of each work session. Please note that in the Pattern Design system, pattern pieces and models can be saved directly to the hard drive but not directly to a removable storage medium.

Renaming Folders or Data

Storage folders and data can be renamed. To do this, follow these steps:

1. Open AccuMark LaunchPad.
2. Select AccuMark Explorer, Utilities.
3. Double click on the AccuMark Explorer icon.
4. Right click on the name of the file or storage area to be renamed. A drop-down menu will appear.
5. Select Rename. The object name will be highlighted; delete the existing name, and type in a new name.
6. Hit Enter on the keyboard or click in an empty space on the screen.

Deleting

Storage area folders and files can be deleted as described below.

1. Open AccuMark LaunchPad.

8

2. Select AccuMark Explorer, Utilities.
3. Double click on the AccuMark Explorer icon.
4. Right click on the name of the file or storage area to be deleted. A drop-down menu will appear. Select Delete.
5. The Confirm Delete dialog box will appear. Select Yes or Yes to All.

Note: The following files cannot be deleted: P-CUTTER, P-LAYRULE-SRCH, P-MARKER-PLOT, P-NOTCH, P-PIECE-PLOT, and P-USER-ENVIRON.

Copying Data from One Storage Area to Another

Data can be copied in two ways: clicking and dragging or copying and pasting. However, Gerber software does not allow for the copying of pattern pieces from Release Version 8 to Release Version 7.

Click and Drag

To copy data by clicking and dragging it into a storage area, follow these steps:

1. Open AccuMark LaunchPad.
2. Select AccuMark Explorer, Utilities.
3. Double click on the AccuMark Explorer icon.
4. Click on the plus sign to the left of C: to see all of the folders on the C: drive. See Figure 1.5.
5. Click on the folder that contains the information you wish to copy. The contents of that folder will appear in the right-hand column.
6. Click once on the item to be copied to highlight it. To select more than one item, hold down the Ctrl key and click on each item individually. To select all of the items in the storage area, use Select All from the Edit drop-down menu on the toolbar or press Ctrl + A on the keyboard.
7. Click once on the highlighted object (or, for multiples, one of the highlighted objects), keep the mouse button depressed, and move the arrow until the accepting storage area is highlighted. Release the mouse button.

8. If the data folder has the same name as one already in your storage area, the Transfer dialog box will ask if you wish to overwrite it. See Figure 1.7.

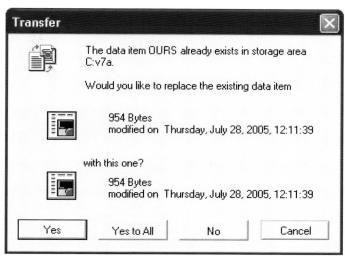

Figure 1.7 Transfer dialog box

9. If you decide to overwrite it, click on Yes or Yes to All. Click on the accepting storage area to confirm that the object has been successfully copied. If you do not wish to overwrite the folder, you must rename the folder to be copied and retry copying the folder to the storage area.

Copy and Paste

Here are instructions for copying data from one storage area to another using copy and paste.

1. Open AccuMark LaunchPad.
2. Select AccuMark Explorer, Utilities.
3. Double click on the AccuMark Explorer icon.
4. Click on the plus sign to the left of C: to see all the folders in the C: drive. See Figure 1.5.
5. Click on the folder that contains the information you wish to copy. The contents of that folder will appear in the right column.
6. Left click on the item to be copied. It will be highlighted. To select more than one item, hold down the Ctrl key and click on each item individually. To select all of the items in a storage area, use Select All from the Edit drop-down menu on the tool-bar or press Ctrl + A on the keyboard.

7. Select Edit>Copy. Alternatively, while the cursor hovers over the highlighted areas, right click to see a drop-down menu, which also includes the Copy command.
8. Click to highlight the accepting storage area in the left column.
9. Select Edit>Paste. Alternatively, while the cursor hovers over the highlighted storage area, right click to see a drop-down menu, which also includes the Paste command.
10. If a data folder has the same name as one already in your storage area, a Transfer dialog box will ask if you wish to overwrite it. See Figure 1.7.
11. The total list of objects in the accepting storage area will appear on the right.

Saving Data to a Removable Storage Medium

Exporting data involves moving data from the computer's hard drive in the Gerber system to a removable storage medium or to the hard drive outside the Gerber system. Importing data involves moving data from a removable storage medium or the hard drive to the Gerber system. (Data can be imported from a CD in this manner.)

Exporting Data

Data can be exported directly to zip disks and memory cards. AccuMark data that is saved to the C: drive using the Gerber software can only be opened with the Gerber software application and is inaccessible directly from the hard drive. To burn AccuMark data onto a CD, it is necessary to export the data to the hard drive (your desktop or some other easily accessible site). From there, it can be burned onto a CD. However, data on a CD can be directly imported into an AccuMark storage area.

To export data to a removable storage medium, follow these steps:
1. Place your removable storage medium in your computer.
2. Open AccuMark LaunchPad.
3. Select AccuMark Explorer, Utilities.
4. Double click on the AccuMark Explorer icon.
5. Click on the plus sign to the left of C: to see all the folders on the C: drive.
6. Select a storage area or a selection of data within a storage area to be exported by clicking once on it. To select more than one item, hold down the Ctrl key and click on each object individually. To select all of the objects within a storage area, use Select All from the Edit drop-down menu or press Ctrl + A on the keyboard.

7. Select File>Export Zip. From the dialog box that appears, select the appropriate removable storage medium. In the File Name field, type in the name of your file. It is suggested that you use your initials and the date as the name of the file. See Figure 1.8a.

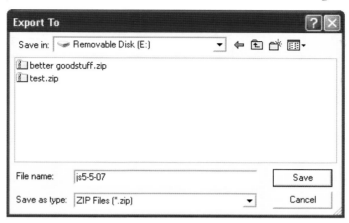

Figure 1.8 a. Exporting data: Export To dialogue box

8. Click on Save. The data will be saved as a zip file. This does not require a zip disk. Zip-file opening software is not required to access this data in the Gerber system.

9. An Export Summary dialog box will appear that states the number of items to be exported, their origin, and their destination. Click on OK. See Figure 1.8b.

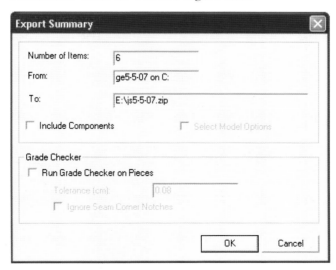

Figure 1.8 b. Exporting data: Export Summary dialogue box

10. Click on OK.
11. Highlight any storage area in the column on the left, and select File>Import Zip to view the files on your disk. If the data are saved on the storage medium, click on Cancel to close the dialog box. If the data has not been saved, click on Cancel and repeat the exporting process.

Importing Data

To import data, a storage area is required. An existing one can be used, but it is recommended that you create a new one for each work session. This way, existing data are not overwritten and lost. Note that data on a CD can be directly imported into an AccuMark storage area.

To import data from a removable storage medium, follow these instructions:

1. Place your removable storage medium in the computer.
2. Open AccuMark LaunchPad.
3. Select AccuMark Explorer, Utilities.
4. Double click on the AccuMark Explorer icon.
5. Select a storage area in the column on the left of the screen. This storage area will receive the imported data.
6. Select File>Import Zip.
7. A window will appear. From the Look In section, select the drive that contains the removable storage medium with your data.
8. Highlight the zip file to be imported. Select Open.
9. A list of folders to be imported will appear; click on OK to select all. To import specific data, select the folders individually, then click on OK.
10. In the Import dialog box, select Yes or Yes to All to import the data, overwriting the defaults that had been automatically placed in the folder.
11. A Process Completed box will appear. Click on OK.

User Environment

The User Environment is used to determine the parameters that will be applied in a folder. A **parameter** is a property that defines a system and determines or limits its performance. Parameters can be thought of as sets of rules that can be changed. Gerber software is used by many different companies, each of which has its own way of making markers, and so each company requires its own different rules or parameters. For example, on one hand, in the United States, we use the Imperial system of measurement, which includes inches, feet, and yards. On the other hand, in Europe, patternmakers work with the Metric system, which uses centimeters and meters. Thus, a patternmaker in the United States will use different parameters than the ones used by a patternmaker in Europe.

The User Environment form is used to give the computer information about work in a particular storage area. Different parameters may be selected for each project, but generally, patternmakers will use the same parameters for all of their work. Unless several user environment forms are planned, it is best to keep the table default name, P-USER-ENVIRON.

Opening and Completing the User Environment Form

The User Environment form can be accessed in two different ways: either by double clicking on P-USER ENVIRON or the name of any other user environment table in the contents of a storage area in the AccuMark Explorer window or by selecting AccuMark Explorer, Utilities on the Gerber LaunchPad and double clicking on the User Environment icon. See Figure 1.9.

Figure 1.9 User Environment icon

The User Environment form will appear. See Figure 1.10.

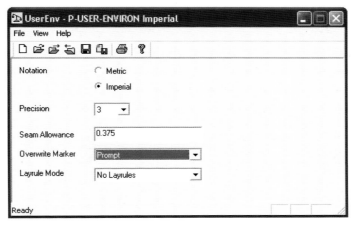

Figure 1.10 User Environment form

14

To complete the User Environment form follow these instructions:

1. *Notation*: This field indicates the system of measurement used. Select either Metric or Imperial. The default is Metric. Those working in the United States should select Imperial.

2. *Decimal Precision Places*: This field specifies how many decimal places the system will recognize. Usually it is best to select 2 or 3 when working in the Imperial system and 1 or 2 when working in the Metric system.

3. *Seam Allowance*: This field specifies the amount of seam allowance that will be added to a pattern piece that is split in marker making (for instance, when a very wide skirt has to be cut in two pieces because the fabric is not wide enough). This field has no effect on the normal perimeter seam allowance that is added during patternmaking. When using the Imperial system and three decimal places, the default amount for this field is 0.375. However, it can be changed.

4. *Overwrite Marker*: This field determines what will happen if a marker order is processed more than once.
   a. *Yes* means that if a marker with the same name as one previously used is processed, the original marker will be overwritten and lost.
   b. *No* means that an order cannot be reprocessed.
   c. *Prompt* means that if an order is processed a second time, the system will ask if you wish to overwrite the original. Prompt is the recommended choice for student work.

5. *Layrule Mode*: No Layrules is the recommended choice for student work.

6. It is necessary to save the changed form. Select File>Save As. It is recommended that you leave the file name as P-USER-ENVIRON. In the Save In field, select the appropriate storage area. Click on Save. A dialog box will appear, informing you that a data file P-USER-ENVIRON already exists in the storage area and asking if you wish to replace it. Select Yes. (Whenever a storage area is created, it contains a P-USER ENVIRON file set with the software defaults that may not be appropriate for your project.)

Notch Editor

The Notch Editor defines the properties of the notches in a pattern piece and is used to enter the dimensions of desired notches. **Notches**

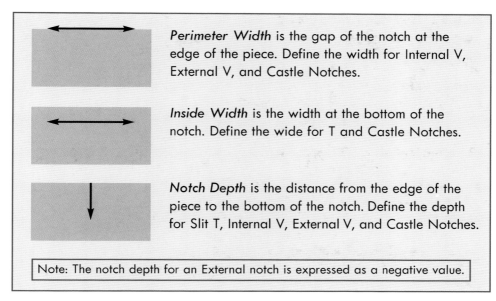

Perimeter Width is the gap of the notch at the edge of the piece. Define the width for Internal V, External V, and Castle Notches.

Inside Width is the width at the bottom of the notch. Define the wide for T and Castle Notches.

Notch Depth is the distance from the edge of the piece to the bottom of the notch. Define the depth for Slit T, Internal V, External V, and Castle Notches.

Note: The notch depth for an External notch is expressed as a negative value.

Figure 1.11 Notch properties (from *AccuMark Training Guide,* page 19).

are used to mark pattern pieces so that they can be fitted together properly when sewn. There are several styles of notches. Notches have a perimeter width, an inside width, and depth. See Figure 1.11. Table 1.1 indicates commonly used notch sizes.

On many commercially cut garments, the notches are small slashes cut into the fabric. If the fabric is cut by a computer-controlled cutter, only V notches can be used. For this use, the perimeter width of the notch (the width across the gap at the edge of the notch) must be twice the depth of the notch. AccuMark software allows for 99 different types or sizes of notches.

Filling in the Notch Editor

The Notch Editor form can be accessed in two different ways: either by double clicking on P-NOTCH or the name of any other notch table in the contents of a storage area in the AccuMark Explorer window or by selecting Marker Creation, Editors on the Gerber LaunchPad and double clicking on the Notch Editor icon. See Figure 1.12.

Figure 1.12 Notch Editor icon

Table 1.1 Commonly Used Notch Sizes

Type of Notch		Perimeter Width		Inside Width		Notch Depth	
Slit notch		0		0		3/16	0.188
T notch		0		1/8	0.125	3/16	0.188
U or Clicker notch		1/16	0.062	1/16	0.062	3/16	0.188
Castle notch		3/16	0.188	3/16	0.188	−3/16	−0.188
Internal V		1/4	0.25	0		1/8	0.125
External V		1/4	0.25	0		−1/8	−0.125
Left Check		3/16	0.188	0		3/16	0.188
Right Check		3/16	0.188	0		3/16	0.188

The Notch Editor will appear. See Figure 1.13.

	Notch Type	Perimeter Width	Inside Width	Notch Depth	
1	Slit	0.000	0.000	0.188	
2	T	0.000	0.125	0.188	
3	U	0.062	0.062	0.188	
4	Castle	0.188	0.188	-0.188	
5	V	0.250	0.000	0.125	
6	V	0.250	0.000	-0.125	
7	Left Check	0.188	0.000	0.188	
8	Right Check	0.188	0.000	0.188	
9	None	0.000	0.000	0.000	
10	None	0.000	0.000	0.000	
11	None	0.000	0.000	0.000	
12	None	0.000	0.000	0.000	

Notch - C:\JS5-5-07\P-NOTCH - Imperial

File   Edit   View   Help

Ready

Figure 1.13 Notch Editor form

This is the procedure to complete the Notch Editor form.

1. Check that you are in your storage area and that Imperial appears on the title bar.

2. Select the name of your notch type by clicking in a notch type field. This is a toggle field and a look-up field. Click in the field until the desired notch type appears or click on the down arrow to select the desired notch type from the list provided.

3. Fill in the remaining fields of the Notch Editor with the appropriate dimensions. Table 1.1 can be used as a guide. The notch depth of castle and external V notches is entered as a negative number. Note that all of the measurements are in decimals. If necessary, please refer to the Fraction/Decimal Conversion Chart in Appendix 1.

4. It is necessary to save the changed form. Select File>Save As. It is recommended that students leave the file name as P-NOTCH. In the Save In field, select the appropriate storage area. Click on Save. A dialog box will appear informing you that a data file P-NOTCH already exists in the storage area and asking if you wish to replace it. Select Yes. (Whenever a storage area is created, it contains a P-NOTCH data file set with the software defaults, which may not be appropriate for your project.)

Summary

AccuMark is used for copying pattern pieces and/or slopers/ blocks into the computer, grading, and marker making. The patternmaker can determine notch types, grading rules, sizes to be produced, and other patternmaking and marker-making parameters.

Storage areas are used to define work spaces. A storage area is used to group related work, such as pattern pieces and a marker for a particular style. Different garment styles will have different storage areas. Managing data in storage areas includes the renaming, deleting, copying, dragging, saving, exporting, and importing of data. It is important to save work on a regular basis to avoid the possible loss of data due to computer problems. Data can be moved from one storage area to another, and it can be saved on the hard drive or a removable storage medium. A parameter is a property that defines a system and determines or limits its performance. Parameters can be thought of as sets of rules that can be changed. The User Environment form is used to give the computer information about work in a particular storage area. The Notch Editor defines the properties of the notches in a pattern piece.

Key Terms

copying	importing
default	look-up field
deleting	notches
digitizer	parameter
digitizing cursor	plotter
digitizing table	renaming
dragging	saving
drop-down menu	storage area
exporting	toggle buttons
hardware	

Review Questions

1. What is AccuMark used for?
2. What is the purpose of a storage area?
3. How is a storage area created?
4. Which notch is used when fabric is cut by a computer-controlled cutter?
5. How are data saved to removable storage mediums?
6. What is the purpose of a User Environment form?

CHAPTER TWO

Introduction to Grading

Objectives

After studying this chapter, you will be able to

- Grade a pattern using a Cartesian graph.

- Complete a Grade Rule Table in Gerber AccuMark.

- Complete a Piece Plot Parameter table and an Annotation table in Gerber AccuMark.

20

Introduction to the Rules of Pattern Grading

In the clothing industry, the sample pattern is made in one size. **Grading** is the process of changing the size of a sample pattern, scaling it up and down to create a range of sizes. The sample-size pattern, or sloper, is graded according to grade rules that are specific to a given manufacturer. The SizeUSA survey published in 2004 by [TC]² (Tailored Clothing Technology Corporation, a not-for-profit industry organization that conducts research and development activities), revealed that the grade rules used by many apparel manufacturers do not accurately reflect the clothing sizes of Americans. As a consequence, many companies are reevaluating their grade rules. The diversity of the American population must be considered when mass producing apparel. Integrated within this chapter are exercises to help reinforce what you learn along the way.

Definitions of Terms Commonly Used in Grading

The following terms are commonly used in the industry:

- **Sloper** A piece needed for a fitted garment with the minimum of ease and no style lines or seam allowances. The darts are shortened to the appropriate distance from the pivot points, but the pivot points are marked. A sloper is used as the basis for flat pattern design or computer-aided design. Several examples of slopers are shown in Figure 2.1.
- **Block** Another name for sloper; the term *block* is commonly used outside the United States.
- **Piece** Used in Gerber Pattern Design to refer to a sloper that is being modified to make a pattern, and to a pattern piece.
- **Sample pattern** A style pattern developed from a basic block or sloper.
- **Master pattern** A style pattern with added fashion details and trued seams. It is usually made only in the sample size.
- **Production pattern** The final perfect pattern. It is created in all of the sizes that are to be made, and each piece has the appropriate seam allowance. To reduce costs, production patterns are often simplified versions of the master pattern.
- **Perimeter** The outer edge of a pattern.
- **Point** A defining mark on a pattern or sloper.

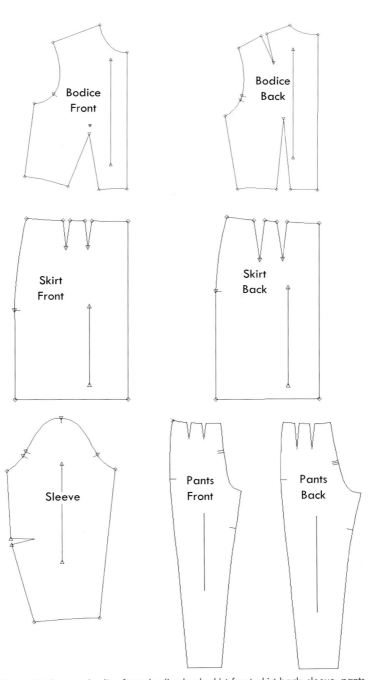

Figure 2.1 Slopers: bodice front, bodice back, skirt front, skirt back, sleeve, pants front, and pants back

22

- **Cardinal points** The points on the perimeter of the pattern where dimensional changes occur during grading.
- **Nested** The stacking of pattern pieces from different sizes on top of one another so that the incremental differences can be seen. See Figure 2.2.

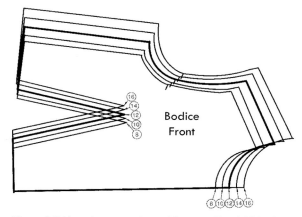

Figure 2.2 Nested pattern pieces. (Courtesy, Fairchild Books.)

- **Grade Rule** The amount of increase or decrease in size at each cardinal point. There will be different rules for different points. (For example, from one size to the next, a shoulder seam may only increase one-eighth inch, but the front of a bodice may increase one inch.)

When to Grade

Traditionally, for any given style, a sample pattern and a sample garment are made. After the sample has been accepted, a production pattern is created and graded to different sizes.

With the introduction of computer-aided design, companies may grade at various points in the product development process. Companies using AccuMark software without computer-aided pattern-making create the sample pattern by draping or traditional flat pattern methods. After the sample pattern is accepted, it is digitized into the computer using appropriate grade rules. The pattern pieces for the desired sizes are then placed in a marker that is used to cut the fabric.

Companies that use Gerber Technology, Inc.'s AccuMark and Pattern Design software may digitize a sloper using the computer and grade rules. Using Pattern Design, a pattern can be created from the sample-size sloper. The pattern is automatically graded by the system using the preestablished rules. After the pattern is completed, a marker can be made for a range of sizes.

Using the Cartesian Graph

Computer grading is based on the **Cartesian graph** that has two axes that cross at a right angle and divide an area into four quadrants. The horizontal axis is labeled x and the vertical axis is y. See Figure 2.3.

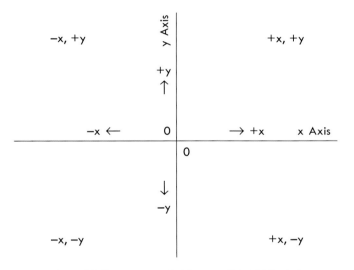

Figure 2.3 Cartesian graph. (Courtesy, Fairchild Books.)

By using the Cartesian graph, locations of specific points can be identified. It is important to understand how numbers define points on this graph.

- The x- and y-axes meet at point (0, 0).
- On the x-axis, numbers to the right of the y-axis are designated plus (+, positive) and numbers to the left are minus (–, negative).

24

- On the y-axis, numbers above the x-axis are plus (+, positive) and numbers below are minus (−, negative).
- By using two numbers and the +/− symbols, it is possible to define any point on the graph.
- The value of the number on the x-axis (the distance along the x-axis from the y-axis to the right or left) is always given first.

Hint for Success

To define or locate a point, go Sideways first and then Up and down. Remember that *S* comes before *U* in the alphabet.

Using the Cartesian Graph for Grading

By placing a sloper on a Cartesian graph, it is possible to define the positions of cardinal points such as neckline, armholes, and dart positions on the pattern. As a pattern is graded, these points are moved. The position of a point for a different size is given by the distance the point is moved along the x- and y-axes relative to the point's original position.

Pattern Orientation

The position of a sloper on the Cartesian graph is important when determining the amount and direction of the movement of cardinal points to produce different sizes of patterns. Slopers can be placed anywhere on the Cartesian graph, but there are some positions that make applying grading rules easier. For this book, we orient the slopers as shown in Figure 2.4.

Numbering Cardinal Points

Cardinal points should be numbered before grading. By convention, the numbering starts at the point on the sloper that is placed on the (0, 0) point on the Cartesian graph. After this point of reference has

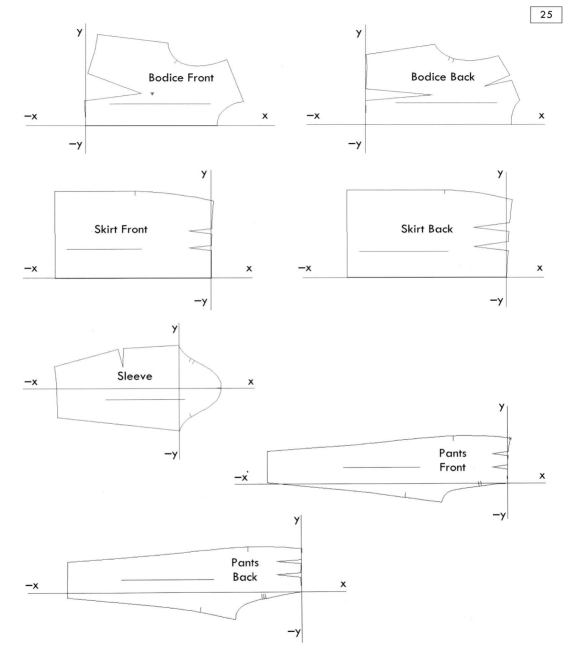

Figure 2.4 Placement of slopers on a Cartesian graph: bodice front, bodice back, skirt front, skirt back, sleeve, pants front, and pants back

been established, all succeeding points are numbered in a clockwise direction as shown in Figure 2.5.

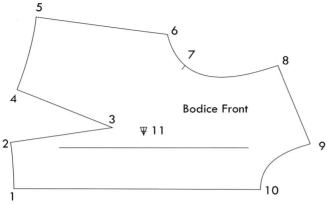

Figure 2.5 Numbering cardinal points

Developing Grade Rules

A **grade rule** is the amount of increase or decrease in size at each cardinal point. A **grade rule table** is where all of the grading measurements are stored. A rule defines how far a cardinal point will move right or left and up or down on the Cartesian graph to change the dimensions of the pattern for the next size. Figure 2.6 shows the (x, y) growth from a small size to a larger one.

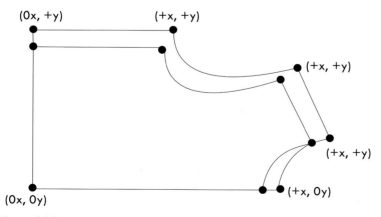

Figure 2.6 Example of *x* and *y* growth from a small size to a larger one.

Each rule is assigned a number, which is how the rule is referenced during digitizing. The same rule can be used in different locations on one piece and on more than one piece when grading. When a piece is digitized (copied into the computer's storage system), the rules stored in AccuMark in a rule table can be used to create similar pieces in different sizes—in other words, graded pieces. When a pattern is symmetrical, the rules are applied only to one side of the pattern as is done in flat pattern design. However, for this book, pattern pieces will be oriented on the Cartesian graph in a manner that makes grading easier. This means that the left side of the backs of the bodice, skirt, and pants will be graded rather than the right side. In this way, the same grade rules may be used for the front and back. If the right side of the backs were to be graded, an additional set of grade rules would be needed. These would have the same dimensions as the grade rules for the fronts, but all of the signs (+ or −) in the y-direction would have to be reversed. This is consistent with the grading methods described in several recent grading textbooks and with some of the examples included with the Gerber training software.

Each grade rule may have more than one set of size changes. For example, the difference between sizes 2 and 4 is not the same as the difference between sizes 18 and 20. A size 2 bust may be 32 inches, and a size 4 bust may be 33 inches, a difference of 1 inch; whereas a size 18 bust may be 44 inches and a size 20 bust may be 46 inches, a difference of 2 inches. The sizes at which the grade rules change are called **break points**. They are usually at size 10 and 16 in Missy sizes. Junior sizes typically break at size 9.

Creating a Rule Table in AccuMark

In the Gerber system, all rules are written in decimals. Fractions are not used. (For help with converting fractions to decimals, refer to the Fraction/Decimal Conversion Chart in the Appendix 1 on page 302.) It is important to open or create a storage area and define the user environment parameters before creating a rule table. The process for creating a rule table is as follows:

1. Select Pattern Processing, Digitizing, PDS from the Gerber LaunchPad.
2. Double click on the Grade Rule Editor icon. See Figure 2.7.

Figure 2.7 Grade Rule Editor icon

3. The first window of the Grade Rule Editor dialog box will appear. See Figure 2.8.

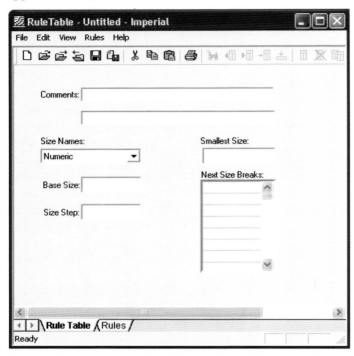

Figure 2.8 The Rule Table window of the Grade Rule Editor dialog box

Check that you are using the Imperial system of measurement. (The system of units used in the Rule Table editor will be the one that was used in the last user environment table accessed. To change from the Metric system to the Imperial system, check Imperial in the user environment table in your storage area.)

4. To fill in the fields of the first window of the Grade Rule Editor, follow these steps:

  a. *Size Names*: This is a look-up field. The choices are Numeric (i.e., sizes 2, 4, 6, and so on) or AlphaNumeric (i.e., sizes XS, S, M, L, XL, and so on).

  b. *Base Size*: This is the size of the pieces on which all of the grade rule data are based. It is your sample size.

  c. *Size Step*: This is only used with the Numeric system—usually the size step is two (e.g., if the sizes used are 8, 10, and 12, the size step is two; if sizes 29, 30, and 31 are used, then the size step is one). The size step need not be related to actual differences in size. As noted before, the differences between sizes 2 and 4 are not the same as the differences between sizes 18 and 20. If the AlphaNumeric system is selected, this field cannot be filled in.

d. *Smallest Size*: The patternmaker selects the smallest size to be made.

e. *Size Break*: This is the size that grades differently from the previous one. If the Numeric system is selected, specify your base size, smallest size, break sizes, and largest size. If there are to be no break sizes, then list your base size, smallest size, one other size, and largest size. If the AlphaNumeric system is selected, specify your base size, your smallest size, and each additional size (e.g., base size: M, smallest size: XS, next size: S, next size: L, next size: XL).

5. To fill in the second window of the Grade Rule Editor, follow these steps:

a. Select the Rules tab in the lower left-hand corner of the first window. See Figure 2.9.

Figure 2.9 The Rules window of the Grade Rule Editor dialog box

b. *Rule Number*: Numbers should be entered sequentially (1, 2, 3, and so on).

c. *Comment*: This is an optional field. Leave this field empty at this point.

d. *Point Attribute*: Leave this field empty.

e. *Breaks*: The computer will automatically fill in the breaks that you have indicated in the first window of the Grade Rule Editor.

f. Fill in the x- and y-coordinates for each rule. If you do not want breaks then the x- and y-coordinates will be the same for all sizes. You need only fill in the top line for the smallest size; the other spaces will be filled in with the same coordinates automatically when you move to the next grade rule. If you have break points, the coordinates for the movement of each cardinal point must be filled in for each break section.

g. After a rule has been entered, scroll to the right to enter the next rule.

h. When all of the rules have been entered, return to the Rule Table window by selecting the Rule Table tab in the lower left-hand corner of the window.

6. It is necessary to save the form to a storage area. Select Save As from the File drop-down menu. In the Save In field, select the appropriate storage area. Enter an appropriate file name for the rule table. Click on Save.

Hint for Success

Hard copies of all the completed rule tables should be printed for easy reference (select File>Print>OK).

Hint for Success

After adding data to a storage area, the data does not immediately show up in the right-hand section of the AccuMark Explorer screen. You must go to another storage area and then reopen the original storage area to see the newly added data. This is particularly important when exporting data to a removable storage medium because all information to be exported *must* be visible on the right-hand side of the screen.

Accessing and Modifying a Rule Table

A storage area may have many rule tables so long as each has a different name. However, a rule table may have several hundred rules: enough for any possible requirement.

Existing rule tables can be modified, and the values for each rule can be changed. Additional rules can be added. There are two ways to view an existing rule table:

1. Double click on the name of the rule table in the contents of a storage area in the AccuMark Explorer window.
2. Select Gerber LaunchPad>Pattern Processing, Digitizing, PDS> Grade Rule Editor icon. This will bring you to the first window of the Grade Rule Editor. From the File drop-down menu, select Open. In the Look In box, select the storage area containing the desired rule table. Select the name of the rule table to be opened. Either select Open or double click on the name of the rule table.

Applying Grade Rules to a Sloper

The rules for a basic rule table named OURDATA are provided in Appendix 2 on page 303. They are sufficient to grade the seven basic sloper pieces. Students/faculty can use these rules to develop a Gerber rule table for use when grading slopers digitized as described in Chapter 3. Figures 2.10a through 2.10g show the basic sloper pieces and the appropriate application of our OURDATA grade rules to these pieces.

Grade Rule Exercise

For this exercise, students will create grade rules and a grade rule table that can be applied to a rectangle. In the next chapter, this graded rectangle will be digitized.

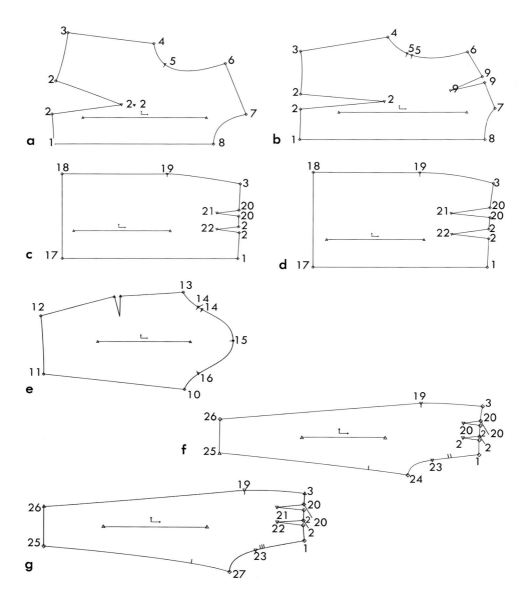

Figure 2.10 Basic slopers with grade rules: a. bodice front, b. bodice back, c. skirt front, d. skirt back, e. sleeve, f. pants front, and g. pants back

a. The rectangle in Figure 2.11 represents an 8½ × 11 inch sheet of paper. It will be used as a pattern piece sized M. For each larger size, the rectangle will grow one inch along the x-axis and one-half inch along the y-axis. For smaller sizes, the rectangle shrinks by one inch along the x-axis and one-half inch along the y-axis.

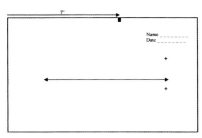

Figure 2.11 Pattern piece for the grade rule exercise

b. Label a piece of 8½ × 11 copy paper with your name and the date. This is your pattern.

c. Using a red pencil, mark each corner of the rectangle with a grade rule number, starting at one in the bottom left-hand corner and continuing around the rectangle in a clockwise direction.

d. Then, in each corner write (using a green pencil) the distance the corner must be moved in the x- and y-directions to create the larger size.

e. Now fill in the rule table. See Table 2.1.

Table 2.1

Rule number	1	2	3	4
X				
Y				

f. Draw a grain line parallel to the long side of the paper.

g. Along the top of the paper and seven inches from the left, draw a notch.

h. Wherever you want, draw two crosses for drill holes that will represent the placement of a pocket.

    i. When the pattern is changed to the next larger size, the notch and drill holes are going to move. The notch should move three quarters of an inch along the x-axis (to the left) and one-half inch along the y-axis so that it is still on the edge of the pattern.

    j. The pocket placement marks will move in the same manner as the notch.

    k. In red pencil, label the notch and drill holes grade rule 5.

    l. Next to the rule number on the paper, write in green pencil the distance each point must be moved along the x- and y-axes to create the next larger size.

    m. Fill in the rule table. See Table 2.2.

Table 2.2

Rule number	
X	
Y	

    n. To create a Grade Rule Table in AccuMark for this rectangle, begin by creating a new storage area specifically for this project. Label it with your initials and REC (e.g., JSREC).

    o. Set up your User Environment parameters so that you are working with the Imperial system. (Double click on P-USER ENVIRON in the contents of your storage area, fill in the form, and save the changes to your storage area.)

    p. Open the Grade Rule Editor: Select Gerber LaunchPad>Pattern Processing, Digitizing, PDS>Grade Rule Editor.

    q. Confirm that you are still using the Imperial system. If not, check your User Environment table and change it if necessary.

    r. Complete the rule table. For this exercise, AlphaNumeric sizes will be used. See Figure 2.12.

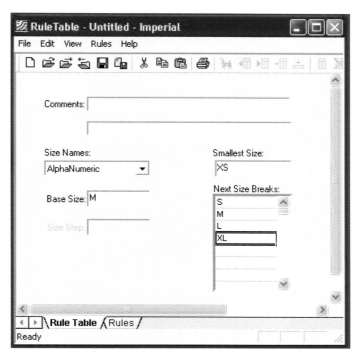

Figure 2.12 Rule Table using AlphaNumeric sizes

   i. *Size Name*: Select AlphaNumeric.
   ii. *Base Size*: This is your sample size. For this exercise students will use M.
   iii. *Smallest Size*: For this exercise, use XS.
   iv. *Size Break*: For this exercise, use sizes S, M, L, and XL.
 s. Select the Rules tab in the lower left-hand corner to go to the second window of the Grade Rule Editor.
 t. Enter rule numbers sequentially, and fill in the x- and y-coordinates for each rule. You only need to fill in the top line XS–S. The other spaces will be filled in automatically.
 u. Save As in your storage area. Label the rule table REC. (It is recommended that you use a short name as it will be entered into the digitizer. The longer the name, the greater the chance of errors occurring in digitizing.)

Completing a Piece Plot Parameter Table

The Piece Plot Parameter table is completed as part of the preparation for digitizing, which is discussed in Chapter 3. The Piece Plot Parameter table determines various factors that affect the manner in which a piece is plotted. Pieces can be plotted individually or as part of a marker (see Chapter 10). This table determines the specifics of plotting individual pieces. Pieces may be plotted in a variety of ways, such as smaller or larger than the original digitized piece or nested. The Piece Plot Parameter table can be accessed two ways:

1. Double click on P-PIECE-PLOT or the name of any other piece plot parameter table in the contents of a storage area in the AccuMark Explorer window.
2. Select the Plotting and Cutting button on the Gerber LaunchPad, and then double click on the Piece Plot Parameter icon. See Figure 2.13.

Figure 2.13 Piece Plot Parameter icon

The process to complete the Piece Plot Parameter table is as follows:
1. Access the Piece Plot Parameter table. See Figure 2.14.

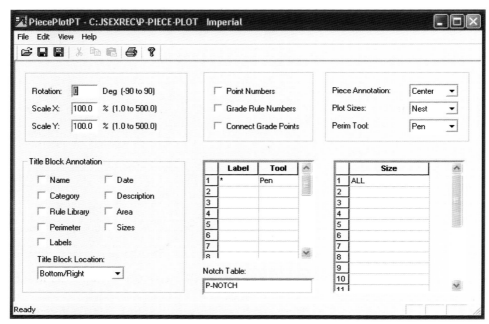

Figure 2.14 Piece Plot Parameter window

2. *Rotation*: This is a fill-in field. Zero degrees (0 Deg) indicate that a piece will be plotted with the grain lengthwise on the plotting paper. Sometimes, to save paper, pieces may be rotated up to 90 degrees. For example, an evening dress may be plotted across the paper rather than lengthwise on the paper.

3. *Scale X*: This is a fill-in field that changes the scale of the piece along the x-axis.

4. *Scale Y*: This is a fill-in field that changes the scale of the piece in the y-axis. Usually Scale X and Scale Y are the same so larger or smaller copies of a piece may be plotted. For actual-size piece plots, the settings for Scale X and Scale Y are 100 percent.

5. *Point Numbers*: When this field is selected, point numbers assigned during digitizing will be printed during plotting.

6. *Grade Rule Numbers*: When this field is selected, grade rule numbers assigned during digitizing will be printed during plotting.

7. *Connect Grade Points*: This field is only relevant if nested pieces are being plotted. When it is selected, grade points will be connected from pattern piece to pattern piece in the nest.

8. *Piece Annotation*: This field, with a drop-down menu, determines whether the piece annotation (labels) is located in the center of the piece or on the grain line of the piece. The information included in Piece Annotation is determined by the Annotation Editor (see page 38).

9. *Plot Sizes*: A drop-down menu, this field determines whether single pieces or a graded nest are plotted.

10. *Perim Tool*: This is a drop-down menu that determines whether the piece perimeter is cut with a knife or drawn with a pen.

11. *Title Block Annotation*: This field enables users to choose which labels are placed as a title to a piece but not on the actual piece. The options are Name, Category, Rule Library, Perimeter, Labels, Date, Description, Area, and Sizes.

12. *Title Block Location*: This drop-down menu provides four options for the placement of the title block annotation outside the perimeter of the piece: Bottom/Left, Top/Left, Bottom/Right, Top/Right.

13. *Notch Table*: The default P-NOTCH automatically appears in this field, but it can be changed.

14. *Sizes to Plot*: The default setting in this field is ALL. Different sizes can be selected. By selecting BASE in the first box, only

the base size will be plotted. To plot an assortment of sizes, select each size desired in a different box by using the drop-down menu.

15. Save or Save As in the storage area being used. Each table must have a unique name; however, the same parameters are usually used for most products a company makes so the same table is used most of the time.

The default piece plot parameter table, P-PIECE-PLOT, is appropriate for most uses and generally will not need to be changed.

Retrieving an Annotation Editor

Annotations are notes plotted on the pattern pieces. It is useful to have information, such as model, size, quantity, piece name, and category, on the plotted pattern piece. The Annotation Editor determines what information is plotted. A series of abbreviations separated by commas is used to designate the information. See Table 2.3.

Table 2.3 Annotation Table Abbreviations

SZ1-6	Size
BD1-3	Bundle
MSQ	Model/Size/Quantity
AP	Add-piece bundle
WI	Marker width
L	Length
U	Utilization
PS	Plaid/Stripe
SY6925	SY = Symbol
	69 = Plot a drill hole as a star
	25 = $1/4$ inch across
PN1-20	Piece name
PC1-20	Piece category
ON1-20	Order number
MK1-20	Marker name

The Annotation Editor also determines the layout of the information. Annotations to be plotted on separate lines are separated by comma, forward slash, comma (,/,). Generally speaking, an annotation table provided with Gerber training data is acceptable for student work. The settings that the authors prefer for student use are shown in Figure 2.15.

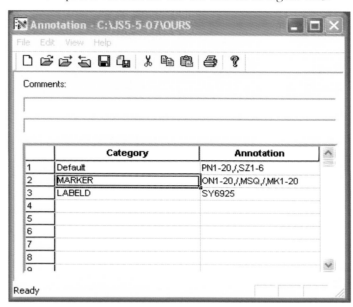

Figure 2.15 Annotation Editor, with the authors' preferred annotation data

This data can be inputted into an annotation table and saved by using the File drop-down menu (use Save As and give the file a new name to avoid overwriting the default annotation editor). To see an annotation table, click on its name in the contents of a storage area.

To add the Gerber default annotation table to a storage area, follow these steps:

1. Select Marker Creation, Editors on the Gerber LaunchPad.
2. Double click on the Annotation icon. See Figure 2.16.

Figure 2.16 Annotation icon

3. Select File>Save As. Select your storage area. Enter a file name and select Save.

40

Piece Plot and Annotation Exercises

1. Look at the piece plot parameter table in your storage area EXREC. Check the grade rule numbers, name, category, and date. Save the table in your storage area with the file name: MyPiecePlot.
2. Import an annotation table to your storage area EXREC.
3. If necessary, save your storage area EXREC to a removable storage medium so that it can be used in the exercises in Chapter 3. Also, have your paper rectangle pattern available for Chapter 3.

Summary

Grading is the process of changing the size of a sample pattern to create a range of sizes. A sample-size pattern or a sloper is graded according to grade rules that are specific to a given manufacturer. Computer grading is based on the Cartesian graph that has two axes that cross at a right angle and divide an area into four quadrants. By using the Cartesian graph, locations of specific points can be identified.

A grade rule is the amount of increase or decrease in size at each cardinal point. A rule table is where all the grading measurements are stored. A rule defines how far a cardinal point will move right or left and up or down along the Cartesian graph. Each rule is assigned a number.

The Piece Plot Parameter table determines various factors that affect the manner in which a piece is plotted. For example, pieces may be nested, rotated, or plotted smaller or larger than the original digitized piece. The Annotation Editor determines the notes that will be plotted on the pattern pieces. These notes can include model, size, quantity, and piece name.

Key Terms

annotations	master pattern
block	nested
break points	perimeter
cardinal points	piece
Cartesian graph	point
grade rule	production pattern
grade rule table	sample pattern
grading	sloper

Review Questions

1. What is grading?
2. What is a grade rule?
3. How are slopers used in the apparel industry?
4. What is the purpose of the Piece Plot Parameter table?
5. What are the differences between a sample pattern, a production pattern, and a master pattern?
6. What is a Cartesian graph? How is it used in grading?

CHAPTER THREE

Digitizing

Objectives

After studying this chapter, you will be able to

- Input a sloper into a computer using a digitizing table and cursor.
- Solve common digitizing errors.

Introduction

In Chapters 1 and 2, we explained how to define parameters and create grade rules and a grade rule table. It is now possible to enter slopers, or pieces, into the computer. This is usually done by digitizing. Digitizing is the process of tracing a sloper/pattern piece into the computer and entering information about that sloper/pattern piece. Once a piece has been digitized and stored on a computer's hard drive or a removable storage medium, it is easily accessible and does not deteriorate with use. Complete libraries of slopers and pattern pieces can be stored indefinitely.

Digitizing Hardware

A digitizer is a device that is used to enter information into a software system. It consists of a digitizing table, a cursor, and a digitizing menu. Figure 3.1 shows a technician working at a digitizing table. An alternative to the digitizing table is the **silhouette table**. This table, as

Figure 3.1 A technician working with a digitizing table.

Figure 3.2 A silhouette table

shown in Figure 3.2, is more technologically advanced, allows for more flexibility, and is easier to use than the digitizing table. As a result, digitizing tables are being replaced by Silhouette tables in the industry. Most educational settings still have digitizing tables.

The Digitizing Table

The digitizing table is a large, electronic work area that can be adjusted by height and angle. A diagram of a digitizing table is shown in Figure 3.3.

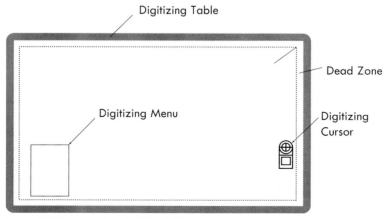

Figure 3.3 Diagram of a digitizing table

It is connected by cables to the computer and to the digitizing cursor. Pieces to be digitized are taped onto the digitizing table. The computer receives signals from the digitizing cursor. The outer three inches of the table are known as the "**dead zone**;" they do not respond to the cursor signals. On the digitizing table, there is a holder for the cursor and an application selection area. There is also a **digitizing menu** that is rather like a keyboard, where specific instructions can be given to the computer.

The Digitizing Cursor

The digitizing cursor is used to enter information into the computer. It has two functions:

1. To trace the outline of the piece and input information that is included on the piece.
2. To be used on the digitizing menu, like your fingers on the keyboard of a computer, to give the computer information about the stages of the digitizing process.

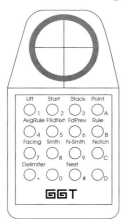

The digitizing cursor, as shown in Figure 3.4, has two parts: the crosshairs and the buttons. The crosshairs are used to determine exact coordinates of a piece on the digitizing table and to select instructions on the digitizing menu. The buttons are used to enter information about the coordinates or to select keys on the digitizing menu. There are 16 buttons on the cursor: letters A, B, C, and D, numbers 0–9, a delimiter (*), and a number symbol (#). The functions of the buttons are described in Table 3.1.

Figure 3.4 Diagram of a digitizing cursor

Hint for Success

To work properly, the digitizing cursor must always be in contact with the digitizing table.

Instructions for Using the Digitizing Cursor

1. Always start at the bottom left-hand corner of the piece and work around the piece in a clockwise direction.
2. Place the crosshairs over the point to be entered and press the A button.
3. If the point is to be graded, press A>B>the grade rule number.
4. If the point is a notch press A>C>the notch type number.
5. If the notch is graded press A>B>the grade rule number>C>notch type number.
6. If a line is straight, it is only necessary to digitize the points at the ends.
7. For curves, more points must be entered. The computer will automatically create curves. If too many points are entered, the curves will be "wiggly."
8. When close to corners that are more than 90 degrees, digitize a point close (a quarter of an inch) to the corner, a point on the corner, and a point just after the corner (a quarter of an inch).

Table 3.1 Cursor Button Functions

Button	Function
A	1. Used to enter menu information 2. Used to enter information on the digitizing table, such as grain line, perimeter points, notches, and internal points
B	Used to indicate that a grade rule is being added a. It is always preceded by pressing button A to define where the grade rule will be applied. b. It is always followed by the grade rule number from the grade rule table. For example, A>B>1 where A is the point on the sloper, B indicates that a grade rule is to be applied, 1 is the specific grade rule to be applied.
C	Used to indicate a notch a. It is always preceded by an A. b. It may be preceded by A>B and a rule number if the notch is to be grade. c. It is always followed with the notch type number from the Notch Parameter Table. For example, A>C>3 for an ungraded Type 3 notch, A>B>1>C>3 for a Type 3 notch graded according to grade rule 1.
D	1. Used to indicate an **attribute**, or special characteristic applied to a point a. It is followed by an attribute code. b. The only attribute that will be used in this introductory book is coded 9. D>9 is used on a corner that is more than 90 degrees to ensure that it is not automatically smoothed into a curve. For example, A>D>9 where D>9 is the instruction to leave the point as digitized or A>B>1>D>9 for a graded non-smoothed point. 2. Used to indicate placement of a drill hole (for example, pocket placement). It may be followed by a B and a grade rule.
Delimiter	Indicates the end of a command or set of commands

The Digitizing Menu

The digitizing menu, as shown in Figure 3.5, is located on the digitizing table, usually on the lower left-hand corner, though it may be placed elsewhere on more sophisticated tables. It is used to enter identification data, such as style name, piece category, and piece description. It is also used to indicate which rule table is to be used. Data are entered by placing the crosshairs of the cursor on an instruction or letter on the menu and pressing the A button on the cursor.

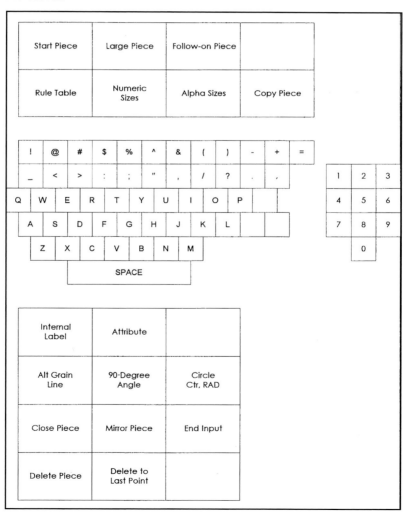

Figure 3.5 A digitizing menu

48

Preparing a Sloper/Pattern for Digitizing

Traditionally, finished production patterns were graded. As more companies are using computer-aided design, it is now common for slopers to be graded before patterns are made. In this chapter, slopers will be digitized into the computer using grade rules. Some people find it easier to add grades in the Pattern Design system after a piece has been digitized.

Before digitizing, it is necessary to give a sloper a name and category, and to determine the grade rule to be used for each grading point and the location of notches and internal points. This information should be clearly specified on the sloper so that it can be easily accessed during digitizing.

By convention, in flat pattern and draping, pattern pieces are always designed using the right (as opposed to the left) side of the body of the potential wearer. The exception is an asymmetrical piece, which requires a full pattern piece. Sloper pieces are usually placed on the digitizing table with the center front at the bottom and the top of the garment at the right; therefore, all notations should be written on the piece so they can be read from this orientation. This convention is different from traditional patternmaking. It allows the patternmaker to use the same rule on front and back pieces.

Hint for Success

Mark the sloper pieces so notations can be easily read. Remember that the sloper or pattern pieces are displayed as they were on the Cartesian graph in Chapter 2. *pg 25*

Marking the Sloper for Digitizing

Please refer to Figure 3.6 while marking the sloper for digitizing. It is suggested that each sloper or pattern piece be marked with the following information:

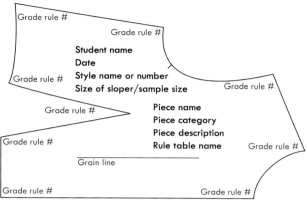

Figure 3.6 Diagram of a sloper ready for digitizing.

1. Designer or patternmaker's name, which will not be digitized but will aid in identification of the piece.
2. Style name or number.
3. Size of the sloper.
4. Piece name, which must be unique for every piece within a storage area. The piece name may have up to 20 alphanumeric characters. It is best to have a convention for naming pieces (for example, the patternmaker's initials, the style number, and the piece type—js123ftsk). Fabric type can also be added: *L* for lining, *I* for interfacing, and *M* for main fabric. Keep the name to as few characters as possible while still providing adequate and unique information. The longer the name, the more time it takes to enter it into the computer and the greater the chance for errors.
5. Piece category, which should be unique for each piece within a **model** (garment or item). Like piece names, there should be a convention for naming categories. They can be used on different models. For example, *skbk* can be used for skirt back in all models. A category cannot be duplicated within a model (i.e., you can only have one skbk in a model). The category name may have up to 20 alphanumeric characters, but it is best to keep the number as low as reasonably possible.
6. Piece description, which does not have to be included in digitizing, but it may be used to identify sloper size, alternative style numbers, and so on. It may have up to 20 alphanumeric characters and does not have to be unique.

7. The name of the rule table to be used to grade the sloper.
8. Grain line.
9. Numbered cardinal points.
10. Grade rule number at each cardinal point.
11. Notch type number.
12. Drill holes and internal lines.

Preparing the Software and Hardware for Digitizing

It is important to follow the exact procedure for digitizing a sloper. Before you start to digitize, check the information in your storage area and make sure that the digitizer is functioning correctly.

Checking the Data in Your Storage Area

In the AccuMark Explorer window, check that the storage area contains the following files: appropriate P-USER-EVIRON, appropriate rule table, appropriate annotation table, appropriate P-NOTCH table. These files should contain the appropriate data in the appropriate units of measure.

Checking the Digitizer

To test the digitizer, place the cursor on the digitizing table and press button A. You will hear a beep if there is communication between the computer and digitizer. If there is no beep, you may have to restart. Right click on the Edit Digitize icon (in the lower right-hand corner of the screen). See Figure 3.7.

Figure 3.7 Edit Digitize icon

Click on Restart in the menu. If there is still no beep or if the digitizing table/silhouette table or computer has been turned off, the following procedure should be followed:

1. Turn off the digitizer.
2. Turn off the host computer.
3. Remove all metal, objects, and miscellany from the digitizer table top.

4. Start the digitizer again.

5. Place the crosshairs of the 16-button cursor over the Application 2 box (for a Silhouette table, use the Application 1 box) on the lower right-hand side of the tabletop. You should hear a series of quick chirps. Press and hold the 2 button on the 16-button cursor until you hear a long tone followed by a short beep. This should take five to seven seconds.

6. Turn on the computer.

Test the digitizer by placing the 16-button cursor over the Start Piece box on the lower left-hand side of the digitizer and press the A button. You will hear a beep if communications have been restored between the computer and the digitizer. For the silhouette table, you may test if it is functioning properly by entering Pattern Design system at the tabletop and selecting draft mode.

Digitizing Troubleshooting

When inputting a sloper on the digitizing table, a beep should be heard each time a button on the cursor is pressed. The beep signals that the computer is acknowledging receipt of the digitizer's signal. No beep may result when the digitizing storage area is full or the files where the digitizing data are stored are corrupt.

The following is the procedure for deleting the raw digitized data and repairing the digitizer control file:

1. Select Gerber LaunchPad>AccuMark Explorer, Utilities. Double click on the AccuMark Utilities icon, then select Storage Area>Delete Digitizer Files. (See Figure 3.8.)

Figure 3.8 AccuMark Utilities icon

2. The system will prompt you that this will delete raw digitized data and ask if you are sure you want to continue. Click on OK. This will delete the raw digitized data.

3. Once again, from AccuMark Explorer, Utilities, select Storage Area. From the resultant drop-down menu, select Check. On the lower right-hand part of the screen, click once in the little box beside Digitizer, then select OK. This procedure will repair the control file (i.e., a directory file) for the raw digitizer files that were deleted above.

> ## Hint for Success
>
> Static buildup on the surface of the digitizer can result in a loss of data and configuration. It is possible that static build-up created by the digitizing cursor moving over the table may cause the digitizer to malfunction. This will result in the loss of data and require starting the process again. Touching the computer's case periodically may help to dissipate static on your body. It is recommended not to wear acrylic sweaters or combinations of wool and nylon. This problem will be especially prevalent in the winter due to lower humidity.

Digitizing a Sloper Piece

Before beginning the digitizing process, set up your computer so that your digitized pieces are saved in your storage area. To do this, follow these steps:

1. Select Gerber LaunchPad>AccuMark Explorer, Utilities>AccuMark Explorer icon.
2. From the View menu, select Process Preferences. In the Process Preferences box, select Digitize Processing. See Figure 3.9.

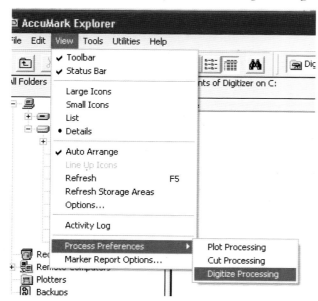

Figure 3.9 Digitize Processing drop-down menu

This produces the Verify Options dialog box. Click on the button to the right of the storage area name in the Verify Storage box. This produces a look-up table with a list of all the storage areas available in the C: drive. Select your storage area and click on Open. The name of your storage area should appear in the Verify Options box. If it is correct, click on OK. If it is not correct, create a new storage area and import your tables and other data into that storage area.

Tape your pattern piece to the digitizer table with the orientation as shown in Chapter 2, at least three inches from the edge of the table. You are now ready to start digitizing. Review the instructions in the box on page 46 on how to use the digitizing cursor. The complete process for digitizing a sloper is summarized in Table 3.2.

Accessing and Storing Digitized Data

After digitizing, the data are temporarily stored in the digitizer file. The raw digitized data can be saved in the digitizer storage area on the C: drive as "raw digitized data." Data must be retrieved, verified, and saved in a storage area before it can be used for patternmaking or plotting. It is also advisable to display the piece graded to ensure that the grade rules have been properly applied. First, the steps in these processes will be presented as though there have been no errors in the process or in the data that were entered. The steps for correcting errors will be discussed later in the chapter.

Retrieving and Verifying a Digitized Piece

When a piece is digitized, the information received from the digitizing table is stored in the Digitizer storage area, a temporary storage area. After you have finished digitizing one or more sloper/pattern pieces, it is necessary to check the accuracy of the digitizing process. This is known as **piece verification**. Pieces must be retrieved before they are verified. If a piece can be retrieved, then the process of digitizing has been correctly performed. Note that there may be other errors, such as the application of wrong grade rules or notch identifications. These errors can be corrected later. The steps in retrieving a digitized file are as follows:

1. Select Gerber LaunchPad>AccuMark Explorer, Utilities>AccuMark Explorer icon.
2. Click on Digitizer in the left-hand column of the window. The name of the digitized piece should appear in the Contents of Digitizer in the right-hand column of the window. If the name is not there, there is a problem with the process, and it may have to be repeated.

Table 3.2 Order for Digitizing Pieces

Order	Button	Location	Procedure
1	A	Menu	Click on Start Piece
2	A	Menu	Spell out piece name
3	*	Anywhere on table	
4	A	Menu	Spell out piece category
5	*	Anywhere on table	
6	A	Menu	Spell out piece description If not wanted, skip, and go to #8 (press * for #5 followed by * for # 7)
7	*	Anywhere on table	
8	A	Menu	Click on Rule Table
9	A	Menu	Spell out rule table name
10	*	Anywhere on table	
11	A	Piece	Location of left end of grain line
12	A	Piece	Location of right end of grain line
13	*	Anywhere on table	
14	A	Piece	Starting at the bottom left-hand corner, digitize all the points on the perimeter until you reach the one prior to the first digitized point. For nongraded points, press the A button at each point. For graded points, press A, then B, then the number button that corresponds to the grade rule number. Non graded notches are entered by pressing A>C>notch type number. Graded notches are entered by pressing A>B>grade rule number>C>notch type number.
15	A	Menu	Click on Close Piece or Mirror Piece. Figure 3.10 shows the difference

			If no internal lines go to step 19
16	A	Menu	Click on Internal Label (See note.)
17	A	Menu	Select the label letter or number on the menu. The A label selected from the menu is used for a two point line. The D label selected from the menu is used for a drill hole.
18	A	Piece	Digitize the internal by pressing the A button (add grading if needed, i.e., A>B>grade rule number) After selecting the internal label D on the menu, you may continue pressing the A button on the cursor to mark many drill holes.
19	*	Anywhere on table	
20	A	Menu	Click on End Input

Note: Internal labels are used to indicate the position of drill holes for locating pockets, buttons, and other garment features and for internal lines which may be used for placement of annotations (special notes), and internal cutouts which are beyond the scope of this book. Annotations may be added later in the process.

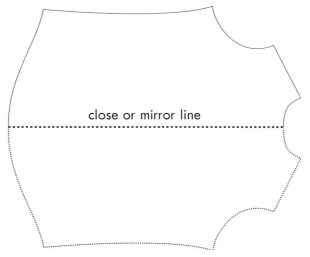

close or mirror line

Figure 3.10 Closing and mirroring digitized pieces. When mirror is used instead of close, only one side of a piece needs to be digitized. The system will create the other half of the piece.

3. Double click on the name of the piece to open the
EditDigitize window. See Figure 3.11.

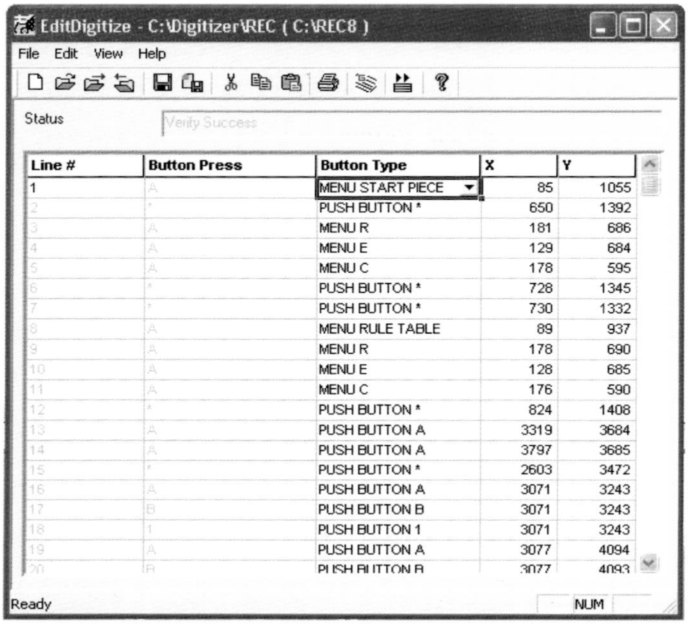

Figure 3.11 EditDigitize window

The EditDigitize window sequentially lists all the buttons
pushed during digitizing except the name of the piece. The
status bar will indicate if the data has been entered correctly.
If not, there will be an error message(s). Errors will be dealt
with in the next section. If the data was entered in the correct
order, the status bar will state "Verify Success." This means that
the process of digitizing was successful; however, there may
still be errors in grade rules applied or notch types.

4. Save the piece in your storage area by selecting File>Save As.
5. Return to the AccuMark Explorer window. Although the piece
   has been saved to your storage area, it may not appear in the
   storage area contents on the screen. To check that it has been
   saved, open a different storage area, and then reopen yours.

Digitizing Errors

Some errors in digitizing can be corrected, though sometimes it is
easier just to redigitize the piece. Basically, there are four types of
errors:

- Missing data
- Misplaced data
- Errors in the process of digitizing
- Errors in the points, grades, or notches digitized

Missing Data

If the name does not appear in the Digitizer contents in the AccuMark Explorer window, this may mean that

- you may have failed to End Input with the cursor in the AccuMark menu. To correct this, simply go to the Digitizer and complete the process by selecting Delimiter>End Input.
- the digitized data are in different storage areas. Select View>Process Preferences>Digitize Processing>Verify Options and select a different storage area (try some of the Gerber training storage areas, such as Data 70).
- the error in the process was so serious that the piece must be redigitized.

Misplaced Data

If the status bar message in EditDigitize is "Could not read RULE TABLE," there is either an error in processing or EditDigitize has not accessed the storage area containing the rule table used in digitizing. The title bar should have the name of the storage area that contains the desired rule table. If it is correct, then there is an error in the digitizing process—see the next section. If it is incorrect, then it is necessary to change the data being used by EditDigitize. To do so, follow these steps:

1. From the AccuMark Explorer screen, select View>Process Preferences>Digitize Processing. See Figure 3.9.
2. In the Verify Options box, click on the button to the right of the name of the storage area in use.
3. In the Lookup dialog box, select the name of the storage area containing the desired rule table. Click on OK. This storage area name will now appear in the Verify Options box. Click on OK again.
4. Click on the name of the digitized piece in the digitizer storage area found in the AccuMark Explorer window. The EditDigitize window will appear with the name of the correct storage area in the title bar. If there are no other errors, then "Verify Success" will appear in the Status field.

58

Errors in the Process of Digitizing

If there is an error in the digitizing process, an error message will appear in the Status field of the EditDigitize window. The error message will indicate the line number of the first (and hopefully the last) error. The line where the error occurs will also be highlighted in red. As each error is corrected, the next error is highlighted. Please note that the location of the error may be one line higher than the box that is highlighted. Read the error message carefully. It does not change when the error is fixed.

Carefully work down the columns of Buttons Press and Button Type. Rows can be inserted or deleted, and button types may be changed. To make corrections, click in the appropriate Button Type box:

1. Right click in the box to access a drop-down menu that contains the following options: Cut, Copy, Paste, Insert Row, Insert Row At End, Delete Row, and Clear Contents. See Figure 3.12.

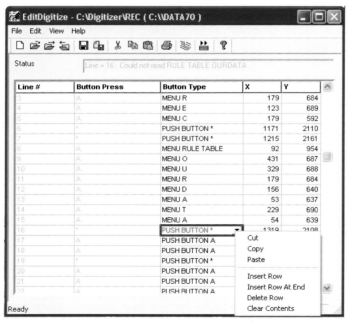

Figure 3.12 EditDigitize Button Type drop-down menu (produced by right clicking)

2. Left click on the arrow for a list of button type options. Function keys can also be used in correcting errors. See Figure 3.13.

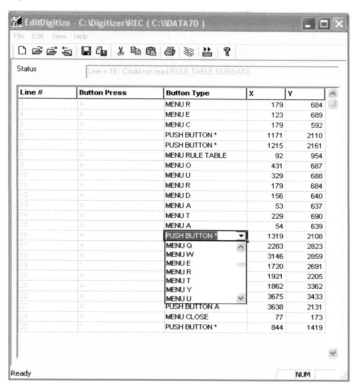

Figure 3.13 EditDigitize Button Type options menu

Use of the function keys is described in Table 3.3. When all corrections have been made, "Verify Success" will appear in the Status field.

Errors in the Points, Grades, or Notches Digitized

After a piece has been verified and stored as a piece (not stored as raw digitized data), there can still be errors in points, grades, and notches. These errors can only be seen when the piece is displayed or displayed graded. To display a piece, click on the piece name in the contents area of the storage area being used. This will open Pattern Design. Errors in points, grades, and notches can be corrected using Pattern Design. Later chapters will address Pattern Design.

Table 3.3 Use of the Function Keys in Correcting Errors (in the Edit Digitize Window)

Function key	Function
F4 = Lookup	The Look Up window will list all the menu buttons and push button choices. See Figure 3.12. The look up window is also accessible as a right click on the mouse. Select the one you need and press Enter. This will take you back to the EditDigitize window. If there are more errors, the cursor will automatically highlight the next error.
F6 = Truncate	This button will delete from the field anything that is to the right of the cursor.
F8 = Insert a row	This button will insert a row. The row is inserted above the row in which the cursor is placed. If you forgot to put in a push button or a * or missed any steps during digitizing use F8 followed by F4 (The Lookup window is also accessible by right clicking the mouse) to select what to insert.
Shift + F8 = Delete a row	If you put in an extra letter or * you can delete the whole row and shift the next row up.

Hint for Success

In the EditDigitize window, the columns of button press and Button Type do not show the name of the piece being digitized. Line 1 is Menu Start Piece. The next delimiter and piece name are omitted. Line 2 is the delimiter before Piece Category. Refer to Table 3.2, "Order for Digitizing Pieces."

Digitizing Exercises

These exercises were designed to help you master the skills covered in this chapter. Getting started in AccuMark using these skills as your foundation will set you on your way to a smooth design process using Gerber software.

1. Digitize a rectangle. For this exercise, students will use the rectangle, rules, and rule table created in Chapter 2.

   a. The following should appear on your rectangular pattern piece:

   Your name

   Date

   Size of the rectangle (M)

   Piece name—this piece should be named REC with your initials (e.g., RECJS)

   Piece category (REC)

   Rule table name—this is the rule table created in Chapter 2. It is labeled REC.

   Grain line

   Cardinal points marked with the grade rule to be used

   A notch labeled with its type and grade rule

   Two drill holes each labeled with a grade rule

   b. At a computer connected to the digitizer, create a new storage area (named with your initials and the date). Import the data required for this exercise:

   Annotation Table

   P-CUTTER

   P-LAY RULE SEARCH

   P-MARKER PLOT

   P-NOTCH

   P-PIECE PLOT

   P-USER ENVIRON

   Rule table (REC)

   c. Digitize this pattern piece. Verify, correct, and store the piece in your storage area. Later, this piece can be printed and plotted.

2. Select a sloper to be used. It can be a bodice, skirt, or sleeve piece. For this exercise, you will need an appropriate rule table, such as one using the rules in Appendix 2. You may need to create your own rule table, or there may be one provided by your instructor.

   a. On the sloper, write the following information:

      Your name

      Date

      Style name or number of the piece

      Size of sloper/sample size

      Piece name

      Piece category

      Piece description

      Rule table name

   b. Check that there is a grain line on the sloper.

   c. Using a suitable grade rule table, mark each of the points to be graded on your pattern with the appropriate grade rule.

   d. At a computer connected to the digitizer, create a new storage area (named with your initials and the date).

   e. In the storage area, check the P-USER ENVIRON to make sure that you are working with the Imperial system. Import your notch table, rule table, and annotation table.

   f. Digitize this pattern piece.

   g. Verify, correct, and store the piece in your storage area. Later, this piece can be printed and plotted or used to make patterns.

Ordering a Piece Plot

After a piece has been digitized, it may be plotted. A piece plot order allows the plotting of individual pieces in the base size or in a selection of sizes. It is usually best to plot a group of pieces using a marker. See Chapter 10, "Marker Making," for more information. It is important that the storage area containing the piece to be plotted has an appropriate annotation table. A table may be copied or dragged from another storage area. There are two ways of ordering a piece plot:

1. Select Gerber LaunchPad>Plotting and Cutting>Piece Plot icon. See Figure 3.14.

Figure 3.14 Piece Plot icon

2. In the AccuMark Explorer window, right click on the name of the piece to be plotted. From the drop-down menu, select Send to Plotter.

Completing the Piece Plot Window

Using the Piece Plot window is the best method to order a piece plot immediately after digitizing a piece. It may also be used for pieces that have been stored. If you are planning to plot previously stored pieces, create a storage area on a computer that is connected to a plotter. Import your data into that storage area. Check that you are in the correct storage area and using the correct units of measurement.

64

Filling in the Piece Plot Window

Follow these instructions to fill out the Piece Plot window:

1. *Selecting a piece*: Pieces are entered into the table at the bottom of the Piece Plot window. See Figure 3.15.

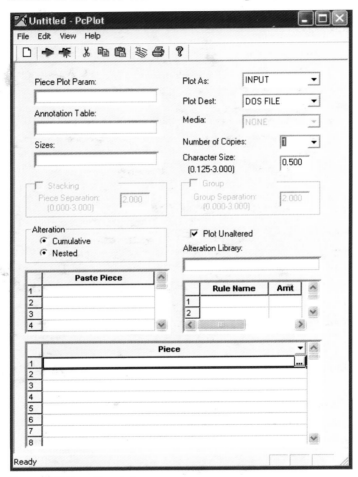

Figure 3.15 Piece Plot window

   a. If the window has been accessed by clicking on a piece in AccuMark Explorer, that piece will automatically be entered in the piece field.

    b. If the window has been accessed from the Gerber LaunchPad, click in the first row of the Piece field to highlight that row, click on the button to the right of the row to select the storage area that contains your piece. Select your piece, and then select Open.

2. *Piece Plot Param*: This is a look-up field. The default is P-PIECE PLOT. If a scaled version of the piece is needed, then a different piece plot parameter table may be created and used.

3. *Annotation Table*: This is a look-up field. Select the appropriate table. Generally, a company will have only one annotation table that is appropriate for all of its work.

4. *Sizes*: From this look-up field, select the sizes desired. The default is to leave the field empty, which means that all of the sizes will be plotted.

5. *Plot As*: Select from the following options:
   a. *Input*: Plots the piece as it was digitized
   b. *F-Rotation*: Plots the piece rotated 90 degrees
   c. *Model*: Plots both left and right sides
   Note that the recommended setting is Input or Model.

6. *Plot Destination*: This field provides two choices:
   a. *LOCAL*: Sends the file directly to the plotter. (If the computer is not attached to a plotter, this option is not available.)
   b. *DOS file*: Saves the plot data as a DOS file

7. *Number of Copies*: This is a fill-in field or drop-down menu. Select the desired number of copies.

8. *Character Size*: This is a fill-in field, and it determines the size of the annotations plotted. It can range from 0.125 inches to 3 inches.

9. *Group*: If Group is checked, all of the pieces sent to the plotter will be plotted in a group.

10. *Group Separation*: This determines the separation of group plotted pieces.

11. *Stacking*: If Stacking is selected, pieces will be plotted side by side. This uses less plotter paper.

12. *Piece Separation*: If Stacking is selected, it is necessary to indicate the desired distance between the pieces by filling in a number in this field. The separation should be small enough to save paper but large enough to still allow the pieces to be cut apart.

After the window has been completed, check that the plotter is ready. Select File>Process.

Piece Plot Exercise

Use each of the methods just described to plot your rectangle and pattern piece.

Summary

Digitizing is the process of tracing a sloper/pattern piece into the computer and entering information about that sloper/pattern piece. A digitizer is a device used to enter information into a software system. It consists of a digitizing table, a digitizing cursor, and a digitizing menu. The digitizing table is a large work area that can be adjusted by height and angle. It is connected by cables to the computer and to the digitizing cursor. Pieces to be digitized are taped on the digitizing table. The computer receives signals from the digitizing cursor. The digitizing cursor has two parts: the crosshairs and the buttons. The crosshairs are used to determine exact coordinates on the sloper and instructions on the digitizing menu.

Before digitizing, it is necessary to give a sloper a name and category and to determine the grade rule to be used for each grading point and the location of notches and internal points. This information is written on the sloper so that it can be accessed easily during digitizing. It is important to follow the exact procedure for digitizing a sloper.

When inputting a sloper at the digitizing table, a beep should be heard each time a button on the cursor is pressed. When a piece is digitized, the information received from the digitizing table is temporarily stored in the Digitizer storage area. After digitizing, it is necessary to verify the piece, which involves checking the accuracy of the digitizing process. The digitized piece can be stored as digitized data, not as a piece, and it cannot be used for plotting or patternmaking, but it can be retrieved, displayed, corrected, and then stored as a digitized piece. Before storing a piece to the AccuMark system, it is advisable to view the information on the computer and check that the shape of the piece, notch placement, grading, and so on are correct.

Some errors in digitizing can be corrected, but sometimes it may be easier just to redigitize the piece. Basically, there are two types of errors: errors in the process of digitizing and errors in the points or grades digitized. Errors in the process of digitizing can be corrected using the EditDigitize window. Errors in points, grades, and notches can be corrected using Pattern Design.

Key Terms

attribute   piece verification
dead zone   silhouette table
model

Review Questions

1. List the three parts of a digitizer.
2. What are the two functions of the digitizing cursor?
3. List five pieces of information that should be marked on each sloper piece before digitizing.
4. What is piece verification?
5. Why is it advisable to view a piece on the computer before storing it in AccuMark?
6. What are the two main types of digitizing errors?

CHAPTER FOUR

Getting Started in Pattern Design

Objectives

After studying this chapter, you will be able to

- Open and customize the pattern design screen.
- Use the commands in the File menu.
- Understand the different cursor shapes.
- Use the Piece icon drop-down menu and manage pieces on the screen.
- Customize the working environment further using Preferences/Options.

Introduction to Pattern Design

Gerber Pattern Design is used to create and alter pattern pieces. Patterns are not created from scratch, but rather by using slopers to develop patterns in a way similar to the flat pattern process.

For Pattern Design, the storage areas created for AccuMark are used. The User Environment table, Notch Parameter table, and Rule table will be the same as those used in AccuMark for digitizing sloper pieces. The tables created previously need not be changed.

As you read the book, follow the learning activities using pattern pieces or slopers. These may be ones you produced by digitizing, ones your instructor has provided, or samples from the Gerber training library (these may be named Data 70, Data 70 AE, or Silhouette 2000). Some of the Gerber pieces have been linked together in a model. A **model** is all the pattern pieces required for a particular style.

The Pattern Design Screen

The pattern design screen is the area in which patterns are created. There are two ways to access this screen.

1. Select Gerber LaunchPad either from your desktop shortcut or the All Programs menu of your computer. Select Pattern Processing, Digitizing, PDS from the LaunchPad, then select the Pattern Design icon shown in Figure 4.1.

Figure 4.1 Pattern Design icon

2. Select AccuMark Explorer, Utilities from the LaunchPad. Click on the AccuMark Explorer icon. Select your storage area to show a list of rules and pattern pieces in your storage area. Click on the name of a pattern piece to be used. This will take you to the Pattern Design screen.

Screen Layout

The screen layout can either be left as the default or customized to meet individual preferences. The default layout, as shown in

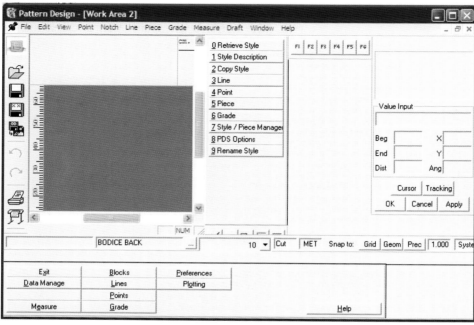

Figure 4.2 Default layout of the Pattern Design work area

Figure 4.2, contains many toolbars and a relatively small work area.
The most useful elements for patternmaking are:

Work area The drafting of patterns is done in this area. See
Figure 4.3.

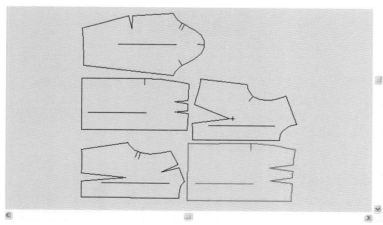

Figure 4.3 A work area

Function menu bar The function menu bar is located at the top of the screen. It organizes the features used in patternmaking. Each function has a drop-down menu that contains a list of related commands that appear when that function is selected. See Figure 4.4.

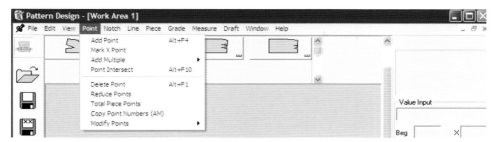

Figure 4.4 The Function menu bar with an example of a drop-down menu

Toolbar Depending on personal preference, the toolbar can be located at either side, the top, or the bottom of the screen. It can be customized to hold the items that are used frequently, such as zoom in, zoom out, undo, and redo. See Figure 4.5.

Icon bar The icon bar may be located at the top or bottom of the screen. It shows the pieces selected for use. See Figure 4.6.

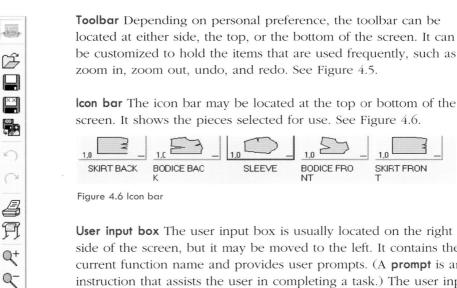

Figure 4.6 Icon bar

User input box The user input box is usually located on the right side of the screen, but it may be moved to the left. It contains the current function name and provides user prompts. (A **prompt** is an instruction that assists the user in completing a task.) The user input box is also used to input specific measurements and other options required by the current command. This box is very important, as it

Figure 4.5 Toolbar

provides instructions and information needed to perform a command. See Figure 4.7.

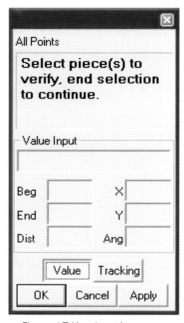

Figure 4.7 User input box

Information bar The information bar is usually located below the scroll bar at the bottom of the screen but can be placed at the top of the screen. See Figure 4.8.

Figure 4.8 Information bar

This bar contains the following information:
- Model or style name—If the piece being worked on is not part of a model or style, then this field will be empty.
- Name of currently selected piece.
- Current pieces button—Clicking on this button provides a list of all the pieces currently in the work area.
- Size of the current piece.

- Cut or Sew—indicates which type of line is currently on the outside of the piece.
- Unit of Measurement chosen—This will be either IMP for the Imperial system or MET for the Metric system. This depends on the user environment parameters and rule table located in the storage area you are using. It is very important to be working in the appropriate measurement system.
- The remaining buttons are used for advanced projects.

Customizing the Pattern Design Screen Layout

Other elements seen on the default screen are not generally used for learning Pattern Design. When they are removed from the screen, a larger work area is available. To customize the screen, go to View on the Function menu bar and select Screen Layout. Figure 4.9 lists the preferences for the layout that will be appropriate for use in this chapter.

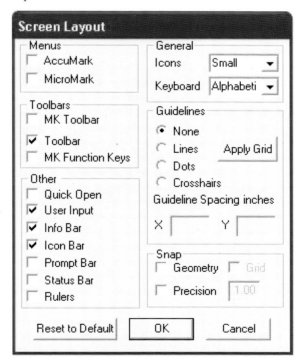

Figure 4.9 Screen Layout dialog box

74

Figure 4.10 illustrates the recommended screen layout.

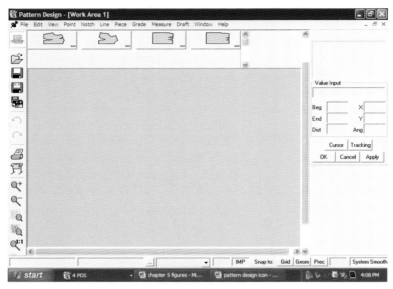

Figure 4.10 Recommended settings for screen layout

File Menu

The File menu is a drop-down menu accessed from the toolbar at the top of the screen. See Figure 4.11. The following commands are the most useful ones in this menu:

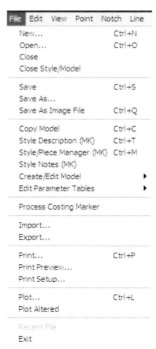

New: New will open a new work area. It is possible to have multiple work areas open at the same time. Work areas can be minimized, maximized, or resized using the buttons at the upper right-hand corner of the screen. Work areas are identified by the last piece or model opened.

Open: Clicking on Open produces a dialog box. It allows for the selection of pieces to be brought into the work area.

Figure 4.11 File drop-down menu

Close: This option closes the current work area. It is also possible to close a work area by using the *X* in the upper right-hand corner of the work area screen. By clicking on this *X*, Pattern Design will close and all work not previously saved will be lost. There is no prompt asking if you wish to save your work. It is advisable to save before closing.

Save: Choose this option to store pieces or models using their original names. This may cause overwriting and the loss of pieces that may be needed in their original form. It is usually best to use the Save As command.

Save As: This command is used to save a piece or model with a new name or in a different location.

Create/Edit Model: This command is used for putting pattern pieces together as a model. Its use will be covered in a later chapter.

Print: The Print command is used to print what is displayed in the work area.

Print Preview: Print Preview allows for the viewing of the screen as it will appear when it is printed.

Plot: The Plot command is used to plot an individual pattern piece or a selection of pattern pieces directly from Pattern Design. However, in many academic situations, student work stations may not be directly connected to a plotter.

Cursor Shapes

The shape of a cursor will change according to its purpose at a given time. Table 4.1 has diagrams of different cursor shapes and indicates the role of each shape. Understanding the function of each type of cursor can prevent irritation. For example, if the software is not functioning as expected, checking the cursor shape may indicate that the selected command is not correct for the expected use.

When the cursor appears as a cross with a small box to the bottom right, it indicates that there are additional right-button options. These options will change according to the command being used. Often the right-button options are simply OK or Cancel and can be used as a quick way to select an option. Other times the list of options is extensive and allows for accurate location of lines, points, and other features.

Table 4.1 Cursor Shapes

Cursor Shape	Indicates
↖	Normal mode.
↔ (four-way arrow)	Selected point, piece, or thumbtack can be moved.
✳	Object closest to the cursor is selected.
+	A command is active.
+▤	A command with additional right menu button options.
⊕ (magnifier)	Zoom in command is currently selected.

Opening, Saving, Printing, and Closing

Commonly used commands in the File menu are Open, Save, Save As, Print, and Close.

Opening

After accessing Pattern Design, it is necessary to find the models or pieces needed and to bring them into the icon bar. From the icon bar, they can be moved into the work area.

Bringing Pieces to the Icon Bar

To bring pieces into the icon bar, follow this process:

1. Select File>Open. See Figure 4.12.

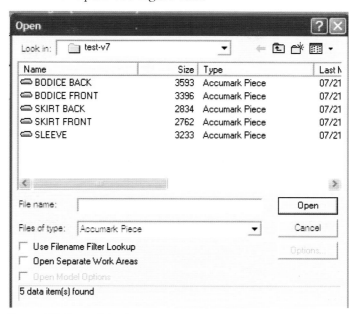

Figure 4.12 Open dialog box

2. In the Look in: field, use the down arrow to display the storage areas available. Highlight and select the desired storage area.
3. In the Files of type: field, use the down arrow to display the types of files available. The files appropriate for student pattern-making are AccuMark Piece and AccuMark Model. AccuMark Piece will produce a list of pieces available in the selected storage area. AccuMark model will show a list of models in the storage area. Select either AccuMark Piece or AccuMark Model.
4. Select the model or pieces needed by highlighting them. Click on Open to place the pieces into the icon bar. (To select more than one piece, press the control key while clicking on each piece in turn.) Alternatively, a model name or pattern piece name can be typed into the File name: field, and Open selected to place the model or piece in the icon bar.

Moving Pieces from the Icon Bar into the Work Area

Select a piece in the icon bar by clicking once on it. *Do not drag.* Using the mouse, without holding any buttons down, move the piece into the work area. Click again to release the piece.

To move multiple pieces into the work area, press and hold the control key on the keyboard, click on each of the pieces needed, and release the control key. Click on one of the pieces or press the space bar, and the pieces will automatically move into the work area. To clear the work area, press F10.

Saving Pieces

It is usually best to use the Save As command. The Save and Save As commands are in the File drop-down menu. The Save command saves a piece, but the original version is overwritten. There is no prompt asking if you wish to overwrite the original. The Save command produces the prompt "Select piece(s) to save, end selection to continue" in the user input box. It is necessary to select the piece or pieces to save by clicking on them. Then click on OK in the user input box or right click on the mouse and select OK from the drop-down menu.

Selecting the Save As command produces the prompt "Select piece to Save As." Selecting a piece by clicking on it opens the Save As dialog box. See Figure 4.13.

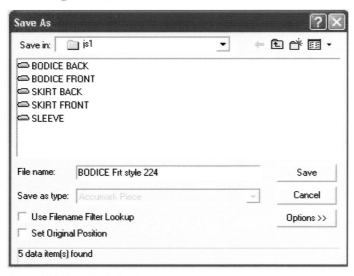

Figure 4.13 Save As dialog box

In the Save in field, select your storage area. In the File name field, type in the new name of your piece. Once a new name is created and a storage area selected, click on Save.

Pieces saved in Pattern Design should also be saved on a removable storage medium. To do so, open AccuMark Explorer and check that the newly saved pieces are in your storage folder. If the names of the new pieces are not in your folder, close the folder by selecting the C: drive, and then reopen the folder. The names of the newly saved pieces should be visible. Export the storage folder to a removable storage medium as described in Chapter 1.

Print

The Print command is in the File drop-down menu. Selecting the Print command produces the Print dialog box shown in Figure 4.14.

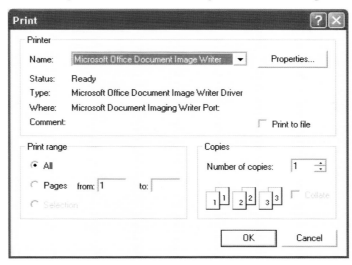

Figure 4.14 Print dialog box

Select the printer to which the computer is connected. Select the number of copies required. Although the dialog box may indicate that several pages can be printed, the system only prints what is visible on the screen. To print, select OK.

Closing

It is important to Save or Save As before closing. To close a work area, select File>Close. To close Pattern Design, click the *X* icon at the top right of the screen.

80

Piece Icon Drop-Down Menu

Right clicking on a piece icon in the icon bar produces a drop-down menu. See Figure 4.15.

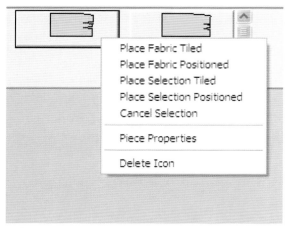

Figure 4.15 Piece icon drop-down menu

Selecting Piece Properties from the drop-down menu opens a window that contains all of the relevant information about the piece, such as its name, category, storage area, and the rule table used. See Figure 4.16.

Piece Properties - SKIRT BACK

Property	Setting
Device	C:
Storage Area	TEST-V7
Model/Style	Model not found.
Rule Table	OURDATA
Piece Name	SKIRT BACK
Category	SKBACK
Description	
Fabric	
Digitized Boundary	
Grade Seam / Co...	
Auto Update Seam	
Adjust Seam Grad...	
Seam Extensions	
Move End Points	Yes
Points	Boundary = 33; Total...

Figure 4.16 Piece Properties drop-down window

When you select Delete icon from the drop-down box, the icon is removed from the icon bar. Note that if the piece is newly created and has not been saved, it will be lost.

Managing Pieces on the Screen

Pieces can be managed by using function keys, toolbar icons, and the piece drop-down menu. These commands allow you to move pieces around the work area, zoom in and out, remove pieces from the work area, return pieces to the icon menu, undo and redo commands, identify pieces, and find information about piece properties.

Function Keys (F keys)

The **function keys** on the keyboard can be used as shortcuts for certain functions. The function keys are located above the numbers on a standard keyboard.

F2: Separates pieces that overlap and locates all pieces so that they can be seen together in the work area.

F3: Returns the work area to a full screen that shows all the pieces in use.

F4: Fills the screen with a piece that has been identified. Do not click on the desired piece. Place the cursor over a piece and its outline will change color, indicating that it has been selected, then press F4.

F7: Brings the zoom in cursor into the work area. The functioning of the zoom in cursor is explained later in this chapter.

F8: Zooms out

F10: Clears all work from the work area.

Toolbar Icons

The toolbar icons provide shortcuts to some commands for managing pieces. Some frequently used icons are presented in Table 4.2.

Table 4.2 Toolbar Icons

Image	Name	How It Functions
	Open	A shortcut to the Open dialog box and equivalent to selecting File>Open.
	Save	A shortcut to the Save command and equivalent to selecting File>Save.
	Save As	A shortcut to the Save As command and equivalent to selecting File>Save As.
	Undo	Clicking this icon will undo the last command; it may be clicked up to 20 times to undo a series of actions.
	Redo	Selecting this icon will redo actions that were undone; it may be clicked several times to redo a series of actions.
	Zoom In	Either press F7 or click on this symbol on the tool bar. Use the mouse and click on a spot near the area you want to enlarge. Move the mouse to create a square and click again. (Do not drag as you might do in other software applications.)
	Zoom Out	Click on the icon to see more of the work area; clicking again allows you to see still more of the work area. This is the equivalent of pressing the F8 key.
	Full Scale	A shortcut for F3 that returns the work area to a full screen that shows all pieces.

Piece Drop-Down Menu

Right clicking on a piece in the work area produces the piece drop-down menu, as shown in Figure 4.17.

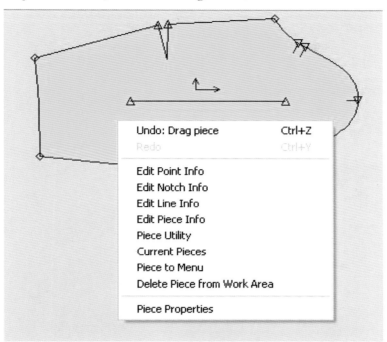

Figure 4.17 Piece drop-down menu

When no command has been selected, the drop-down menu allows you to undo the last command. The following is a list of some of the important functions in the piece drop-down menu:

Undo: Undoes the last action. The software allows for 20 "undos."

Redo: Redoes the last undo.

Current Pieces: Provides a list of pieces in the work area.

Piece to Menu: Removes a piece from the work area and sends it to the icon bar. This piece is not automatically saved.

Delete Piece from Work Area: Erases the piece from the work area. If the piece has not been saved, it is permanently deleted, unless it is recovered immediately by using the Undo command.

Piece Properties: Produces the Piece Properties drop-down box. See Figure 4.16.

84

Preferences/Options

In addition to providing options for the screen layout, the View menu can be used to select preferred working criteria and to customize elements of the screen environment. Selection of Preferences/Options in the View drop-down menu produces a dialog box labeled Preferences/Options. Information about the Paths, General, Color, and Display tabs will be discussed.

Paths Tab of Preferences/Options

The Paths tab of the Preferences/Options dialog box provides the opportunity to confirm that the correct storage area is in use (see Figure 4.18).

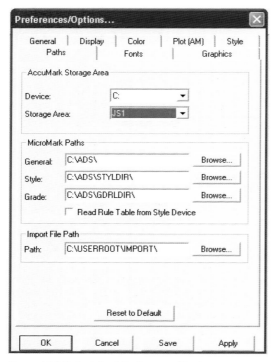

Figure 4.18 Paths tab of Preferences/Options

By using the drop-down menu in the Storage Area: field, it is possible to select a different storage area. This will automatically change the rule table and user environment parameters to the ones in that storage area. Selecting default in this tab will take you to a training storage area (Data 70) provided with the software. Generally, it is best to avoid this storage area because it may function in the Metric system. If settings are changed, it is necessary to click the Apply button, and then click the Save button to make the settings permanent.

General Tab of Preferences/Options

Figure 4.19 shows the General tab of the Preferences/Options dialog box.

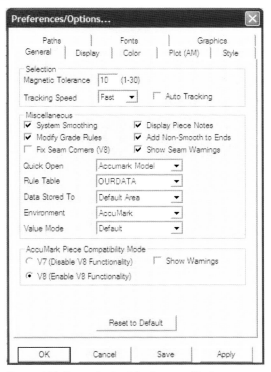

Figure 4.19 General tab of Preferences/Options

The default settings under the General tab are appropriate in most instances. The Rule Table: field is the only field on this tab that may need to be changed. It is a drop-down menu that allows you to select the correct rule table. If your rule table cannot be found, then it will be necessary to go back to the Paths tab and confirm that you are in the correct storage area.

86

Color Tab of Preferences/Options

The Color tab of the Preferences/Options dialog box allows you to select piece, nest, text, and miscellaneous colors. See Figure 4.20.

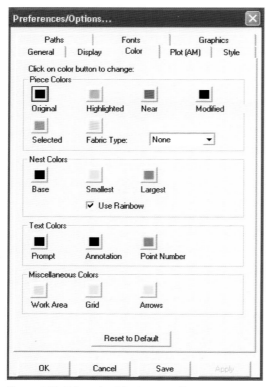

Figure 4.20 Color tab of Preferences/Options

Clicking on a color button produces a dialog box with color options. When a new color has been selected, click on OK in this box, then select Apply on the Color tab. Color choice is a matter of personal preference, but many people find it easier to read the prompts and annotations if they are in dark colors.

Display

See Figure 4.21 for an example of the Display tab of Preferences/ Options.

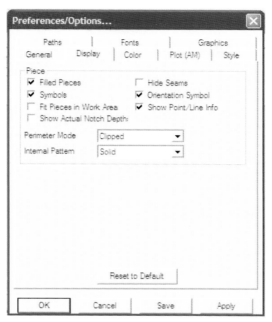

Figure 4.21 Display tab Preferences/Options

Selecting Filled Pieces shows the pieces on the screen in a different color from the work area, rather than as an outline of the shape. Some people prefer to work with filled pieces. Selecting Symbols means that symbols will be shown on pieces to indicate graded points and line ends. If Orientation Symbol is selected, a grain arrow will appear. If Show Point/Line info is selected, line and point information will appear in the work area when a point or line on a piece is selected.

Summary

Gerber Pattern Design is used to create and alter pattern pieces. Patterns are not created from "scratch" but rather by using slopers. The Pattern Design screen is the area in which patterns are created. The screen layout can be left as the default or customized to meet individual preferences.

Selecting File, located on the toolbar at the top of the screen, opens a drop-down menu that features the following commands: New, Open, Close, Save, Save As, Create/Edit Model, Print, Print Preview, and Plot.

Right clicking on a piece icon in the icon bar produces a drop-down menu. Selecting Piece Properties produces a box containing all the relevant information about the piece such as its name, category, storage area, and rule table used.

Pieces can be managed using function keys, toolbar icons, and the piece drop-down menu. These commands allow you to move pieces around the work area, zoom in and out, remove pieces from the work area, return pieces to the icon menu, undo and redo commands, identify pieces, and find information about piece properties.

In addition to providing options for the screen layout, Preferences/Options in the View menu, can be used to select preferred working criteria and to customize elements of the screen environment.

Key Terms

function keys

function menu bar

icon bar

information bar

model

prompt

toolbar

user input box

work area

Review Questions

1. What should you do if you have deleted all the pieces from the work area and want them back?
2. Describe two ways to access Pattern Design.
3. Why is it important to customize the Pattern Design screen?
4. Explain the function of the user input box.
5. Why does the cursor change shape? Why is this important?
6. Why is it usually best to Save As instead of Save?

CHAPTER FIVE

Measure, Edit, and View Functions

Objectives

After studying this chapter, you will be able to

- Use the Measure function.
- Use the View function.
- Use the Edit function.

Introduction

The Measure and View functions allow patternmakers to find information about pieces and measurements, such as distances between points and lines and the placement of points, notches, and graded points. The Edit drop-down menu provides information about points, lines, and pieces. It also allows users the opportunity to edit points, lines, and pieces.

Hint for Success

It is usually possible to change from one function to another by selecting the new function. Sometimes, it may be necessary to close one function/command before opening another. This can be done by clicking on Cancel in the user input box or by selecting Cancel from the drop-down menu that appears when you right click. Sometimes a dialog box will appear and sometimes a menu will appear, depending on the command.

Measure Function

By using the Measure function, it is possible to accurately measure lines, distances, angles, and areas. This is very useful when trueing slopers or patterns that have been made by draping and digitized into the computer. Accuracy is also necessary when new designs are being created, and pattern pieces are altered or cut into two or more pieces. Figure 5.1 shows each of the commands found under the Measure function.

Hint for Success

It is important that you work in the correct system of units (Imperial or Metric). To ensure that you are in your storage area and using your rule table, select View>Preferences/ Options. Refer to Chapter 4 for discussion of options in the Path and General tabs.

To use this command, complete the following steps:
1. Select Measure>Perimeter 2 Pt/Measure Along Piece.
2. Select the first point.
3. Select the second point.
4. A line and the measurement of the shortest distance between the two points will appear.
5. To continue using this command, select OK. If you do not select OK, then the measurement will disappear from the screen the next time the mouse is clicked.

Distance to Notch/Measure Along Piece

The Distance to Notch/Measure Along Piece command can be used to measure the distance between two sets of notches or the distance from a corner of a piece to a notch as shown in Figure 5.6.

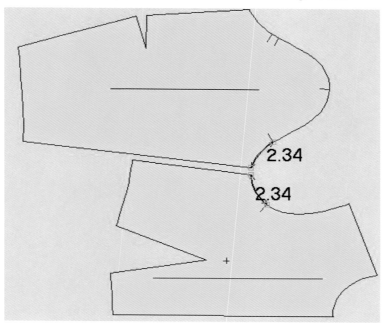

Figure 5.6 Pieces showing Distance to Notch/Measure Along Piece dimensions.

To access this command, complete the following steps:
1. Select Measure>Distance to Notch/Measure Along Piece.

2. Select a portion of a line between notches or between a notch and the end of a line.
3. A line and the measurement of the shortest distance between the two points will appear.
4. To continue using this command, select OK. If you do not select OK, then the measurement will disappear from the screen the next time the mouse is clicked.

Distance 2 Pt/Measure Straight

The Distance 2 Pt/Measure Straight command can be used to measure the shortest distance between any two points on a piece, such as from a dart tip to the bust apex. See Figure 5.7.

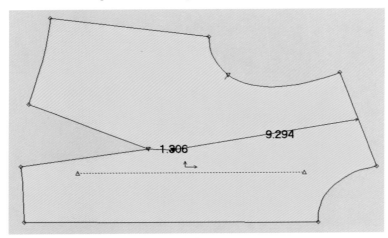

Figure 5.7 A piece showing Distance 2 Pt/Measure Straight dimensions

To use the command, complete the following steps:
1. Select Measure>Distance 2 Pt/Measure Straight.
2. Select the first point.
3. Select the second point.
4. A line connecting the two points and the measurement of the distance between them will appear automatically.
5. Select OK.

This command has a cursor right click drop-down menu. See Figure 5.8.

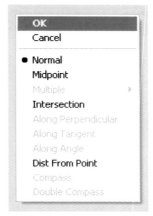

Figure 5.8 Right click drop-down menu for Distance 2 Pt/Measure Straight

This menu can be used to place the end of the line being measured at an intersection, at the midpoint of another line, or at a distance from a point. To do so, follow the prompts in the user input box. Note that if a midpoint or an intersection has been used, you must click on Normal to place the other end of a line to be measured at a visually selected point.

Piece Perimeter

The Piece Perimeter command measures the distance around the pattern piece. To use this command, complete the following steps:
1. Select Measure>Piece Perimeter.
2. Select the piece to be measured.
3. Select OK. The perimeter measurement will be displayed inside the piece.

Piece Area

The Piece Area command measures the area of a piece. To use this command, complete the following steps:
1. Select Measure>Piece Area.
2. Select the piece to be measured.
3. Select OK. The area measurement will be displayed inside the piece.

98

Angle

The Angle command enables you to measure the size of an angle within a piece. However, it will not measure the size of an angle in a dart because a dart is considered one line. To use this command, complete the following steps:
1. Select Measure>Angle.
2. Select the two lines that form the angle to be measured.
3. The measurement will appear in the Angle field in the user input box. Note that to measure a second angle, you need to repeat the process. If OK is selected, then the command will be terminated.

Clear Measurements

To immediately remove all measurements from the work area, select Clear Measurements from the Measure drop-down menu. The measurements can be restored using the Undo icon in the toolbar, the Undo command from the Edit drop-down menu, or selecting Undo in the cursor right click drop-down menu.

Hide/Show Measurements

Select Measure>Hide/Show Measurements to immediately hide all visible measurements or to show ones that have been hidden.

Measure Function Exercises

Before you begin the following two exercises, check that you are using the Imperial system of measurement.
1. Using a bodice front piece with a dart, find the following information:
   a. What is the length around the perimeter of the piece?
   b. What is the distance down the center front of the piece?
   c. How long is the shoulder seam?
   d. What is the distance from the bust point horizontally to the shoulder seam?
   e. What is the shortest distance from the bottom of the arm hole to the center front of the piece?
   f. Are the two sides of the dart the same length?
2. Using other pieces, find the following information:
   a. What is the difference between the length of the center front and the center back of the skirt?

b. What is the length of the skirt side seam?

c. What is the total distance around the skirt at the level of the notch?

d. What is the size of the waist of the skirt?

e. What is the size of the waist of the bodice?

f. On the sleeve, what is the distance from the underarm seam to the back notch?

g. On the bodice back, what is the distance from the armhole seam to the back notch?

h. On the skirt front, what is the angle between the waist and the side seam?

i. On the skirt back, what is the angle between the waist and the side seam?

View Function

The View function is used to determine the appearance of the screen and the content of the work area. The View menu is used to create customized toolbars. This process is not included in this book, but customized toolbars can be created by experienced patternmakers. The View menu also allows patternmakers to see information about the pieces in the work area. Many of the choices in the View menu, as shown in Figure 5.9, have additional drop-down menus that provide more options. Some of those options include the following commands: zoom, point, notch points, and grade.

Figure 5.9 View function drop-down menu

Zoom

The Zoom commands permit the patternmaker to zoom in, zoom out, see full-scale pieces, zoom to a selected piece, and separate the pieces. These commands work in the same way as the function keys described in Chapter 4. Additionally, the command 1:1 shows pieces on the screen so that one inch on a piece is displayed as one inch on the screen. The Zoom drop-down menu is shown in Figure 5.10.

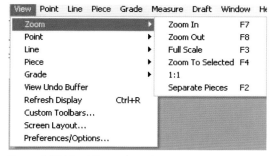

Figure 5.10 View>Zoom drop-down menu

Point

A point is a defining mark on a piece. Points are created when the sloper or pattern is digitized into the computer. They may also be added or deleted during patternmaking. They are used to define the perimeter of a piece. Some points have grade rules. There also may be points inside a piece that are used to define the location of pockets, buttons, and other details. The View>Point menu, shown in Figure 5.11, allows patternmakers to see All Points, Intermediate Points, Point Numbers (AM), Grade Rules, Point Types/Attributes, and Total Piece Points.

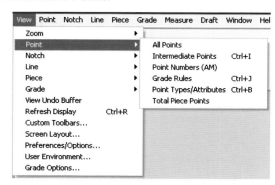

Figure 5.11 View>Point drop-down menu

Table 5.1 Point Symbols

Symbol	Meaning
Circle	Represents a **smoothing point**, a point inserted by the computer to create curved or smooth lines as they would appear when plotted; this point cannot be graded.
Square	Indicates an **intermediate point**, a digitized point located between graded points, often on curves; grade rules can be applied to these points.
Triangle	
Point-up triangle	Indicates the end of a line and cannot be deleted except when two lines are merged. These points can be graded.
Point-down triangle	Indicates a graded point.
Diamond	A combination of point-up and point-down triangles. Diamonds indicate the ends of lines and graded points. They cannot be deleted except when two lines are merged. Merging two lines will leave a graded point triangle that can be deleted.

The types of symbols used to define different types of points are shown in Table 5.1. To see any point symbols, it is necessary to have the Symbols box selected in the Display Path of the Preferences/ Options dialog box.

All Points

The All Points command is used to show all of the graded points, notches, and darts, but this command does not show intermediate points, such as those used to define curves. To use this command, complete the following steps:

1. Select View>Point>All Points.
2. To see points, select pieces in the work area by clicking on them. All pieces can be highlighted using a marquee box, as explained previously on page 92.
3. Select OK in the user input box, or right click and select OK from the cursor drop-down menu.

4. When a new piece is selected, the intermediate points shown on other pieces will disappear.
5. To conceal the displayed points, go back to View>Point>All Points. The points will disappear when the cursor is placed in the work area.

Intermediate Points

The Intermediate Points command is used to show all of the points that are part of a piece. See Figure 5.12.

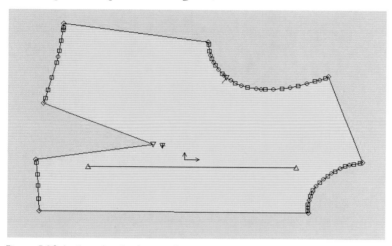

Figure 5.12 A piece showing intermediate points.

To use this command, complete the following steps:
1. Select View>Point>Intermediate Points.
2. To see points, select pieces in the work area by clicking on them. All or a selection of pieces can be highlighted using a marquee box.
3. Select OK in the user input box, or right click and select OK in the cursor drop-down menu.
4. When a new piece is selected, the intermediate points shown on other pieces will not disappear as they do when using the All Points command.
5. To conceal the displayed points, repeat the process of selecting View> Point>Intermediate Points, then select the piece and click on OK.

Point Numbers (AM)

When the Point Numbers (AM) command is selected, point numbers will automatically appear. See Figure 5.13.

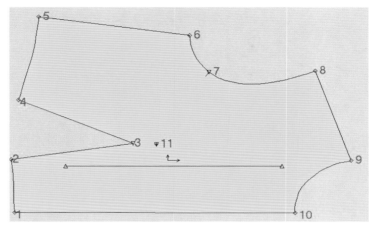

Figure 5.13 A piece showing point numbers.

AM is an abbreviation that indicates that this command is specific to AccuMark. To access this command, select View>Point>Point Numbers (AM). To remove the numbers, just repeat this process.

Grade Rules

When the Grade Rules command is selected, a grade rule number will automatically appear next to each graded point. See Figure 5.14.

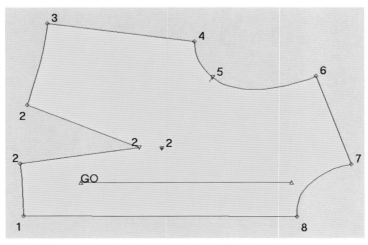

Figure 5.14 A piece showing the grade rule used for each graded point.

To access this command, select View>Point>Grade Rules. To remove the numbers, access the command again. The grade rule numbers will automatically disappear. Note that **GO,** as seen in Figure 5.14, refers to grain orientation.

Point Types/Attributes

Attributes are characteristics applied to a point during digitizing. For example, N means "nonsmoothing point." Students will not need to use the Point Types/Attributes function at this time.

Notch Points

Within the View menu, the Notch command has two options: Types and Shapes. The Types option places the notch-type number (for example, 1 = slit notch) next to each notch. The Shapes option shows the shape of each notch in the work area. To use the Notch command, complete the following steps:

1. Select View>Notch>Types.
   a. Select pieces in the work area by clicking on them. All pieces can be highlighted using a marquee box.
   b. Select OK in the user input box, or right click and select OK from the cursor drop-down menu. The notch-type number will appear next to each notch. See Figure 5.15a.

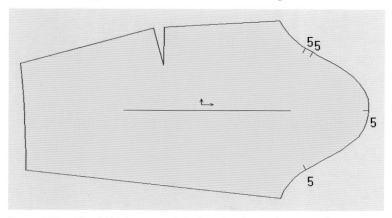

Figure 5.15 a. View>Notch command: A piece showing notch type numbers.

This number will disappear from the screen once the mouse is used again.

2. Select Shapes.

    a. All pieces in the work area will automatically show the shape of the notch type used. See Figure 5.15b.

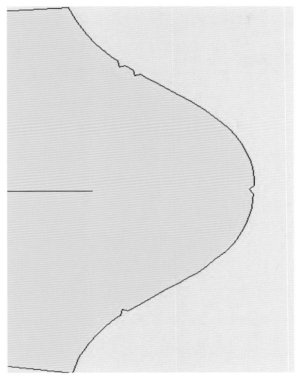

Figure 5.15 b. View>Notch command: A piece showing the notch shapes.

    b. The shape will return to a slash once the mouse is used again.

Grade

Using the View menu, it is possible to see graded pieces—either in all sizes or selected sizes. The following options are included in the View>Grade menu: Show All Sizes, Show Selected Sizes, Show Regular/Break Sizes, Stack On/Off, and Clear Nest. See Figure 5.16.

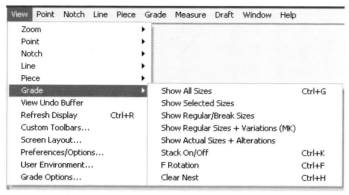

Figure 5.16 View>Grade drop-down menu

The procedure for changing the base size is included in this section, even though the commands are in the Grade menu on the function toolbar.

Show All Sizes

By selecting the Show All Sizes command, all of the sizes of a piece will be shown in the work area. To distinguish the sizes from one another, it is possible to change the outline colors of the different pieces. This can be done by using the Preferences/Options command (page 84). To use the Show All Sizes command, complete the following steps:

1. Select View>Grade>Show All Sizes.
2. Select a piece or pieces in the work area by clicking on them. All pieces can be highlighted using a marquee box.
3. Select OK in the user input box, or right click and select OK from the cursor drop-down menu. All sizes will be shown nested in the work area, as seen in Figure 5.17.

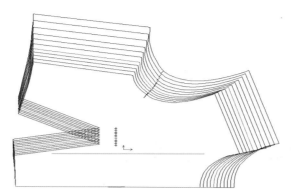

Figure 5.17 A piece with all sizes shown nested.

Show Selected Sizes

By using the Show Select Sizes command, user-specified sizes of a
pattern piece will be shown in the work area. To use this command,
complete the following steps:

1. Select View>Grade>Show Selected Sizes.
2. Select a piece or pieces in the work area by clicking on them.
   All pieces can be highlighted using a marquee box.
3. Select OK in the user input box, or right click and select OK
   from the drop-down menu.
4. The Show Selected Sizes dialog box will appear. See Figure 5.18.

Figure 5.18 The Show Selected Sizes dialogue box

Push the buttons of the sizes to be shown. Hold the Ctrl key down while you click to select more than one size.

5. Click on OK in the dialog box. The selected sizes will be shown nested in the work area.

Show Regular/Break Sizes

By selecting the Show Regular/Break Sizes command, regular/break sizes of pattern pieces will be shown in the work area. See Figure 5.19.

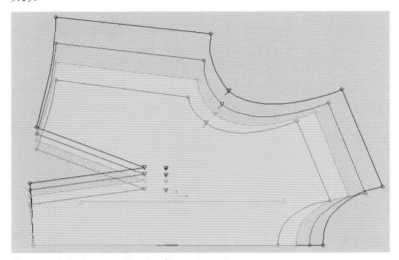

Figure 5.19 A piece with Regular/Break Sizes shown

To use this command, complete the following steps:
1. Select View>Grade>Regular/Break Sizes.
2. Select a piece or pieces in the work area by clicking on them. All pieces can be highlighted using a marquee box.
3. Select OK in the user input box, or right click and select OK from the cursor drop-down menu.
4. Regular/Break sizes will be shown nested in the work area.

Stack On/Off

Stack On/Off is used to select a new base point for stacking or nesting. To use this command, complete the following steps:
1. Select View>Grade>Stack On/Off.
2. Select a new stacking point on each individual piece. Note that

the original stacking point can be seen when all sizes are shown. See Figure 5.20a.

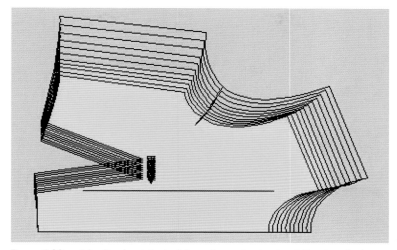

Figure 5.20 a. A bodice front stacked from: the center front waistline (cardinal point 1).

Select OK in the user input box, or right click and select OK from the cursor drop-down menu. No changes will be apparent in the work area.

3. Select the Show All Sizes command (page 106) to see the sizes nested from the newly selected stacking point. See Figures 5.20b and 5.20c.

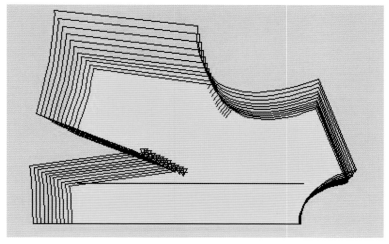

Figure 5.20 b. A bodice front stacked from: the center front neck.

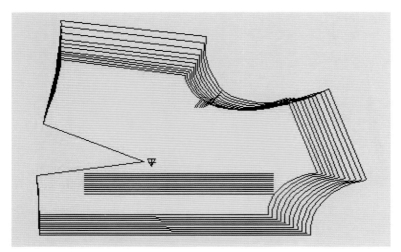

Figure 5.20 c. A bodice front stacked from: the bust apex.

4. It is also possible to change the stacking point of a piece when All Sizes are being shown on the screen. To do this, select View>Grade>Stack On/Off, and a new stacking point.

Clear Nest

Select View>Grade>Clear Nest to instantly remove all sizes, except the base size, from the work area. Note that if a nonbase size has been selected for use, it will remain in the work area.

Changing Base Size

To change the base size of a piece, follow these steps:
1. Click on Grade on the function toolbar.
2. Select Edit Size Line>Change Base Size. See Figure 5.21.

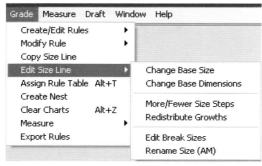

Figure 5.21 Grade function drop-down menu

3. Select the piece(s) to change.
4. Select OK. The Change Base Size dialog box will appear. This is similar in appearance to the Show Selected Sizes dialog box that you saw in Figure 5.18.
5. Select the new base size (only one size can be selected at a time).
6. Click on OK in the dialog box.

View Function Exercises

Using the Pattern Design software, answer the following questions. With the help of your instructor, select pattern pieces that are graded. Refer to your user input box for help.

1. What options appear under the menu for View>Point?
2. How is it possible to show all of the points of several pieces?
3. How are point numbers viewed?
4. What is the point number of the center front waist of the skirt?
5. How are point numbers removed from the work area?
6. What does the Intermediate Points command allow users to see?
7. Place the sleeve in the work area. Show the Intermediate Points, and print a hard copy.
8. What does the Grade Rules command allow users to see?
9. Which grade rule is used for the point of the front bust dart?
10. Which grade rule is used for the bodice center back waist point?
11. Which grade rule is used for the skirt center back waist?
12. Place a bodice front and a bodice back in the work area. Show the Grade Rules for each point. Print a hard copy.
13. How are grade rule numbers removed from the work area?
14. What appears when View>Notch>Shapes is selected?
15. What type and shape of notch is used in your piece?
16. How is Notch Point information removed from the work area?
17. Place a skirt front in the work area. Show All Sizes and print a hard copy.
18. Describe how to remove nested sizes from the work area.
19. Using two identical pieces, change the base size of one piece to

the smallest available size and the base size of the other piece to largest available size. Place the smaller piece on top of the larger, and print a hard copy.

20. How do you select a new stacking point when viewing nested sizes?

Edit Function

The Edit function provides information about pieces in the work area, the ability to undo and redo previous commands, and the opportunity to edit point, line, and piece information. The Edit menu is found on the function toolbar and is also available as a drop-down menu when the mouse is right clicked in the work area (when not working in a command). See Figure 5.22.

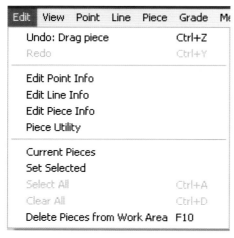

Figure 5.22 Edit function drop-down menu

Edit Point Information

The Edit Point Information command provides information about points and enables users to change grade rules. To use this command, follow these steps:

1. Select Edit>Edit Point Information.

2. The Tracking Information window will open on the Point tab. See Figure 5.23.

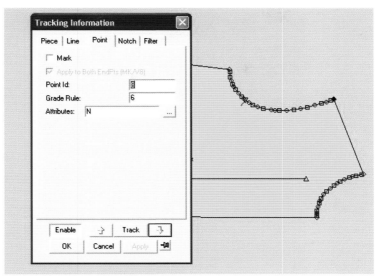

Figure 5.23 Tracking Information window—Point tab

3. Select a point on a piece. When the word Track is visible at the bottom of the window, use the arrows to highlight each point in turn until the desired point is reached. When the word Stop is visible, each point on the piece will be highlighted in turn, and the information about each point will appear in the dialog box. To change the information about a specific point, click on Stop in the window. (This button will be now be labeled Track.)
4. The grade rule can be modified by changing the number in the appropriate box, and then selecting Apply. Apply must be selected after each change is made for the change to take effect.
5. To confirm that the grade rule has been changed, select View>Show All Sizes.

Edit Notch Information

The Edit Notch Information command allows you to change the notch type. To use this command, complete the following steps:
1. Select Edit>Edit Notch Info.
2. The tracking information window will open on the notch tab.
3. Select notches for editing. To change a notch type, select a different number from the Type drop-down menu. Click on Apply.

Edit Line Information

The Edit Line Information command provides names of line types, such as grain line. It numbers the lines in the order in which they were digitized.

To use this command, follow these steps:
1. Select Edit>Edit Line Info.
2. The Tracking Information window will appear and will open on the Line tab.
3. Select a line on a piece. Information about the line will appear in the Tracking Information window. Lines can be selected individually, or if Track is selected, the system displays the information for each line in turn.
4. Names and categories of lines are not usually changed.

Edit Piece Information

The Edit Piece Information command shows the name and category of a piece and allows these to be changed.

To use this command, follow these steps:
1. Select Edit>Edit Piece Info.
2. The Tracking Information window will appear and will open on the Piece tab.
3. Select a piece. Information about the piece will appear in the Tracking Information window in the piece tab. See Figure 5.24.

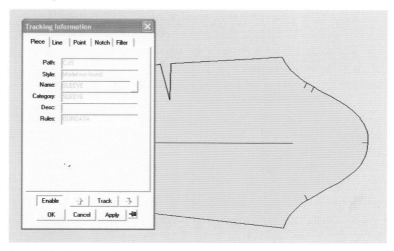

Figure 5.24 Tracking Information window—Piece tab

Pieces can be selected individually.

4. To change the name or category of a piece, type the new name or category in the appropriate box, and click on Apply.

Edit Function Exercises

Working with any pattern or sloper piece complete the following exercises.

1. Select Edit. Practice using the Edit menu.
2. Change the grade rule for a point or points on a piece. Show all of the sizes of the piece nested, and print a hard copy.
3. Return the sloper piece to its original grade rules. Show all of the sizes of the piece nested and print a hard copy.

Summary

By using the Measure function, it is possible to accurately measure lines, distances, angles, and areas. The View function focuses on the appearance of the screen and the content of the work area. Many of the choices in the View menu have additional drop-down menus that provide more options. The base size of a piece can be changed by use of the Grade function. The Edit function provides information about pieces in the work area and enables users to undo and redo previous commands and edit points, lines, and piece information. The Edit function is found in the function bar and is also available in a drop-down menu when the mouse is right clicked in the work area.

Key Terms

AM	intermediate points
GO	smoothing points

Review Questions

1. When is the Measure command especially useful?
2. How are all measurements immediately removed from the screen?
3. What is the purpose of the View menu?
4. How can the Zoom commands be accessed?
5. Explain what a point is.
6. What kind of information does Edit Piece provide?

CHAPTER SIX

Point and Notch Functions

Objectives

After studying this chapter, you will be able to

- Add and modify points to change the shape of a piece.
- Add and modify notches.

Introduction

Points and notches are instrumental in the creation of patterns from slopers. The patternmaker has total control of these two tools to create the desired look or style. Points can be added or moved either specific distances or by using the cursor, until they are correctly located. Notches can be added or moved as needed to indicate how pattern pieces should fit together.

As patterns are modified to create a new style, it is important to save them with appropriate names. It is best to maintain the basic sloper pieces with their original names so that they can be reused. It is advisable to save and name pieces several times during development. New names should be assigned at each stage of development so that you will be able to return to earlier stages if necessary (for example, angled front skirt 1, angled front skirt 2, etc.). The process for saving and naming a piece is described in Chapter 4 (see page 78).

Cursor and Value Modes

For many commands, there are two options in the user input box: Cursor and Value. The Cursor button toggles to Value. When the Cursor is visible, one is in the Cursor mode. Likewise when Value is visible one is working in Value mode. In Cursor mode, points, lines, etc. are placed or changed "by eye." In Value mode, points, lines, etc. are placed, moved, or changed using specific measurements that are entered in the Value Input field or other appropriate fields in the user input box.

Point Function

Points can be added, moved, or deleted to change the shape of a piece. See Figure 6.1 for a list of the commands in the Point function.

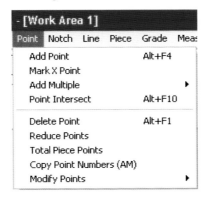

Figure 6.1 Point function drop-down menu

The following commands from this menu will be introduced to you in this chapter: Add Point, Mark X Point, Add Multiple, Delete Point, Reduce Points, and Modify Points.

When in the Point function and using the right click cursor drop-down menu, points may be added by selecting a site, or they may be placed at the midpoint of a line, at the intersection of two lines, or at a specific distance from another point. See Figure 6.2 for an illustration of the right click drop-down menu.

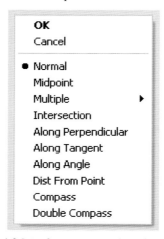

Figure 6.2 Point function, cursor drop-down menu

Multiple points may be added either a specific distance apart along a line, or in space; or they may be spaced proportionally on a line or in space. The Point function is useful for placing buttons, pleats, or trim.

Add Point

These are the steps to use the Add Point command.

1. Select Point>Add Point.
2. Click on a line to add a point; click inside a piece to add drill holes for pockets and other pattern features.
3. To remove points, use either the Undo command or select Point>Delete Point. Highlight points to be removed, and then click on OK in the cursor drop-down box or in the user input

box. If you are using the Delete Point command, you can double click on a point to delete it.

Hint for Success

Before working with points, it is a good idea to show the intermediate points. Select View>Points>Intermediate Points. Check in View>Preferences/Options>Display to make sure that the Symbols box has been checked. Unless a grade rule is applied, added points are intermediate points and not usually visible.

Accurate Point Placement

Drop-down menu options that appear when you right click on the mouse may be used when adding points and marking X-points. **X-points** are visible at all times and may be used as intermediate points or to mark internal locations such as those for button, trim, or pocket placement. After you select Add Point, the user input box will offer the prompt, "Indicate point position." The point position can be indicated by using the cursor or more accurately by selecting the desired command from the right click cursor drop-down menu. Follow the prompt instructions.

Hint for Success

The drop-down menu that appears when you right click should be dragged and placed far from where you are working onscreen, so it does not hide your work.

Following is a list of the commands that right clicking enables you to access and instructions on how to use them:

- *Midpoint*: This command enables you to add a point in the middle of a line.

- *Multiple*: Four options are available in this command. See Figure 6.3.

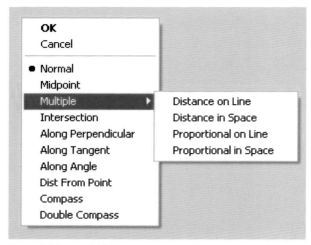

Figure 6.3 Point>Add Point>cursor drop-down menu>Multiple

1. Distance on Line
   a. Select a line to receive the point.
   b. **Thumbtacks** will appear at each end of the line.
       Thumbtacks are used to define the beginning and end
       of a distance. See Figure 6.4.

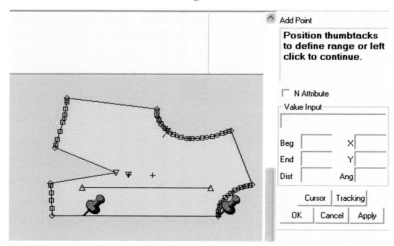

Figure 6.4 Point>Add Point or Mark X Point>Multiple>Distance on Line

To move a thumbtack, click on it, remove your finger from the mouse, and move the mouse (and thumbtack) the desired distance. Click again to finalize its placement. After both ends of the line have been defined, click on OK.

c. A drop-down menu that allows you to choose the ends to receive points will appear. The options are: None, Both, First, and Last. See Figure 6.5.

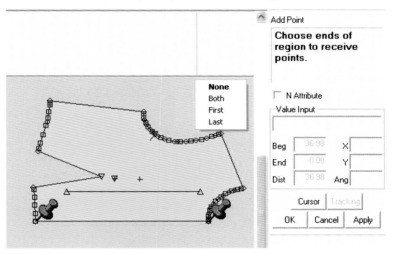

Figure 6.5 Drop-down menu for the selection of end(s) to receive points

- *None*: The ends of the line will not receive a point.
- *Both*: Both ends of the line will receive a point. (This means that the distance between the last and next to last points may not be equal to the distance between any other two adjacent points.)
- *First*: The first thumbtack (working in a clockwise direction) will receive a point.
- *Last*: The last thumbtack (working in a clockwise direction) will receive a point.

    d. Select your choice of ends.

    e. In the Value Input field in the user input box that appears, type the distance desired between the points. Click on OK, and the points will appear on the piece.

2. Distance in Space

    a. Select a starting location—do not click on OK.

      b. Select a finishing location—do not click on OK.

      c. From the drop-down menu, select which ends are to receive points—do not click on OK.

      d. In the user input box, type the desired distance between the points, and click on OK.

3. Proportional on Line

      a. Select a line to receive the points.

      b. Move the thumbtacks as desired, and click on OK.

      c. Select your choice of ends.

      d. Type the number of points desired in the Value Input field, in the user input box and click on OK.

4. Proportional in Space

      a. Select a starting location—do not click on OK.

      b. Select a finishing location—do not click on OK.

      c. From the drop-down menu, select which ends are to receive points.

      d. Type the number of points desired in the Value Input field, in the user input box and click on OK.

Hint for Success

All measurements are made in a clockwise direction. Measurements are made between cardinal points in a clockwise direction. To measure in a counterclockwise direction, enter a negative number. Note that this also applies to thumbtacks.

- *Intersection*: This command allows you to add a point at an intersection. Select two intersecting lines (there is no indication that the lines have been selected). After the second line is selected, the point appears.

- *Along Perpendicular*: This command allows you to add a point perpendicular to a point on a line. For this command, there are two options in the user input box: Cursor mode and Value mode. In Cursor mode, wherever you place the point, it will be moved to be perpendicular to the point of intersection. In Value mode points can be placed a specific distance in a specific direction from a given point. The numbers are entered in the Value Input field, and then OK is selected. See Figure 6.6.

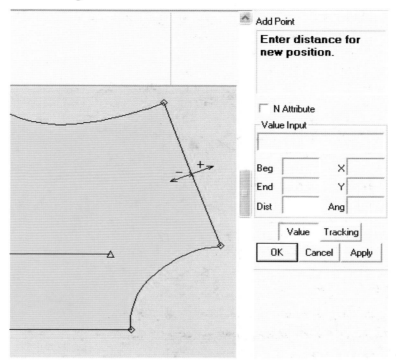

Figure 6.6 Points>Add Point>Along Perpendicular

To use this command, complete the following steps:
1. Select a point of intersection. This should be a point already indicated on a line.
2. If using Cursor mode, click on the line to indicate the new point position, and click on OK. If using Value mode, enter a distance for the new point in the user input box, and click on OK.

- *Along Tangent*: This command allows you to add a point that is on a tangent to a curve. To use this command, complete the following steps:
  1. Select a point of intersection. This should be a point already indicated on a curved line.
  2. Indicate the new point position. If you are in Cursor mode, wherever you place the point, it will be moved to be tangential to the point of intersection. If Value mode is used,

       enter a distance for the new position in the Dist field of the
       user input box, and click on OK.

- *Distance from Point*: Using this command adds a point that is a
  specific distance from another point along the perimeter of the
  piece. (Distances are measured in a clockwise direction. To
  measure in a counterclockwise direction, enter a negative number.) To use this command, follow these steps:
  1. Select a point from which to enter a distance.
  2. Enter the desired distance in the Value Input field, and click
     on OK.

Mark X Point

X Points are useful for marking pieces because they are visible at all
times. They can be used to change the shape of a piece, but they
cannot be graded. The different ways of adding X Points are identical
to the processes for adding points.

Add Multiple

The Add Multiple command works similarly to the commands found
in the drop-down menu produced by right clicking when using the
Add Point and Mark X Point commands. However, for this command,
the choice of which ends receive points is in the user input box.
Check the desired box before selecting any points. Under the Add
Multiple command, you will find the following options:

- Add Drills is the same as adding multiple points using the
  Proportional in Space command.
- Add Drills Dist is the same as adding multiple points using the
  Distance in Space command.
- Add Points Line is the same as adding multiple points using the
  Proportional on Line command.
- Add Points Ln Dist is the same as adding multiple points using
  the Distance on Line command.

Delete Point

The Delete Point command allows for the removal of points. These
may be digitized points or points that were added during the design
process. Points indicating the end of a line (point-up triangles and
diamonds) cannot be deleted. Points shown as circles are created
by the software to smooth curves. These points cannot be deleted.
However, if the square points on either side of them are deleted,
the circles created by the software will disappear, and a straight line
will appear.

Note that deleting points may change the shape of a piece. This command can be used to delete some points if the intent is to move existing points to change the shape of a piece, such as manipulating the shape of a neckline. The process for deleting points is as follows.

1. Select Point>Delete Point.
2. Select the points to be deleted by clicking on them. Multiple points can be selected by clicking on each point individually or by placing a marquee box around them. (Remember to create a marquee box, simply click, let go, move the cursor to create the box, and then click again.)
3. End the selection of the points to be deleted by clicking on OK either in the user input box or from the drop-down menu that appears when you right click.
4. Individual points may also be deleted by double clicking on them when in the Delete Point command

Reduce Points

The Reduce Points command is used to remove unnecessary intermediate points from a line. Sometimes digitized lines can be a little "wobbly," and reducing points will smooth the lines.

1. Select Point>Reduce Points. The number of points reduced is determined by **Reduction Factor** in the user input box. Type in the desired reduction factor. Note that if the factor is too high, many points will be removed and the shape of the piece may be drastically changed. See Figure 6.7.

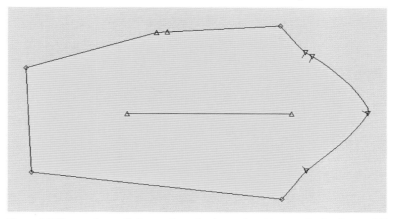

Figure 6.7 Sleeve piece with the number of points reduced by a reduction factor of 5.

2. Select the lines or pieces to reduce points.

3. End the selection by clicking on OK either in the user input box or in the drop-down menu that appears when you right click.

Modify Points

The Modify Points commands are used to move points on a piece to change its shape. Figure 6.8 shows commands found in the Modify Points drop-down menu.

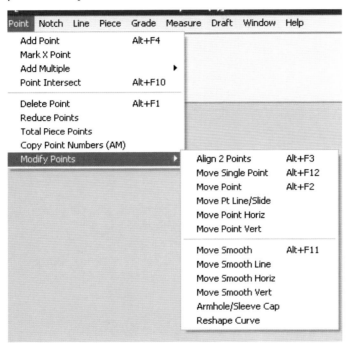

Figure 6.8 Modify Points drop-down menu

Selected commands in Modify Points will be discussed. Points are moved in Cursor or Value mode. Most of the following instructions apply when in Cursor mode. To move points specific distances, use Value mode and enter numbers/distances in the appropriate fields.

Move Single Point

The Move Single Point command is very useful when changing the shape of a piece. A square point can be moved without moving adjacent square points. See Figures 6.9a and 6.9b.

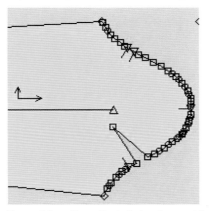

Figure 6.9 a. Move Single Point: sleeve with a single point moved in the sleeve cap.

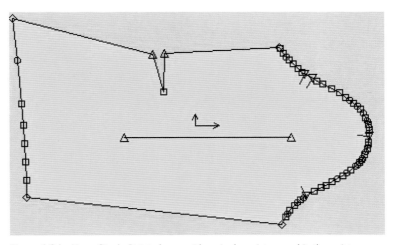

Figure 6.9 b. Move Single Point: sleeve with a single point moved in the wrist corner.

To move a single point, follow these steps:

1. Select Point>Modify Points>Move Single Point.

2. Select the point to be moved. Place the cursor at the desired new location and left click. Alternatively, Value mode can be used to define the new location of the point.

Move Point

The Move Point command allows for the unified movement of a group of points. To do this, follow these steps:

1. Select Point>Modify Points>Move Point.
2. Select the point(s) to move, and click on OK.
3. Place the cursor at the desired new location, and click. The location of the cursor will be the new site of the last point selected. All other selected points will be located in reference to that point. Alternatively, Value mode can be used to define the new location of the last selected point.

Move Point Line/Slide

Using this command, selected points can be moved only by sliding them along an existing line or an extension of an existing line.

1. Select Point>Modify Points>Move Point Line/Slide.
2. In the user input box, select the line you wish to move the point along: the first line, the second line, or the closest line. The first line is the one that was digitized first—i.e., the one on the counterclockwise side of the point. The second line is the line digitized after the first. If the closest line is selected, the point will move along the line closest to the cursor.
3. Select the point to move. Select the new location by clicking on it. Alternatively, when using Value mode, the Value Input field in the user input box can be used to define the new location of the point. The new location can be determined as a measurement from the beginning of the line (Beg) or the end of the line (End) or as a distance from the point (Dist). Arrow prompts appear in the work area.

Move Point Horiz and Move Point Vert

These commands allow for selected points to be moved only in a horizontal or vertical direction.

1. Select Point>Modify Points.
2. Select Move Point Horiz or select Move Point Vert.

3. Select the point to move, and click on OK.
4. Points can be moved either by using Cursor or Value mode. Points will move either horizontally or vertically depending on the command being used. Perimeter points will move the perimeter line between adjacent square points. When Value mode is used, the point will move the specified distance in the appropriate direction (horizontally or vertically).

Move Smooth

The Move Smooth command is used to move a point in any direction. Other points along a defined range of the line containing the point also move. Smooth curves are created. To use this command, follow these steps:

1. Select Point>Modify Points>Move Smooth.
2. Select the point to move, and click on OK.
3. Thumbtacks will appear. Move these to define the range. It is easier to move these with the cursor rather than with values. When the thumbtacks are correctly placed, either click in an open space or click on OK.
4. Place the point at its new location either by using the cursor or by providing x- and y-coordinates for the new position.

Move Smooth Line

The Move Smooth Line command is used to move a point along a line so that other points along the line will also move to form a smooth curve. It may be used to make armholes or necklines deeper or smaller. With this command, using values is particularly useful to make equal changes to front and back pieces.

The procedure for using this command is as follows.

1. Select Point>Modify Points>Move Smooth Line.
2. In the user input box, select the line you wish to move the point along: the first line, the second line, or the closest line. Alternatively, this selection may be made after the point to move has been selected.
3. Select the point to move, and click on OK.
4. Thumbtacks will appear. Move these to define the range, and click on OK.
5. Place the point at its new location either by using the Cursor mode or if using Value mode, by typing in the distance the

point should be moved from a specified point, using a negative number if necessary. See Figure 6.10 a–c.

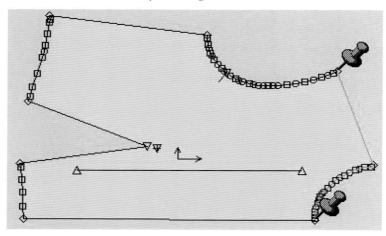

Figure 6.10 a. Steps to change a neckline using the Smooth Move Line command: piece with thumbtacks.

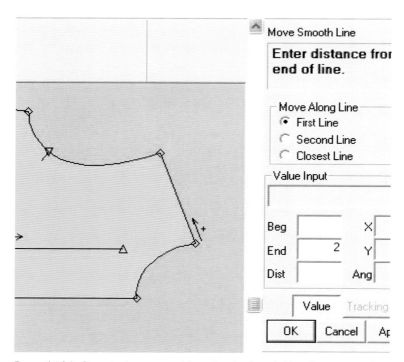

Figure 6.10 b. Steps to change a neckline using the Smooth Move Line command: piece showing value arrow.

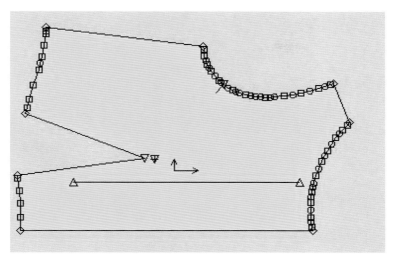

Figure 6.10 c. Steps to change a neckline using the Smooth Move Line command: piece with new neckline.

Move Smooth Horiz and Move Smooth Vert

The Move Smooth Horizontal command is used to move a point along the x-axis. The Move Smooth Vertical command is used to move a point along the y-axis. To use these commands, follow these steps:

1. Select Point>Modify Points.
2. Select Move Smooth Horiz or Move Smooth Vert
3. Select the point to move, and click on OK.
4. Thumbtacks will appear. Move these to define the range, and click on OK.
5. Place the point at its new location either by using the cursor or by providing the x- or y-coordinate for the new position, depending on the mode in use.

Point Function Exercises

Using sloper pieces, perform the following exercises:

1. Add points:
   a. Mark the midpoint of a bodice front shoulder with an X point. (Point>Mark X Point>cursor drop-down menu>Midpoint.)

132

    b. Mark the placement of seven hooks (or eyes) down the front of a bodice so that they are equal distances apart and there is a hook at the top of the piece and one at the bottom. (Point>Mark X Point>cursor drop-down menu>Multiple>Proportional on Line.)

    c. Arrange your altered pieces on the screen so that they fill the screen but are still totally visible.

    d. Print a hard copy.

2. Move, delete, and add points: (There are several correct ways of doing some of the following exercises.)

    a. Shorten the length of the front and back shoulder seam lines at the armhole by one-half inch by selecting Point>Modify Points>Smooth Move Line.

    b. Create a square neckline on front and back bodice pieces. Remember that the front and back shoulder seam lines must be the same length. Keep a record of the commands used and how they were used.

    c. Alter skirt front and back pieces to create a flared skirt. Which commands did you use?

    d. Arrange your altered sloper pieces on the screen so that they fill the screen but are still totally visible.

    e. Print a hard copy.

Notch

A notch is a mark, usually a slash or a V-shaped cut, on a piece perimeter that is used as a guide for matching garment sections during construction of the garment. Using the Notch function, notches can be added, moved, or removed; the type of notch in a piece may be changed; or a notch angle may be changed so that it can be accommodated in narrow pieces or near a sharp angle on a piece. The different ways of adding notches are identical to the processes for adding points. However, it is very important that a notch type be indicated in the user input box. Figure 6.11 shows the commands available within the Notch Function.

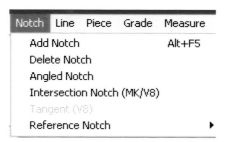

Figure 6.11 Notch function drop-down menu

Add Notch

To add a notch to a pattern piece, do the following:
1. Select Notch>Add Notch.
2. In the user input box, specify the notch type to be used.
3. Select the new notch position. The drop-down menu that appears when you right click provides options for accurately placing notches and for placing multiple notches at the same time. Usually, notches are added at the midpoint of a line or at a specific distance from a given point. Notches can then be used to match pattern pieces.

Delete Notch

In order to delete a notch, complete the following steps:
1. Select Notch>Delete Notch.
2. Select notches for deletion by clicking on them. Multiple notches can be selected by clicking on each point individually or by placing a marquee box around them.
3. Click on OK.
4. Individual notches may also be deleted by double clicking on them when in the Delete Notch command.

Angled Notch

To ensure accuracy in the selecting of a notch to be angled, use the zoom command to enlarge the area and pick carefully on the notch. If the perimeter is selected, a new notch will be created.

1. Select Notch>Angled Notch.
2. Select the notch to angle.
3. Place the cursor so that the notch is at the desired angle and click.

Reference Notch

Every notch is attached to a **reference point**, which may be the notch itself, a different notch, a line, or an intersection of lines. When a reference point is modified, the notch is also modified. The Reference Notch drop-down menu, shown in Figure 6.12, provides access to six different commands. Several of these commands work in similar ways to notch commands already discussed.

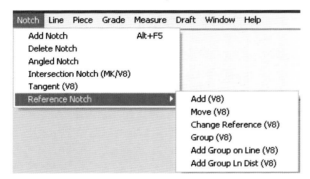

Figure 6.12 Reference Notch drop-down menu

Adding a Notch and Copying a Notch Location

To add and copy a notch location, follow these instructions:

1. Select Notch>Reference Notch>Add.
2. In the user input box, select the notch type to be used and make sure that the Copy Distance field is not checked.
3. Select the reference point for the new notch.
4. If the cursor is being used to select the position of the new notch, place the cursor in the desired location and click on the mouse. If Value mode is being used, enter the distance from the reference point to the new location, and click on OK.
5. To position a notch so that its location matches that of another notch, select Copy Distance in the user input box.
6. Select the reference point for the new notch.
7. Indicate the line for the new notch placement.
8. Select the notch to match.

Move

To move a notch, complete these steps:

1. Select Notch>Notch Reference>Move.
2. Select a notch to move.
3. Place the cursor at the new location and click. Alternatively, Value mode can be used to define the new location of the notch.

Add Group on Line

The Add Group on Line command is used to add a group of notches spaced proportionally along a line or section of a line. Here is how to use this command.

1. Select Notch>Notch Reference>Add Group on Line.
2. In the user input box, select a notch type to be used.
3. Select the line to receive the notches.
4. Move the thumbtacks to define the line section to receive the group of notches, and click on OK.
5. In the user input box, select your choice of ends to receive notches.
6. Type the number of notches desired in the Value Input field, and click on OK.
7. Select a reference point for the new notches. This point must be outside the group of notches being added.

Add Group Ln Dist

The Add Group Ln Dist command is used to add a group of notches spaced a specified distance apart along a line or section of a line. Follow these steps to use this command.

1. Select Notch>Notch Reference>Add Group Ln Dist.
2. In the user input box, select a notch type to use.
3. Select the line to receive the notches.
4. Move the thumbtacks to define the line section to receive the group of notches, and click on OK.
5. In the user input box, select your choice of ends to receive notches.
6. In the user input box, type the desired distance between notches, and click on OK.
7. Select a reference point for the new notches. This point must be outside the group of notches being added.

Notch Function Exercises

There are a few different, yet correct, ways to complete these exercises.

1. On a sleeve sloper, place a notch on each side seam, five inches from the armseye. Which commands did you use?
2. Select one of the notches on the sleeve and angle it.
3. Place a notch on the side seams of a skirt back. Then place a notch to match it on the side seam of a skirt front. Which commands did you use?
4. Print a hard copy.

Summary

Points and notches are instrumental in creating patterns from slopers. They can be changed using either Cursor or Value mode. The patternmaker has control of these tools to create the desired look or style. As pieces are modified to create a new style, it is important to save them with appropriate names. It is best to maintain the basic pieces with their original names so they can be reused. It is advisable to save and name pieces several times during development.

Points can be added, moved, or deleted to change the shapes of a piece. The Modify Points command is used to move points in a piece to change its shape. Points are moved by using Cursor or Value mode. The type of notch in a piece may be changed or a notch angle may be changed. It is very important that a notch type be indicated in the user input box. Notches can be also added, moved, or removed.

Key Terms

reduction factor

reference point

smooth factor

thumbtacks

Review Questions

1. Why are X points useful? What is their limitation?
2. What are notches used to indicate?
3. Why is it important to show intermediate points?
4. Why may a notch angle be changed?
5. How can wobbly lines be smoothed?
6. Describe the two ways points can be moved.

CHAPTER SEVEN

Line Function

Objectives

After studying this chapter, you will be able to

- Create a line, a perpendicular line, and conics.
- Delete, replace, and swap lines.
- Modify lines.

Introduction

Lines can be created, moved, added, split, joined, straightened, lengthened, and shortened. Being able to manipulate lines is an important design tool for patternmakers. As with points and notches, it is important to save new pieces with appropriate names.

All lines are initially created as internal lines. Perimeter lines are made by swapping or replacing them with internal lines. The Line function drop-down menu is shown in Figure 7.1.

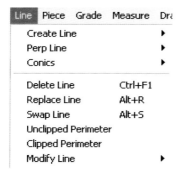

Figure 7.1 Line function drop-down menu

Selected commands from the Line drop-down menu will be presented in this chapter.

Create Line

Lines can be created in many different ways, including digitizing and by placing two points to indicate the ends of a line. Figure 7.2 shows the Line>Create Line drop-down menu.

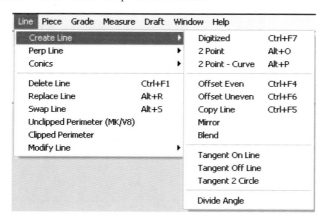

Figure 7.2 Line>Create Line drop-down menu

Digitized

The Digitized command allows the patternmaker to draw lines with more than two points. For this command, there is a cursor drop-down menu that allows for curves to be created and for the accurate placement of lines. The default commands are Normal and Line. To utilize this command, complete the following steps:

1. Select Line>Create Line>Digitized.
2. Click the cursor at the starting point of the line. Move the cursor clicking at various points. To end the line, click on the final point, and click on OK.

To create a horizontal line, a vertical line, a curved line, or an accurately placed line, use the cursor right click drop-down menu (see Figure 7.3).

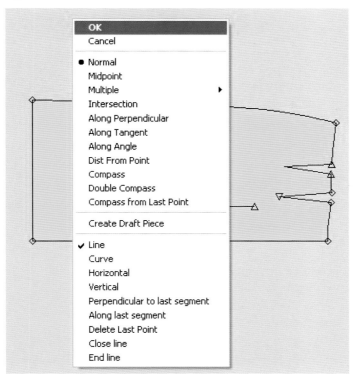

Figure 7.3 Line>Create Line>Digitized cursor drop-down menu

Table 7.1 lists and describes most of the commands that can be accessed through this drop-down menu.

2 Point

The 2 Point command allows the designer to create a straight line using two points. The procedure for using this command is below.

1. Select Line>Create Line>2 Point.
2. Click the cursor at the starting point of the line. Move the cursor to the end of the line and click again.
3. Lines of a specific length can be created by selecting Value mode in the user input box and then typing the appropriate numbers in the Value Input fields in the user input box.
4. The cursor drop-down menu for this command is the same as that for the Digitized command. See Figure 7.3 and Table 7.1.

2 Point Curve

The 2 Point-Curve command allows the patternmaker to create a curved line using two points.

1. Select Line>Create Line>2 Point Curve.
2. Select the first point of the line.
3. Select the final point of the line.
4. Move the cursor until the line has the desired curve, and left click.

Offset Even

The Offset Even command allows for the creation of one or more lines parallel to and the same length as an existing line; or in the case of a curve, parallel to the original curve and maintaining the same arc. An offset line may be placed by using the cursor or more accurately placed in Value mode. The Offset Even command is particularly useful when creating facings, plackets, and pockets.

To create Offset Even lines, follow these instructions:

1. Select Line>Create Line>Offset Even.
2. An offset line may be added or may replace an existing line by selecting the appropriate button in the user input box. Offset lines may also be extended to adjacent lines by selecting the appropriate button in the user input box.
3. Select a line to be offset, and click on OK.

Table 7.1 Selected Commands from the Create Line, Digitized and 2 Point Drop-Down Menu

Note: To use this drop-down menu, one item must be selected from each section. (For example, if you select Normal from Section 1, then you may choose Line from Section 2.)

Command	Use
Section 1	
Normal	Selection of points by use of the cursor
Midpoint	Starts or finishes a new line at the midpoint of an existing line
Multiple	Allows for the creation of several parallel lines. There are four options within this command: Distance on Line Distance in Space Proportional on Line Proportional in Space Use of these commands is similar to Adding Multiple Points (see Chapter 6).
Intersection	Selecting an intersection of two lines as the first and/or last point of a new line
Along Perpendicular	Allows for the creation of a line that is perpendicular to an existing line
Along Tangent	Creating a line at a tangent to another line
Dist From Point	Allows for the beginning or end of a line to be located at a specific distance from an existing point (the Value mode should be used).
Section 2	
Line	Creates a straight line
Curve	Creates curves
Horizontal	Creates a horizontal line
Vertical	Creates a vertical line
Perpendicular to last segment	Creates a line that is perpendicular to the last segment of a newly created digitized line
Delete Last Point	Removes the last digitized point
Close line	Draws a line from the last digitized point to the first digitized point, creating an enclosed polygon
End line	Ends the line, but the command is still functional

4. The location of the offset line can be selected using the Cursor or Value mode. An example of offset lines is shown in Figure 7.4.

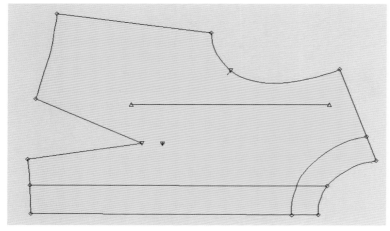

Figure 7.4 Piece showing two offset even lines.

    a. When using Cursor mode, move the cursor and the line to the desired position and click.

    b. When using Value mode, select the line to offset and click on OK. In the user input box enter the distance to offset and click on OK. A negative number will be required to offset the line in one of the directions.

5. To create multiple evenly spaced offset lines in Value mode, enter the desired number of lines in the Number Offsets field of the user input box and input the offset amount in the Value Input field.

Offset Uneven

The Offset Uneven command is used to create a new line that is not parallel to an existing line. This command is useful when modifying curved lines or when changing the slope of a shoulder. To use this command, follow these steps:

1. Select Line>Create Line>Offset Uneven.

2. The offset line may be added or may replace an existing line, and it may be extended to adjacent lines by selecting the appropriate buttons in the user input box. See Figures 7.5a and b.

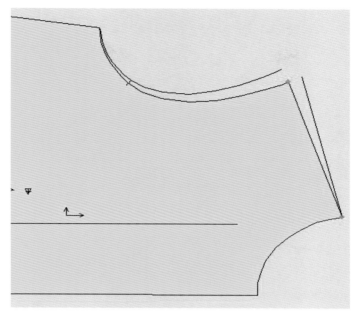

Figure 7.5 a. Offset Uneven: adding offset uneven lines

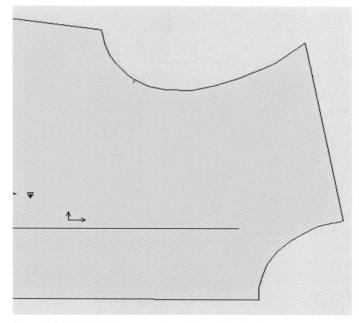

Figure 7.5 b. Offset Uneven: replacing lines with offset uneven lines

3. Select the first point of the line to be offset uneven by clicking on it. Enter an appropriate distance for it to be offset in the Value Input field and click on OK.

4. Select the second point on the line to be offset uneven by clicking on it. Enter the appropriate distance for it to be offset in the Value Input field and click on OK to see the line. Click on OK a second time to complete the function.

Copy Line

The Copy Line command is used to copy one or several lines from one piece to another or within a piece. It can be used to transfer necklines, pockets, and other garment features from one piece to another. Copied lines can be placed in their new locations either by using Cursor or Value mode; however, it is difficult to copy lines from one piece to another using Value mode. To use this command, follow these steps:

1. Select Line>Create Line>Copy Line.
2. Select the lines to copy either by clicking on them individually or by creating a marquee box around the desired lines, and then click on OK. The point at which the lines are selected will be the reference point used to move the lines.
3. Select the piece or pieces to receive the copied lines, and click on OK.
4. If Select Reference Location is checked in the user input box, an extra step will be added to the process. It requires the user to select a reference point for moving the line.
5. With the cursor, move the line(s) to the desired location and click once. (If you click on OK, you will lose your line.) If using Value mode, enter the distance the lines are to be moved or the new x and y coordinates, and click on OK.

Tangent On Line

The Tangent On Line command allows for the drawing of an internal line tangential to a selected point on a curve. (An internal line is one that is not a perimeter line; however, an internal line may be located outside of a piece.) This command can be used in conjunction with other commands to change the flare on a piece. The procedure for using this command is as follows:

1. Select Line>Create Line>Tangent On Line.
2. Select the point of intersection. This should be on a curved line.

3. Select the end point of the new line, either by moving the cursor or entering a value, and click on OK. Figure 7.6 shows a tangent line on a piece.

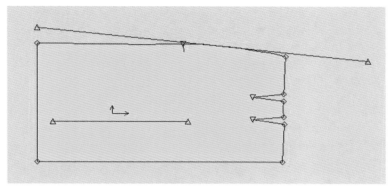

Figure 7.6 Piece showing a Tangent On Line.

Divide Angle

The Divide Angle command is used to create one or more lines that divide the angle between two lines. To use this command, follow these steps:

1. Select Line>Create Line>Divide Angle.
2. Select the first line, defining the angle to be divided.
3. Select the second line that forms the angle.
4. In the user input box, enter the Number Of Divisions desired.
5. Move the cursor to define the direction and length of the new line(s).
6. Click once to set the line.

Perp Line

There are three commands in the Perp Line function. They are used to create lines that are perpendicular to other lines. There are two options for Perp Line in the user input box: Half and Whole. Selecting Half will create a new line that will not extend past the intersecting line. Selecting Whole will create a new line that will extend past the intersecting line.

146

Perp On Line

The Perp On Line command is used to create a line that is perpendicular (at 90 degrees) to a specific point. To use this command, complete the following steps:

1. Select Line>Perp Line>Perp On Line.
2. Select the point of intersection on the line.
3. Select the end point of the new line, either by using the Cursor or Value mode and then click on OK.

Perp Off Line

The Perp Off Line command is used to create a line that is perpendicular to a perimeter line and intersects it at a particular point. To use this command, follow these steps:

1. Select Line>Perp Line>Perp Off Line.
2. Select the point where you want the new line to begin.
3. Select the line that the new line will intersect.
4. The new line will be created.

Perp 2 Points

This command creates a perpendicular line midway between two points on a line. To use this command, follow these steps:

1. Select Line>Perp Line>Perp 2 Point.
2. Select two points on the same line.
3. Enter the new line endpoint, either by using the Cursor or Value mode and click on OK.

Conics

The Conics function contains commands for creating circles and ovals. See Figure 7.7.

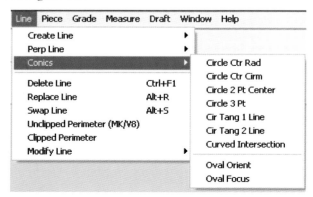

Figure 7.7 Line>Conics drop-down menu

The parts of a circle are shown in Figure 7.8.

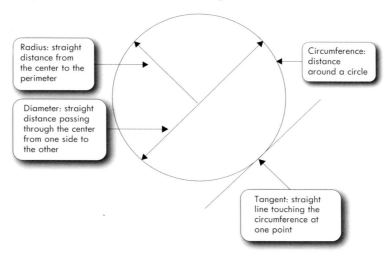

Radius: straight distance from the center to the perimeter

Circumference: distance around a circle

Diameter: straight distance passing through the center from one side to the other

Tangent: straight line touching the circumference at one point

Figure 7.8 Parts of a circle

Circles can be created as internal lines in a piece or as separate pieces. They may be created by defining the radius, the circumference, or points on the circumference, or they may be based on a tangential line. Table 7.2 illustrates the different ways circles can be created. When a new circle is created, a triangle symbol indicates the point at which the circle can be said to begin.

Circle Ctr Rad and Circle Ctr Cirm

The Circle Ctr Rad and Circle Ctr Cirm commands are used to create circles by establishing the center of the circle first. Circles can be created using the Cursor or Value mode. To use these commands, follow these steps:

1. Select Line>Conics.
2. From the drop-down menu, select Circle Ctr Rad or Circle Ctr Cirm.
3. If a new piece is being created, select Create as a New Piece from the user input box and type in the name of the new piece in the Name field.
4. To show the center of the circle, select Drill or Mark from the user input box.
5. Select either Radius or Circumference from the user input box.

Table 7.2 Different Ways to Create Circles

	Circle Ctr Rad Used to create a circle by selecting the center point and length of the radius
	Circle Ctr Cirm Used to create a circle by selecting the center point and the circumference
	Circle 2 Pt Center Used to create a circle by selecting two points along the circumference and the approximate center point
	Circle 3 Pt Used to create a circle by selecting three points on the circumference
	Cir Tang 1 Line Used to create a circle that touches an existing line
	Cir Tang 2 Line Used to create a circle that touches two adjacent perimeter lines or two internal lines
	Curved Intersection Used to replace a corner with a curve

6. Using the cursor select the center of the circle.
7. To determine the size of the circle, either move the cursor (if using the Cursor mode) and click once, or enter a distance (if using the Value mode), and click on OK.

Circle 2 Pt Center

This command is used to create a circle by using an approximate center point and two points along the circumference.

1. Select Line>Conics>Circle 2 Pt Center.
2. Using the cursor, select two points on the circumference of the circle.
3. To determine the size and location of the circle, either move the cursor (if in Cursor mode) and click once or enter a + or – symbol for the location and a value for the radius in the user input box (if in Value mode), and click on OK.

Circle 3 Pt

The command is used to create a circle by selecting three points on the circumference of the circle as follows:

1. Select Line>Conics>Circle 3 Pt.
2. Select three points on the circumference of the circle.

Cir Tang 1 Line

As described below, this command is used to create a circle that is a tangent on an existing curved line.

1. Select Line>Conics>Cir Tang 1 Line.
2. Using the cursor, select a tangent point on a line.
3. To determine the size of the circle, either move the cursor (if in Cursor mode) and click once or enter a radius value in the Value field (if in Value mode) and click on OK.

Cir Tang 2 Line

As described below, this command is used to create a circle that is tangential to two lines.

1. Select Line>Conics>Cir Tang 2 Line.
2. On a piece, select two internal lines or two adjacent perimeter lines.
3. To determine the size of the circle, either move the cursor (if in Cursor mode) and click once or enter a radius value in the Value Input field (if in Value mode) and click on OK.

Curved Intersection

The Curved Intersection command is used to replace a corner (intersection of two adjacent lines) with a curve.

1. Select Line>Conics>Curved Intersection.
2. From the user input box, select the line type: perimeter or internal.

3. From the user input box, select one of the following options:
   a. *Add/Change Radius*: Creates a curve that can be restored to an intersection by using the Delete option. This is usually the best option to create a curved intersection.
   b. *Add Severed*: Creates a curved section that is separate from adjacent lines; therefore, the curved section cannot be restored to an intersection by using the Delete option.
   c. *Delete*: Causes a selected curved section to return to an intersection unless it has been severed from adjacent lines.
   d. *Sever*: Severs a curved section from adjacent lines.
4. Select a corner to convert to a curve.
5. To determine the size of the circle, either move the cursor (if in Cursor mode) and click once or enter a radius value in the Value Input field (if in Value mode) and click on OK.

Delete Line

The Delete Line command is used to delete a single internal line or a group of internal lines. Perimeter lines cannot be deleted, but all of the intermediate points on a perimeter can be deleted using this command. To delete line(s), follow these steps:

1. Select Line>Delete Line.
2. Select a line to delete by clicking on it, or select a group of lines to delete by clicking on each in turn and click on OK. If a piece is selected and then OK clicked, all internal lines and internal points will be deleted. Double clicking inside a piece will delete all internal lines from the piece.

Replace Line

The Replace Line command is used to change an internal line into a perimeter line. The internal line must intersect the perimeter.

1. Select Line>Replace Line.
2. Select the internal line that will become a perimeter line and click on OK.
3. Select a start point for the perimeter replacement. This is the point at which the internal line intersects the perimeter. Select the point carefully. The intersection selected will determine which segment of the pattern is retained. Work in a clockwise direction.
4. If the internal line crosses a perimeter at more than two points, it will be necessary to select an end point for the perimeter replacement.

Swap Line

The Swap Line command is used to change internal lines into perimeter lines. Unlike the Replace Line command, the Swap Line command can be used for lines that do not intersect the perimeter. The system automatically extends or shortens adjacent lines to close the perimeter. To use this command, follow theses steps:

1. Select Line>Swap Line.
2. If desired, select Delete Original Line and Maintain Graded Nest in the user input box.
3. Using the cursor, select the internal line(s) to swap and click on OK.
4. Select the perimeter line(s) and click on OK. Figures 7.9a and b show lines swapped on a piece.

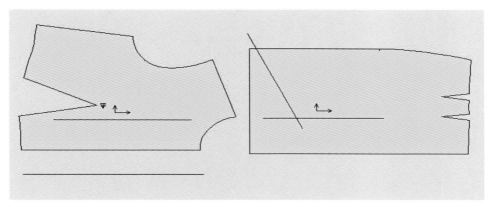

Figure 7.9 a. Swapping lines: pieces showing internal lines.

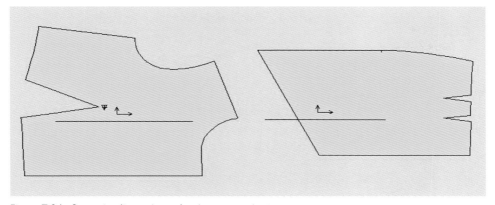

Figure 7.9 b. Swapping lines: pieces showing new perimeters.

Modify Line

By using the commands in the Modify Line function, lines can be moved, rotated, changed in length, split, or combined, and curved lines can be smoothed. See Figure 7.10.

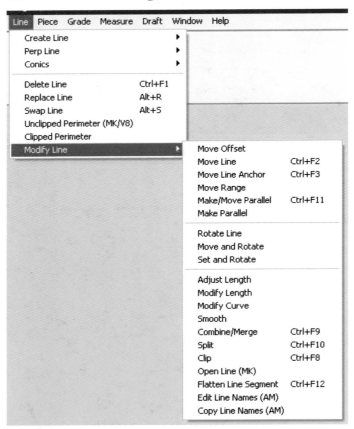

Figure 7.10 Line> Modify Line drop-down menu

Move Offset

The Move Offset command is used to create an offset line that then becomes the perimeter. To use this command, follow these steps:

    1. Select Line>Modify Line>Move Offset.

2. Using the cursor, select the line to offset and click on OK.
3. The location of the offset line (new perimeter) can be selected either by moving the cursor and clicking (when in Cursor mode) or by entering specific values in the Value Input field and clicking on OK (when in Value mode).

Move Line

A line can be moved in any direction, but the line orientation is not changed. If a perimeter line is moved, it remains a perimeter line, but the shape/size of the piece may be altered. Lines cannot be moved from one piece to another using this command. To use this command, complete the following steps:

1. Select Line>Modify Line>Move Line.
2. Using the cursor, select the line to move and click on OK.
3. The new location of the line can be selected either by using the Cursor or Value mode.

Make/Move Parallel and Make Parallel

The Make/Move Parallel and Make Parallel commands can be used to make a line parallel to another line. In the case of Make/Move Parallel, after a line has been made parallel to another, it can be moved. To use these commands, follow these steps:

1. Select Line>Modify Line>Make/Move Parallel or >Make Parallel.
2. Using the cursor, select the line to be made parallel and click on OK.
3. Select the line to be used as a guide by clicking on it.
4. On the line to be made parallel, use the cursor to select a point to remain stationary.
5. If the Make/Move Parallel command is in use, the new parallel line can then be moved to a new location using the Cursor or Value mode.

Rotate Line and Move and Rotate

These commands are used to rotate a line or to move and then rotate a line, as described below:

1. Select Line>Modify Line>Rotate Line or >Move and Rotate.
2. Using the cursor, select the line(s) to rotate and click on OK.

154

3. If the Move and Rotate command is in use, move the line to the appropriate location by using the Cursor or Value mode and click on OK.
4. Using the cursor, select the point (on that line) to remain stationary when the line is rotated.
5. The rotation angle of the line can be selected by either moving the cursor in Cursor mode and clicking once, or by using the Value mode and entering a specific angle value in the Value Input field, and then clicking on OK.

Set and Rotate

Using the Set and Rotate command, a line can be moved so that a point selected on it is placed on a point set on a different line. The moved line can then be rotated. To use this command, follow these steps:
1. Select Line>Modify Line>Set and Rotate.
2. Select the Match Point on the line to move.
3. Select Match Point on the target line.
4. The rotation angle of the line can be selected by either moving the cursor in Cursor mode and clicking once, or by using the Value mode and entering a specific angle value in the Value Input field, and then clicking on OK.

Adjust Length

This command is used to change the length of a line. The procedure to do so follows:
1. Select Line>Modify Line>Adjust Length.
2. Using the cursor, select the line that will be adjusted.
3. Select the end point to change by clicking on it.
4. The change in line length can be determined by using the Cursor or Value mode.

Modify Length

The Modify Length command is used to change the length of a curved line and, as such, to make the curve either greater or smaller.

See Figures 7.11a and b for an example of a modified length of a curve.

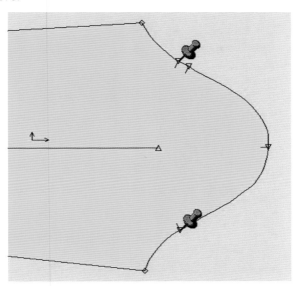

Figure 7.11 a. Modify Length: original sleeve cap with thumbtacks defining distance to modify

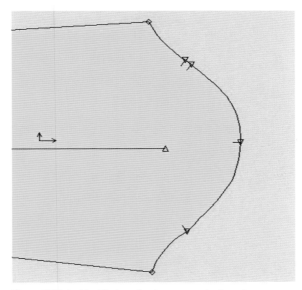

Figure 7.11 b. Modify Length: sleeve cap shortened

1. Select Line>Modify Line>Modify Length.
2. Using the cursor, select a curved line to be modified.
3. Position the thumbtacks to define the section of line to be modified and click on OK.
4. The number in the Value Input field in the user input box is the length of the line to be modified. Enter the new line length in this field and click on OK. The shortest line that can be achieved is a straight line.

Modify Curve

The Modify Curve command is used to curve a line or a section of a line.

1. Select Line>Modify Line>Modify Curve.
2. Using the cursor, select a point on a line to modify.
3. Define the section of the line to be curved by using the thumbtacks.

Hint for Success

Reminder: To move a thumbtack, click on it, remove your finger from the mouse, and move the mouse (and thumbtack) the desired distance. Click again to finalize the placement of the thumbtack.

---

4. Move the line to create the desired curve and click on OK. See Figures 7.12a and b for an example of a curved line.

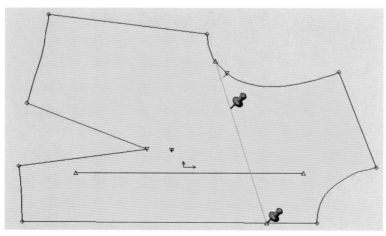

Figure 7.12 a. Modify Curve: defining line section to be curved

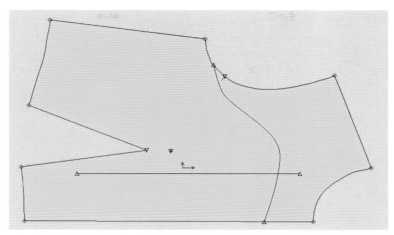

Figure 7.12 b. Modify Curve: line curved

Smooth

The Smooth command is used to smooth out "bumps" in lines, and as such, it flattens curves. The rate of smoothing is determined by the **Smooth Factor**. The higher the number, the more quickly smoothing occurs, but lines may change shape more than intended when the number is too high. To smooth lines and curves, follow these instructions:

1. Select Line>Modify Line>Smooth.
2. Enter the Smooth Factor in the user input box.
3. Using the cursor, select a line to smooth.
4. Define the area by moving the thumbtacks and click on OK.
5. Click the mouse in any location, as many times as needed to create the desired level of smoothness.

158

Combine/Merge

The Combine/Merge command allows the patternmaker to combine two or more lines. Lines do not have to be touching to be merged. Internal lines that intersect will create loops when merged. See Figures 7.13a and 7.13b. To merge lines, follow these steps:

1. Select Line>Modify Line>Combine/Merge.
2. Using the cursor, select the lines to merge. If internal lines are to be merged, select near the beginning points of the lines (working in a clockwise direction). Click on OK.

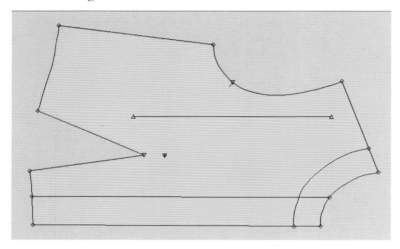

Figure 7.13 a. Combine/Merge Lines: internal lines intersecting

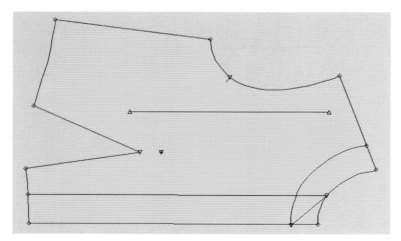

Figure 7.13 b. Combine/Merge Lines: intersecting internal lines merged

Hint for Success

Reminder: Lines are created in a clockwise direction.

Split

The Split command allows the patternmaker to split a straight or curved line. To use this command, follow these steps:

1. Select Line>Modify Line>Split.
2. Select a splitting point on a line to split. An apex-up triangle will indicate the point where the line has been split. This symbol will only be visible when Symbols has been selected in the Display tab of Edit>Preferences/Options or when View>Points>All Points or >Intermediate Points has been selected.

Clip

The Clip command is used to trim and remove the part of a line that is on one side of an intersecting line. Lines that are part of a perimeter cannot be removed. To use this command, follow these steps:

1. Select Line>Modify Line>Clip.
2. Select the line to clip on the side that will not be removed. If this line intersects only one other line, the trimming will automatically occur. If this line intersects several lines, select the intersecting line at which to clip. When using a circle and intersecting lines, it may be necessary to split the circle at several places before the circle or lines can be trimmed.

Line Function Exercises

For each exercise, use a new piece. After completing each exercise, print a hard copy of your results.

1. Mark the placement of a round-bottomed pocket on a bodice front.
   a. Create a horizontal line 2.5 inches long at an appropriate place in the bodice front. Select Line>Create Line and then >2 Point Line>Horizontal from the cursor drop-down menu.
   b. Create a new line two inches away from the previous line. Select Line>Create Line>Offset Even.

c. Create a curved bottom for the pocket. Select
Line>Conics>Circle 2 Pt Center. Click on the left ends of the
two lines to create a circle. Move the cursor until the circle
overlaps the lines.

d. Split the circle at the top and bottom. Select Line>Modify
Line>Split.

   i. Trim away the unwanted lines. Select Line>Modify
Line>Clip. Select the bottom (left curved side) of the pocket to keep and the upper intersecting line to clip.

   ii. Select the bottom (left curved edge) of the pocket to keep
and the lower intersecting line to clip at.

e. Delete the unwanted segments of the circle using
Line>Delete Line.

f. Save this piece (suggested name: front pocket placement). It
will be used for an exercise in the next chapter.

2. Copy the pocket and place it on a sleeve piece. Keep a record
of the commands used and how they were used.

3. Use skirt front pieces to complete the following exercises:

a. Make a skirt front piece five inches longer.
Which commands did you use?

b. On the lengthened skirt front piece, create a curve at the
intersection of the center front seam and the hem.
Which commands did you use?

c. On a new skirt piece, rotate the grain line 45 degrees to create a bias pattern. Move and shorten the grain line so that it
is appropriately located within the pattern piece. Use
Line>Modify Line and so on.

4. Using a new bodice front piece, create a new neckline of your
choice using line commands.
Which commands did you use?

5. Create a facing:

a. Use a front bodice piece.

b. Extend the center front by one inch. Select Line>Create
Line>Offset Even (follow the prompts) Line>Swap Line.
See Figures 7.9a and 7.9b.

c. Create Offset Even lines two inches inside the center front
and the front neckline. Select Line>Create Line>Offset
Even. See Figure 7.13a.

d. Shorten these offset lines by selecting Line>Modify Line>Adjust Length. See Figure 7.14a.

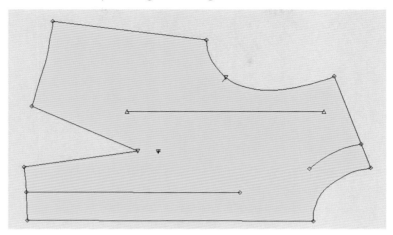

Figure 7.14 a. Combine/Merge Lines: internal lines shortened so that they do not intersect

e. Merge these offset lines to form the outline of the facing. Select Line>Modify Line>Combine/Merge. See Figure 7.14b.

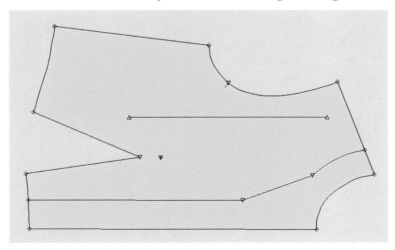

Figure 7.14 b. Combine/Merge Lines: nonintersecting internal lines merged

f. Smooth the merged line. Select Line>Modify Line>Smooth. See Figure 7.14c.

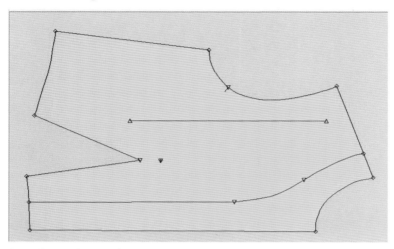

Figure 7.14 c. Combine/Merge Lines: merged lines smoothed

    g. Save this piece. In the next chapter, it will be used to create a separate facing piece.

6. Create a straight sleeve:

    a. Using a sleeve piece, create a 2 Point line horizontally from each underarm point to the wrist.

    b. Swap each newly created internal line with the appropriate perimeter line.

    c. Create a 2 Point vertical line from the wrist point on the front seam line to the back seam line.

    d. Swap the newly created internal line with the perimeter line.

    e. Save this piece (suggested name: straight sleeve). It will be used in the next chapter.

Summary

Lines are important design tools for the patternmaker. Lines can be created, moved, added, split, joined, straightened, lengthened, and shortened. All lines are initially created as internal lines. Perimeter lines are then made by swapping or replacing them with internal lines.

Key Term

Smooth Factor

Review Questions

1. Describe the difference between Digitized lines and 2 Point lines.
2. Describe the uses of the Offset Uneven command.
3. What does the triangle symbol indicate when a new circle is created?
4. What is the difference between Replace Line and Swap Line?
5. What is the purpose of the Smooth Factor?
6. What is made using the Conics function?

CHAPTER EIGHT

Piece Function, Part I

Objectives

After studying this chapter, you will be able to

- Create and modify basic piece shapes through drafting.
- Create new pieces from existing pieces.
- Create, modify, and remove darts.
- Add fullness to pieces.
- Add and modify seam allowances.

Introduction

This chapter presents methods of creating and modifying parts of pieces. The Piece function is used in conjunction with the line and point functions to change basic slopers into stylish patterns. Using this function, darts can be manipulated easily, and seam allowances are added with just a few clicks of the mouse. Selected commands within this function, specifically, Create Piece, Darts, Fullness, and Seam, will be explained. Figure 8.1 shows the Piece function drop-down menu.

Figure 8.1 Piece drop-down menu

Hint for Success

Do not forget to name and save all newly created pieces. Make sure that each new piece has a new name and does not replace an existing piece.

Create Piece

The Create Piece command is a tool used to create very basic piece shapes through drafting. It can be used for collars, waistbands, circles, circle skirts, and ovals. In addition, this command is used to select parts of existing slopers to create new pieces, such as facings. Sometimes the piece being created will automatically appear in the center of the screen and may be hidden behind other pieces. F2 will show all of the pieces in the work area. Figure 8.2 shows the options within the Create Piece drop-down menu.

Figure 8.2 Piece>Create Piece drop-down menu

Rectangle

A rectangle is best made by using the Value mode, not the Cursor mode, in the user input box. In Value mode, rectangles can be made in a specific size for use as waistbands, cuffs, rectangular collars, and other pieces. Following is a list of instructions for creating a rectangle:

1. Select Piece>Create Piece>Rectangle.

2. Click in the work area to select the first corner of the rectangle. In Cursor mode, create the rectangle by moving the cursor and clicking again, or in Value mode, enter values in the X and Y fields in the user input box.
3. Click on OK.
4. Type the name of the rectangle piece in the user input box, and click on OK.

Circle

Circles may be used to create hats and frills such as flared frills around the bottom of skirts or sleeves. Follow these steps to make a circle:
1. Select Piece>Create Piece>Circle.
2. If you wish to create a new circle piece, select Create as a New Piece in the user input box, and type the name of the new piece in the user input box.
3. Click to select the center of the circle.
4. Select Radius or Circumference in the user input box.
5. In Cursor mode, move the cursor to define the circumference of the circle and click once. In Value mode, fill in the Dist field in the user input box with the measurement of the radius or circumference and click on OK.

Skirt

The Skirt command creates a quarter of circle skirt with a defined waist size and length. To create a circle skirt, follow these steps:
1. Select Piece>Create Piece>Circle.
2. Enter a name for the skirt piece in the user input box.
3. Select or type in the appropriate dimensions for the skirt waist and length, in the user input box, then click on OK.

Collar

The Collar command is used to create a convertible roll collar. The measurements for center back to shoulder and shoulder to center front are taken from the bodice piece, using the Line Length command within the Measure function drop-down menu. It will be necessary to create a collar piece for each graded size. (Remember to name each piece with its size.) To create a convertible roll collar, follow these steps:

1. Select Piece>Create Piece>Collar.
2. Enter a name for the collar in the user input box.
3. Type in the appropriate dimensions for the collar, in the user input box, then click on OK.
4. The collar point can be adjusted using Point>Modify Points>Move Single Point. For other roll collar shapes, it will be necessary to add additional points along the outer edge.

Facing

It is usually best if the outline of a facing has been created on the piece (see Exercise 5 in Chapter 7 on page 159). However, it is possible to digitize a line that can be used as the facing outline using the Facing command. To create a facing, at least one of the lines used must be a perimeter line. Follow these steps to use the Facing command:

1. Select Piece>Create Piece>Facing.
2. From the user input box, select Existing Line or Digitized Line:
   a. Using Existing Line, on the piece, select an existing internal facing line. See Figure 8.3a.

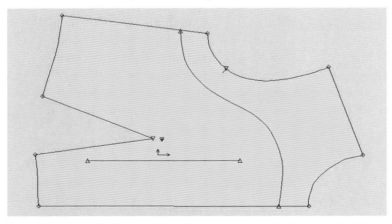

Figure 8.3 a. Using the Facing command: piece with lines indicating the facing shape.

b. Using Digitized Line, create a digitized line to define the facing.

3. A weight icon will appear on the grain line of the facing. Place the cursor on the facing piece and click once. The facing piece will become attached to the cursor and can be moved away from the original pattern piece. Click again to release the facing. See Figure 8.3b and 8.3c.

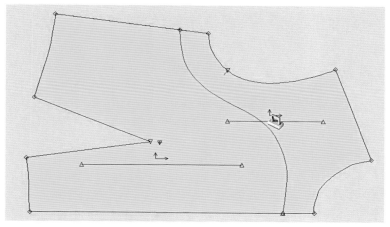

Figure 8.3 b. Using the Facing command: piece after selecting an existing facing line.

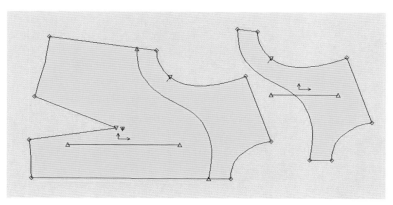

Figure 8.3 c. Using the Facing command: piece after the facing piece has been selected and named.

4. Enter a name for the piece in the user input box.

5. It may be necessary to move the grain line into the facing. To do this, use Line>Move Line. See Figure 8.3d.

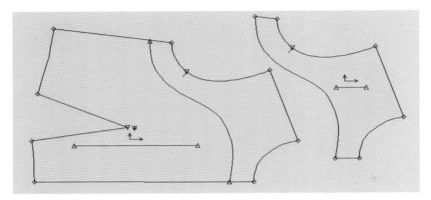

Figure 8.3 d. Using the Facing command: grain line on the facing adjusted to fit within the piece.

Create Binding

The Create Binding command is especially good for creating graded waistbands. To do so, some pieces must be copied and flipped. Here is how to create a binding.

1. Select Piece>Create Piece>Create Binding.
2. Enter the binding width and notch type in the user input box.
3. Using the cursor, select the lines that will be used for the binding. Lines from different pieces can be used together to create one long binding—e.g., front and back armhole, and front and back neckline. However, for the notches to be correctly located, it is necessary to flip one of the pieces. See Figure 8.4.

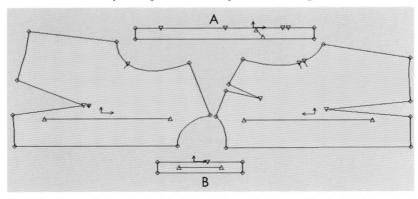

Figure 8.4 Create Binding: Letter A is the armhole and B is the neckline in this piece.

For information on how to flip a piece, see Chapter 9 on page 195.

4. It may be necessary to rotate the grain line 45 degrees so that the piece will be on the bias. To do so, select Line>Modify Line> Rotate Line.

Copy

Use the Copy command when you want to work on a piece while retaining the original copy. To copy a piece, follow these steps:

1. Select Piece>Create Piece>Copy.
2. Select the piece to copy, use the cursor to move the selected piece, and click again to drop the piece.
3. Enter the piece name in the user input box, and click on OK.

Extract

This command is used to extract a section from a piece. The extracted area may be used to make pockets or a garment with sections of different colored fabrics. To extract a region, the original piece must be split into sections. The portion to be extracted must be totally enclosed. See Figures 8.5a and b.

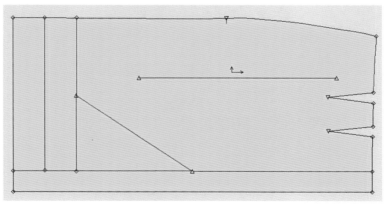

Figure 8.5 a. Extracting a section of a piece: piece ready for the extraction of a section.

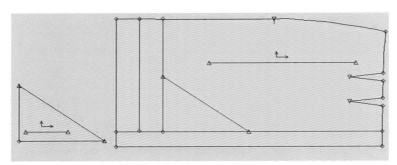

Figure 8.5 b. Extracting a section of a piece: piece with section extracted

Extracting a piece does not leave a hole in the original piece. To use this command, complete the following steps:

1. Select Piece>Create Piece>Extract.
2. Select a piece to extract a region from, by clicking on it.
3. Select a region to extract by clicking the mouse in the selected area. In the same way, additional regions may be selected if desired. Click on OK.
4. Enter a new name for the extracted piece in the user input box.
5. Select any internal lines that must accompany the extracted piece, by clicking on each. (A grain line will automatically be added to the extracted piece.) Click on OK in the user input box or in the cursor right click drop-down box. If no internal lines are desired, click on OK.
6. The extracted piece is attached to the cursor. It can be moved and then dropped by clicking the mouse.

Trace

To trace and create a new piece from an existing piece, the original piece must be split into sections. The portion used to create a new piece using the Trace command need not be totally enclosed. To use the Trace command, follow these steps:

1. Select Piece>Create Piece>Trace.
2. Working in a clockwise direction, select the perimeter lines of the new piece in turn. Click on OK.

Combine Diff Line

The Combine Diff Line command is used to combine two darts located on different lines, such as a waist bust dart and an underarm bust dart. To use this command, follow these steps:

1. Select Piece>Darts>Combine Diff Line.
2. Select the dart point to be combined, by clicking on it.
3. Select the rotation point.
4. Select the hold line.
5. Select the dart point of the target dart.
6. Select the new dart apex.

Change Dart Tip

The Change Dart Tip command simply adjusts the length of the dart by moving the tip (apex). To move the tip to redirect a dart (and change the location of the apex), it is necessary to select Point>Modify Point and use the Move Point command. To change the dart tip, complete the following steps:

1. Select Piece>Darts>Change Dart Tip.
2. Using the cursor, select the dart tip to be changed.
3. To select a new position for the dart tip, either:
   a. In Cursor mode, place the cursor at the new location for the dart tip and click on OK.
   a. In Value mode, add or subtract the distance the tip is to be moved from the distance indicated in the Value field and type that number in the distance field, then click on OK. The distance to the dart apex is measured from the center of the perimeter edge of the dart.

Equal Dart Legs

This command is used to make the two legs of a dart the same length.

To use this command, follow these instructions:

1. Select Piece>Darts>Equal Dart Legs.
2. Select either
   a. The dart tip to balance the dart legs—this will make the legs equal in length (a length that is the average of their original lengths) by moving the apex.
   b. The dart leg to adjust—this will make the selected leg the same length as the other leg by slightly adjusting the shape of the piece.

178

Fold/Close Dart End

Darts can be either cut and stitched or folded and stitched. When a dart is to be folded (during garment construction), the V of the dart is filled with fabric. When darts are shown like this on a piece in the work area, they cannot be manipulated, but they are ready to have seam allowances added. Figures 8.9a and b show open and folded/closed darts. To prepare darts for adding seam allowances, follow these steps:

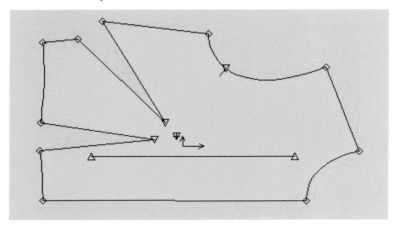

Figure 8.9 a. Piece showing open darts

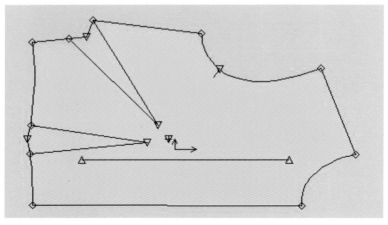

Figure 8.9 b. Piece showing closed darts

1. Select Piece>Darts>Fold/Close Dart End.
2. From the user input box, select Include Fold Lines. You may also wish to select Include Notches, particularly for large, curved darts, and to select the option for including a drill hole at the apex.
3. Select the dart on the side to fold to.

Hint for Success

To create properly closed darts, it is important to know the direction in which darts should be pressed.

Open Dart

This command is used to open a dart that has been folded. Only open darts can be manipulated.

To use this command, follow these steps:
1. Select Piece>Darts>Open Dart.
2. Choose the dart to be opened by selecting any point along the dart perimeter line (the outside edge of the dart).

Smooth Line

Sometimes after a dart has been moved, it may be necessary to smooth the perimeter line from which the dart was removed. The Smooth Line command in Piece>Dart may be used. This works in the same way as the Smooth command accessed by selecting Line>Modify Line. See Chapter 7 on page 152 and Figures 8.10a–d.

Flatten Line Segment

The Flatten Line Segment command makes a curved line straight between graded points. It can be accessed by selecting Piece>Dart>Flatten Line Segment or Line>Modify Line>Flatten Line Segment. To use this command, complete these steps:
1. Select Piece>Darts>Flatten Line Segment.
2. Select the line to be flattened.
3. Move the thumbtacks to define the length of the line, and click once. See Figures 8.10a–d.

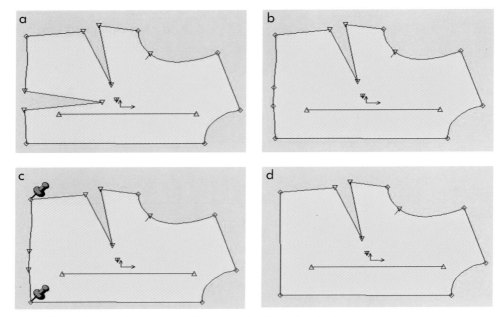

Figure 8.10 a–d. Flatten line segment after closing dart (removing dart).

Permanently Removing Darts

Sometimes fashion styles call for loosely fitted garments with few or no darts, such as a Chanel jacket, elastic-waist skirt or pants, t-shirts, or sweat suits. To remove a dart, follow these instructions:

1. Delete the apex of the dart by selecting Point>Delete Point.
2. Combine/Merge the three line segments (the pattern perimeter before the dart, the dart edge, and the perimeter after the dart) by selecting Line>Modify Line>Combine/Merge. Remember to work in a clockwise direction.
3. Flatten or smooth the line segment as previously described.
4. If underarm darts are removed, it will be necessary to adjust the length of the front bodice side seam so that it is equal to the length of the back bodice side seam.

Fullness

The Fullness commands can be used to add flare or gathers to a piece for design purposes. They can also be used to remove some of the fullness in pieces such as a circle skirt. Using these commands is very similar to the traditional way of modifying slopers using the slash and spread method. After using a fullness command, it may be necessary to smooth lines. The cursor drop-down menu can be used to accurately place slash lines.

1 Point Fullness

This command is used to add a wedge of fullness such as that required to add a flare to a straight skirt. It can also be used to remove a wedge of fullness. To use this command, follow these steps:

1. Select Piece>Fullness>1 Point Fullness.
2. Click on the point on a perimeter line where the added fullness will start. On a different perimeter line, click on the point where the greatest amount of fullness will be added. This will create a slash line.
3. Select the hold line, the line to remain stationary.
4. In the user input box, enter the desired amount of fullness to be added or subtracted, then click on OK. See Figure 8.11.

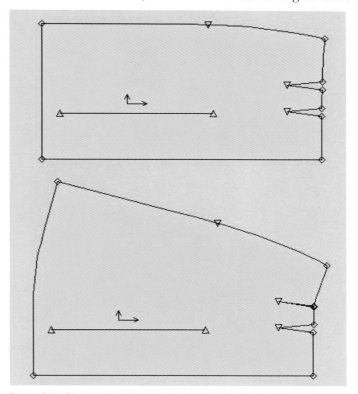

Figure 8.11 Skirt piece before and after adding four inches of fullness between the hem and the dart by using Piece>Fullness>1 Point Fullness.

182

Parallel Fullness

This command is used to add a rectangle of fullness to a piece such as the extra fabric required to convert a straight skirt into a pleated skirt. Here is the procedure for using this command.

1. Select Piece>Fullness>Parallel Fullness.
2. Create slash line(s) by clicking on the desired locations on two different perimeter lines, then click on OK.
3. Select the hold line, the line to remain stationary.
4. In the user input box, enter the amount of fullness to be added or subtracted, then click on OK. Figure 8.12 shows a sleeve with four inches of parallel fullness added.

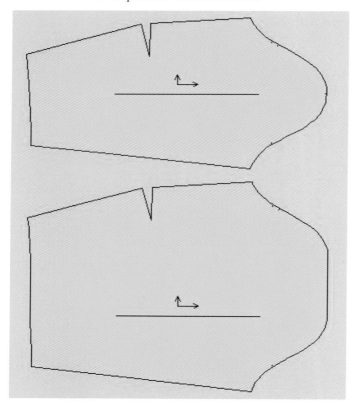

Figure 8.12 Sleeve before and after adding four inches of fullness by using Piece>Fullness>Parallel

Seams

The Gerber Pattern Design software allows for the easy addition of simple seam allowances and for different seam-allowance widths for different seams. For example, a garment hem may have a one-inch seam allowance, whereas the sides may have a half-inch seam allowance. Darts that are going to be folded during construction should be closed before adding seam allowances. There are many options for adjusting corners in the Seam command: Miter Corner, Double Miter Corner, Mirrored Corner, and Turnback Corner.

Although some commands will work after seam allowances are added, usually it is best to add seams only when a piece has been completed. It is possible to move points, notches, and lines after a seam allowance has been added; however, darts may not be manipulated at that point.

Define/Add Seam

This command is used to define the size of a seam allowance to be added to a piece or perimeter line. To define a seam allowance, follow these steps:

1. Select Piece>Seams>Define/Add Seam.
2. Select Manual - Even from the user input box.
3. Using the cursor, select the lines or pieces to which seam allowances will be added. The same seam-allowance will be added to all of the piece perimeter lines if a piece is selected. By selecting specific lines, the patternmaker may customize seam allowances. After selecting the lines, click on OK.
4. Type the desired size of the seam allowance in the user input box, and click on OK. A dotted line indicating the position of the cutting line will appear around the pattern piece. See Figure 8.13.

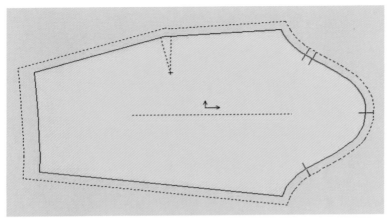

Figure 8.13 Piece with seam allowance defined

After a seam allowance for a piece has been defined, the allowance for a particular line, such as a hem, may be changed by following the process described above for just that line.

The dotted line must be converted to a cutting line by using the Swap Sew/Cut command.

Hint for Success

If the seam allowance is not showing, select View>
Preferences/Options>Display and make sure that the Hide
Seams is not checked.

Swap Sew/Cut

The Swap Sew/Cut command exchanges the added seam allowance line for the piece perimeter line, creating the cutting and sewing lines. The sewing line is shown as a dashed line, while the cutting line is shown as a solid line. To use this command, follow these steps:

1. Select Piece>Seam>Swap Sew/Cut.
2. From the user input box, under Digitized Corners, select Ignore, and from the Grade Rules box, select Ignore. For more advanced work, different selections may be needed, but those are beyond the scope of this book.

3. Select the pieces to Swap Sew/Cut lines, and click on OK. See Figure 8.14.

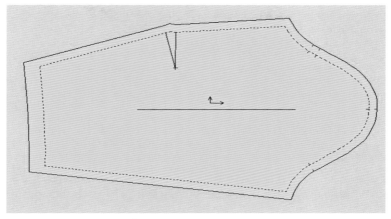

Figure 8.14 Piece with Sew/Cut lines swapped

4. If a seam allowance is changed by using Define/Add after the sew/cut line has been swapped, the outer cut line will remain the same. This will produce a change in the size of the piece.

Add/Remove Seam

The Add/Remove Seam command is used after a seam allowance has been placed around a piece. It removes or returns the appearance of a stitching line on a piece. It cannot be used to create or remove a seam allowance. To use this command, select the command and click on the piece to be changed.

Hint for Success

To remove a seam allowance, use the Swap Sew/Cut command so that the dashed line is on the outside of the piece. In the Define/Add Seam command, select the pieces from which to remove the seam allowance. In the Value field, type in 0 (zero). Click on OK.

Remove Corner

The Remove Corner command is used to revert back to regular a corner that has been altered in some way, such as mitering. To use this command, follow these steps:

1. Select Piece>Seam>Remove Corner.
2. From the user input box, select either Piece or Point. Corner modifications can be removed from an entire piece or selected points.
3. Select either the piece or the points, as appropriate, from which to remove the altered corners, and click on OK.

Mitered Corner

The purpose of a mitered corner is to remove excess fabric. They are most frequently used to remove bulky fabric at a corner or on sharply pointed corners, such as tie-belts and collar points. See Figure 8.15.

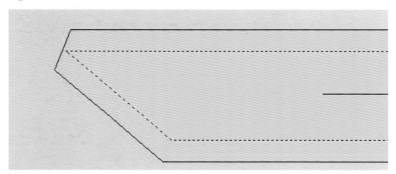

Figure 8.15 Mitered corner

Corners can be mitered before or after the Sew/Cut lines have been swapped. Only corners created by two adjoining lines can be mitered. For example, a corner created by pulling out a point on a straight line cannot be mitered. To use this command, follow these steps:

1. Select Piece>Seam>Mitered Corner.
2. Select the outside point of the corner to miter. If in Cursor mode, determine the correct placement of the seam allowance by adjusting the cursor and clicking on OK. If in Value mode, enter the appropriate amount in the Value field, and then click on OK.

Double Mitered Corner

Corners can be double mitered before or after the Sew/Cut lines have been swapped. The corner must be less than 160 degrees. Only corners created by two adjoining lines can be double mitered. To double miter a corner, complete the following steps:

1. Select Piece>Seam>Double Mitered Corner.
2. On the cutting line (solid line), select the point of the corner to double miter. If in Cursor mode, drag the first portion of the miter line to the desired position, and then click once. Drag the second portion of the miter line to the desired position, and then click once. If in Value mode, enter the appropriate distance in the Value field. Click on OK.

Hint for Success

It is usually best to miter corners after the cut/sew lines have been swapped.

Mirrored Corner

The purpose of a mirrored corner is to create a hem shape that matches the shape of the piece, such as a hem for pegged pants or a flared skirt. This command is used to mirror one corner at a time. See Figure 8.16.

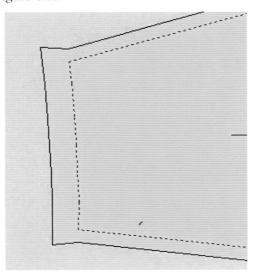

Figure 8.16 Sleeve hem with mirrored corners

To create a mirrored corner, follow these steps:
1. Select Piece>Seam>Mirrored Corner.
2. Select the corner to mirror. The selection must be on the cut line whether it is the perimeter (outer) line or not. Select the cut line before or after the corner to be mirrored.

Turnback Corner

Turnback Corner is an easy method to create a hem shape that matches the shape of the piece. This command will create mirrored corners on each end of the hemline selected. It can be done before or after the seam allowances have been swapped. To use this command, follow these steps:
1. Select Piece>Seam>Turnback Corner.
2. Select the hem line to apply turnback seam corners to. This can be a cut or sew line.

Summary

Stylish patterns can be created from basic slopers by using the Piece function in conjunction with Line and Point functions. Basic slopers can be modified. Simple pattern pieces such as collars, waistbands, and circle skirts can be created using the Create Piece command.

The Darts commands, in the Piece function, allow patternmakers to manipulate darts. For example, a dart can be rotated, distributed on the same line, split and distributed on different lines, combined, added, resized, and removed.

The Fullness commands are similar to the traditional slash and spread method of patternmaking. They are used to add flare or gathers to a piece for design purposes. They can also be used to remove some of the fullness in pieces such as a circle skirt.

The Gerber Pattern Design software also allows for the easy addition of seam allowances and different seam-allowance widths for different seams.

Key Terms

dart apex
hold line

Review Questions

1. Why is it usually best to create a rectangle using Value mode rather than Cursor mode?
2. Which line usually serves as the hold line?
3. Why is it important to know the direction in which darts should be pressed?
4. Which commands are very similar to the traditional way of modifying slopers using the slash and spread method?
5. What is the purpose of a mitered corner?
6. What is the difference between a mirrored corner and a turnback corner?

Piece Function, Part I Exercises

Save and print a hard copy after completing each of the following exercises.

1. Create a facing.

   Use the pattern piece that was created for Exercise 5 in Chapter 7 (see Figure 7.14c).

   a. Move the piece into the work area.
   b. Select Piece>Create Piece>Facing.
   c. From the user input box (Line Type), select Existing Facing Line.
   d. On the piece, click once on a facing line.
   e. Click once on the facing piece. Using the cursor move the piece to a new location and click again to release the piece.
   f. In the user input box, enter the name for the new piece (for example, bodice front facing). Click on OK.
   g. To move the grain line into facing, select Line>Modify Line>Move Line.
   h. Select the line to move (the grain line) and click on OK.
   i. In Cursor mode, place the grain line in the facing. Click once to release the line.
   j. Save the new piece.
   k. Place the front and facing in a corner of the work area for later use.

2. Extract a piece:

Select Open from the File menu. Select the pattern piece that was created in Exercise 1 in Chapter 7.

a. Draw a line across the opening of the pocket placement (Line>Create Line>2Point. From the cursor drop-down menu, select End Line. Then select the first point of the line at the open end of the pocket, and select the second point at the other open end of the pocket).

b. Select Piece>Create Piece>Extract.

c. Follow the prompt instructions in the user input box to extract the pocket.

   i.   Select the bodice front piece containing the pocket.

   ii. Click once inside the pocket, and click on OK.

   iii. Enter a new name for the extracted piece (pocket), and click on OK.

   iv. There are no internal lines to select so click on OK.

d. Move the pocket away from the bodice.

e. Save the new piece.

3. Make a copy of the pocket (Piece>Create Piece>Copy).

4. Add seam allowances.

a. Press F2 on the keyboard to show all pieces in the work area.

b. Close the darts but include the fold line (Piece>Darts>Fold/Close Dart End). Follow the prompts.

c. Place a 1¼-inch seam allowance on the top of the pockets and a ½-inch seam allowance the remaining piece perimeter lines (Piece>Seam>Define/Add Seam).

d. Swap the sew and cut lines. Select Piece>Seam>Swap Sew/Cut Lines and follow the prompts in the user input box.

5. Rotate a dart. Work with a front bodice piece.

a. Move the waistline dart to the side seam. Use Piece>Darts>Rotate, then follow the instructions. Do not forget to move the dart apex. Try this exercise several times using different hold lines to see the different results. Continue working with the front bodice that seems most appropriate.

    b. Smooth the waistline. Select Piece>Darts>Smooth Line and follow the instructions. The line will be smoothed automatically when you click on OK.

6. Create a flared sleeve by adding tapered fullness.

    a. Open the straight sleeve created in Exercise 6 of Chapter 7.

    b. Place three X marks at equidistant intervals on the sleeve cap (Point>Mark X Point, and then from the cursor drop-down menu select Multiple>Proportional on Line).

    c. Add tapered fullness at each X point. Select Piece>Fullness>Tapered Fullness. Create a slash line horizontally from an X point to the wrist, and click on OK.

    d. Select the sleeve cap to remain stationary, as no internal lines need to be moved. Click on OK again.

    e. At the first slash line spread the piece two inches. Repeat the process at the other slash lines.

7. Remove the back shoulder dart.

    a. Rotate the back shoulder dart so that it is located in the back neckline. Use the dart apex as the rotation point.

    b. Close the dart, but do not include fold lines.

    c. Combine/Merge the three lines that now make up the neckline.

    d. Move points and/or smooth the neckline until it is appropriately shaped.

8. Advanced exercise: Create a basic princess-line bodice front. Use a one (waist) dart bodice front piece.

    a. Distribute and rotate the dart so that 50 percent is moved to the midpoint of the shoulder seam. Leave the point of that dart at the bust apex (rotation point).

    b. Move the point of the waist bust dart to the bust apex. (Use the Zoom command to show the piece in large scale to ensure accurate placement.)

    c. Split each dart line at the dart point (Line>Modify Line>Split) so that each leg is a separate line.

    d. Create a circle with a radius of two inches around the bust apex (Line>Conics>Circle Ctr Rad).

e. Create lines to define the centers of the darts (Line>
   Create Line>Divide Angle). See Figure 8.17a.

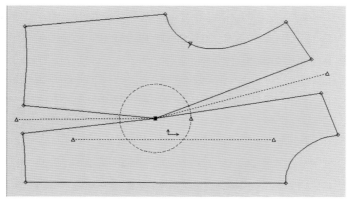

Figure 8.17 a. Creating a princess seam: define the centers

f. Create a line from point A to point B (Line>Create
   Line>2 Point). Create a line from point C to point D.
   See Figure 8.17b.

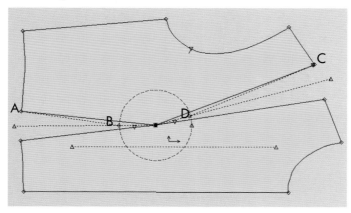

Figure 8.17 b. Creating a princess seam: adding a line

It is important that these lines are accurately placed, so
place the first points by using the cursor drop-down
menu. From this menu, select Intersection. If this is not
done, the tracing of pieces may not be possible as there
may be gaps in the proposed new perimeter.

g. Create a shallow curved line from point B to point D. It is easier to view if the dart center lines are deleted. See Figure 8.17c.

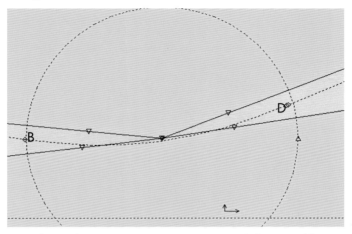

Figure 8.17 c. Creating a princess seam: creating a shallow curved line

The lines will merge more accurately if the line between B and D does not completely reach points B and D.

h. Merge the three newly created lines (Line>Modify Line>Combine/Merge).
i. Trace around the pieces using the newly created lines (Piece>Create>Trace).
j. Smooth the lines if needed.
k. Add matching notches to the pieces. See Figure 8.17d.

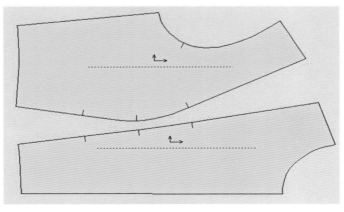

Figure 8.17 d. Creating a princess seam: adding notches

CHAPTER NINE

Piece Function, Part II

Objectives

After studying this chapter, you will be able to

- Modify and split pieces.
- Change the size of pieces in the x and y directions.
- Make allowances for fabrics that are expected to shrink or stretch.
- Create and work with mirrored pieces.
- Add annotations to pieces.
- Add pieces to the icon bar menu.

Introduction

This chapter will describe ways of changing the piece as a whole. Topics presented will include selected command in Modify Piece, and Split Piece, Combine/Merge, Scale, Shrink/Stretch, Mirror Piece, Fold and Unfold mirrored pieces, Annotate Piece, and Piece to Menu.

Modify Piece

Several commands are grouped together within the Modify Piece drop-down menu. They are accessed by selecting Piece>Modify Piece. See Figure 9.1.

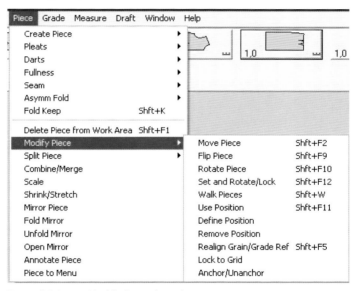

Figure 9.1 Piece>Modify Piece drop-down menu

Flip Piece

The Flip Piece command is used to flip a piece either about a line or in one of four directions.

1. Select Piece>Modify Piece>Flip Piece.
2. From the user input box, select Flip type:

a. *Flip About Line*: Select the line to flip the piece about, and click on OK. See Figures 9.2a and 9.2b.

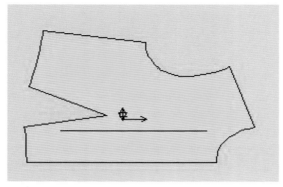

Figure 9.2 a. piece before flipping

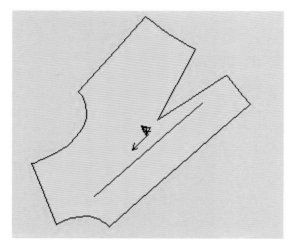

Figure 9.2 b. piece flipped about the shoulder line

b. *Flip About Common Line*: Select pieces to flip, and click on OK. Select a line to flip all of the pieces about, and click on OK.

c. *Flip Piece*: Select the appropriate quadrant for the direction of the flip. See Figure 9.3.

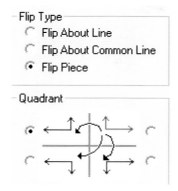

Figure 9.3 Quadrant in Flip command

Select the piece to flip, and click on OK.

Rotate Piece

When a piece is rotated, the grain line rotates with the piece so that the piece is not on the bias. To make a bias piece, it is necessary to rotate a piece and then rotate the grain line. Instructions for rotating a grain line follow later in this chapter.

Pieces can be rotated in three different ways:

1. *Select Reference Location*: This allows the patternmaker to choose a specific location on the piece, as the stationary point during rotation. The amount of rotation can be determined by using the cursor or inputting values in the user input box.
2. *Perform Alignment*: The piece will automatically rotate until the selected reference point lines up with the x or y axis, whichever has been selected. Instructions for this are not presented. This is beyond the scope of this textbook.
3. *Increment*: This command rotates a piece by a selected predetermined amount, in either a clockwise or counterclockwise direction.

Select Reference Location

To rotate a piece by selecting a reference location, complete the following steps:

1. Select Piece>Modify Piece>Rotate Piece.

2. Click Select Reference Location in the user input box. See Figure 9.4.

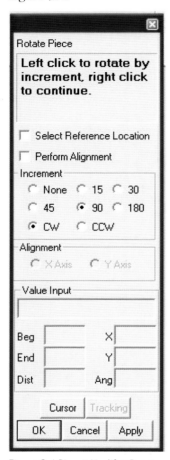

Figure 9.4 Piece>Modify>Rotate user input box

3. Select the piece to rotate, and click on OK.
4. From the user input box, select the Increment of rotation:
   a. Select a given increment from the user input box and either **CW** for clockwise rotation or **CCW** for counterclockwise rotation. Click once to rotate the piece by the selected increment. Each click will rotate the piece by the selected increment each time. Right click to stop using the command.
   b. Select None in the user input box. Select a point on the piece to rotate the piece around. Select a reference point (the point that can be moved by the cursor).

    i. In Cursor mode, the cursor is used to rotate the piece around the rotation point. When the desired degree of rotation is achieved click once.

    ii. In Value mode, inputting a distance or angle in the appropriate field in the user input box will determine the degree of rotation.

Increment

The Increment command is the most useful way of rotating a piece. When using this command, there is no need to select a point about which to rotate. The piece automatically rotates about its center. To use this command follow these instructions:

1. Select Piece>Modify Piece>Rotate Piece.
2. Check that neither Select Reference Location nor Perform Alignment is selected in the user input box. Select the desired angle of rotation and CW or CCW in the Increment field in the user input box.
3. Select the piece to rotate, and click on OK.
4. Click once to rotate the piece by the selected increment. Each click will rotate the piece by the selected increment. Right click to end the command.

Realign Grain/Grade Reference

The Realign Grain/Grade Reference command is used to realign the grain on a piece that has been rotated. It can be used to create bias cut patterns. This command will only function when you work with a piece that has been rotated. Follow these instructions to use this command:

1. Select Piece>Modify Piece>Realign Grain/Grade Reference.
2. Select Realign Grain/Grade Reference in the user input box.
3. Select the grain line to realign in a piece that has been rotated. The grain line will automatically rotate so that it is horizontal in the work area.

Split Piece

Pieces can be split in a variety of ways: on an existing or digitized line, point to point, horizontally or vertically, or diagonally left or diagonally right. Whichever method of splitting is selected, the following options are available in the user input box:

1. Add Piece to Model/Style: This adds a piece that was created by splitting to the model used in marker making.

2. Delete Original Piece.
3. Define Seam on Split Line: This adds a seam allowance on the split line. If the piece already has a perimeter cut line and an internal sew (stitching) line, the new pieces will be similar. The amount of the seam allowance must be entered.
4. Select Internals: This allows users to select which piece retains the internal lines that were in the original piece. If this is not selected, then each new piece will retain the internal lines that are within its boundaries.

In the Grading box, there are three options:

1. *Grade Straight*: Grading is *not* applied to the split line. See Figure 9.5a.

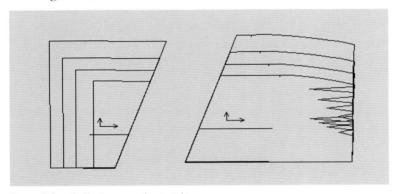

Figure 9.5 a. Split piece: grade straight

2. *Grade Proportional*: Grading is applied to the split line. See Figure 9.5b.

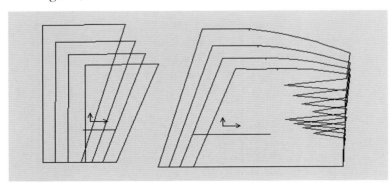

Figure 9.5 b. Split piece: grade proportional

3. *Maintain Graded Nest*: Maintains grade rules or will apply new grade rules to maintain the integrity of the piece.

Split on an Existing Line

Patternmakers can split a piece on an existing line using this command. To use this command, follow these steps:

1. Select Piece>Split Piece>Split on Line.
2. Make appropriate choices in the user input box. It is usually best not to delete the original piece and to select Grade Proportional or Maintain Graded Nest.
3. Select the splitting line. This line may extend beyond the perimeter of the piece. If it does not reach the perimeter of the piece, it will automatically be extended to the perimeter. If a grain line is selected, the piece will split on that line, and new grain lines will be created in each new piece.
4. In the user input box, enter the name for the new piece indicated by the weight icon, and click on OK.
5. Then, in the user input box, enter the name for the other new piece indicated by the weight icon, and click on OK.

Split on a Digitized Line

This command is used to create a digitized line and then to split a piece on that line.

1. Select Piece>Split Piece>Split on Digitized Line.
2. Make appropriate choices in the user input box.
3. Select the first point for the splitting line. A right click on the mouse will produce a drop-down menu with the same line options that were described in Chapter 7 page 139. Select the final point for this line. Double click to end the line. This line may extend beyond the perimeter of the piece. If it does not reach the perimeter of the piece, it will automatically be extended to the perimeter.
4. In the user input box, enter the name for the new piece indicated by the weight icon, and click on OK.
5. Then enter the name for the other new piece indicated by the weight icon, and click on OK.

Other Split Piece Commands

All of the remaining Split Piece commands work in a similar manner to the two previously described. The major difference between those two commands and the other commands within the menu is the way in which the split line is determined. The directions to use these other Split Piece commands are clearly described in the user input box.

Combine/Merge

The Combine/Merge command is used to combine pieces. There are many options available in the user input box for the Combine/Merge command. See Figure 9.6.

Figure 9.6 Combine/Merge user input box

The suggested options are:
- Grade Options-Paste Grading (MK)
- Merge Line Rules-Keep All Rules

When the Convert Mrg Line to Internal is checked in the user input box, there will be an internal line on the merged piece that indicates the location of the merge. It is usually best not to select Delete Original Pieces from the user input box so that it is possible to compare the combined piece with the original pieces. When pieces have been combined, it is advisable to check the grading immediately using View>Grade>Show All Sizes.

Looking at a graded nest of a combined piece can be confusing. Changing the stacking point by selecting View>Grade>Stacking On/Off may provide clarity.

Sometimes it is necessary to rotate or flip one of the pieces to be combined when the combined lines are the same length. When lines are different lengths, it is necessary to select which points will match. If the lines are the same length, the computer will automatically join them, and sometimes noncorresponding points may be joined. See Figure 9.7.

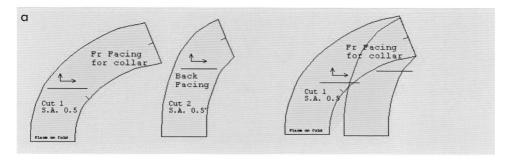

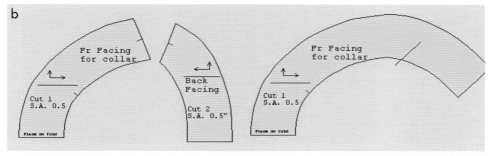

Figure 9.7 Combine/Merge: a. piece not flipped before merging b. one piece flipped before merging.

Although in some cases it is not necessary to flip or rotate pieces or to align them near one another, doing so makes it easier to see the results.

> ## Hint for Success
>
> When pieces are merged, the remaining perimeter lines are not merged. Before performing additional functions, it may be necessary to merge perimeter lines, using Line>Modify Line>Combine/Merge.

To use the Combine/Merge command, follow these steps:

1. Select Piece>Combine/Merge.
2. Select these suggested options from the user input box: Paste Grading, Keep All Rules, and Convert Mrg Line to Internal by checking the boxes next to each one.
3. Using the cursor, select the merge line on the piece to be moved. (Note: Flip pieces if necessary.)
4. Select the target line on the piece to remain stationary.
   a. If the lines are the same length, they will be automatically combined.
   b. If the lines are different lengths, select a match point on the set piece (the piece that will be moved) and select a match point on the target piece, then click on OK.
5. In the user input box, enter a name for the new piece, and click on OK.

> ## Hint for Success
>
> It is necessary to click on Cancel in the user input box to escape from the Combine/Merge command. A new command cannot be opened until Combine/Merge has been closed.

Scale

The Scale command changes the size of a piece in the x and/or y directions. Scale may be used to create petite or long sizes in pants, changing not only the length of the pants, but also the distance from the crotch to the waist. When used on bodice pieces, problems may arise with armhole and sleeve cap sizes. The user input box for this command contains two options: Linear and Percent. Linear asks for the total change in dimension (in inches) in the x and/or y direction. Percent asks for the percentage change in the x and/or y direction. To use this command, complete the following steps:

1. Select Piece>Scale.
2. In the user input box, select either Linear or Percent. Enter the desired amounts in the X and Y fields.
3. Select the piece that will be scaled, and click on OK. See Figure 9.8.

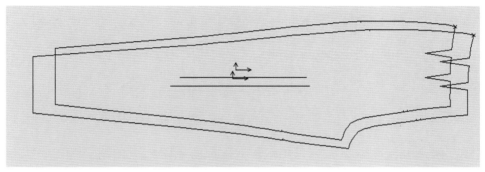

Figure 9.8 Original piece and a piece scaled four inches less in the x direction.

Shrink/Stretch

The Shrink/Stretch command allows the patternmaker to make allowances for fabric that is expected to shrink or stretch. The base-size pattern can be made with an appropriate percent or linear change to allow for fabric dimensional change. The software creates modified grade rules to maintain correct dimensions in all of the sizes of a piece after fabric shrinkage or growth has occurred. If a negative amount is entered in the user input box, the piece will increase in size to allow for shrinkage. If a positive amount is entered in the user input box, the piece will decrease in size to allow for growth. For some fabrics, it may be necessary to allow for shrinkage in one direction and growth in the other.

To use the Shrink/Stretch command follow these steps:

1. Select Piece>Shrink/Stretch.
2. Using the cursor, select the piece to modify. Do *not* click on OK.
3. In the user input box, select Method: Linear or Percent.
4. Enter the Shrink(-) or Stretch(+) amount. Now click on OK.

Mirror Piece

The Mirror Piece command is used to create a piece that has two symmetrical halves. As with traditional flat patternmaking, the patternmaker usually works with one side of the body and then mirrors it to create a complete piece. After a piece has been mirrored, asymmetrical designs can be created. To use the Mirror Piece command, follow these steps:

1. Select Piece>Mirror Piece.
2. In the user input box, if Fold after Mirror is selected, the newly mirrored piece will appear as a half piece with a dashed line indicating the fold line. If Fold after Mirror is not selected, the mirrored piece will be shown in its entirety.
3. The user input box also provides the option of placing notches at one or both ends of the fold line. Notch type can also be selected.
4. Select the mirror line on the piece to mirror, and click on OK. If a notch is to be placed at one end of the mirror line, select the end of the mirror line to be notched.

Hint for Success

An unfolded piece can be worked on as a complete piece, and asymmetrical designs can be created. Changes to one side of a piece will not affect the other side. Note: Perimeter lines must be Combined/Merged using Line>Modify Line>Combine/Merge. Work done on a folded piece will create a symmetrical piece when unfolded.

Fold Mirror

A previously mirrored piece that is still symmetrical can be folded along its mirror line. To use this command, follow these steps:

1. Select Piece>Fold Mirror.
2. Select the piece to fold, and click on OK.

Unfold Mirror

A mirrored piece that has been folded can be unfolded. Follow these steps to unfold a piece:

1. Select Piece>Unfold Mirror.
2. Select the piece to unfold, and click on OK.

Open Mirror

The Open Mirror command allows for returning a mirrored piece to a nonmirrored condition. The piece to be opened must already be folded. To use this command, follow these steps:

1. Select Piece>Open Mirror.
2. Select the piece to open, and click on OK.

Annotate Piece

Annotations (notes) can be added to pieces using the Annotate Piece command. To use this command, follow these steps:

1. Select Piece>Annotate Piece.
2. Select the location for the new annotation or click on the existing annotation to be edited.
    a. In the New Piece Annotation box, type in the annotation. Enter the desired character size.
    b. If the annotation is to be edited, make the changes in the Edit Annotation box. Using the Edit Annotation box, annotations can also be copied (within a piece or from piece to piece), deleted, moved, and rotated. Character size can also be changed in the Edit Annotation box.
3. Click on OK in the New Piece Annotation or Edit Annotation box.

Piece to Menu

The Piece to Menu command allows you to add a piece to the icon bar. The piece is not saved. It is removed from the work area, but it is accessible for use again before the work area is closed. To use this command, follow these steps:

1. Select Piece>Piece to Menu.
2. Select the piece you wish to add to the menu. Right click on the piece in the menu to see the piece properties or to delete the icon from the menu.

Summary

Using the Piece function, a patternmaker can change a piece as a whole by flipping, rotating, and realigning the gain/grade reference. Pieces can also be split and combined or merged. The Scale command changes the size of a piece in the x and/or y directions. Allowances for fabrics that shrink or stretch can be made using the Shrink/Stretch command. The Mirror command is used to create a piece that has two symmetrical halves. The mirrored piece can be folded, unfolded, and opened. Annotations can be added to pieces using the Annotate Piece command. The Piece to Menu command is used to add a piece to the icon bar. The piece is not saved. It is removed from the work area, but it is accessible for use again before the work area is closed.

Key Terms

CW
CCW

Review Questions

1. Why is it usually best not to delete original pieces?
2. Why is it advisable to flip or rotate pieces even when it is not necessary for the Combine/Merge command?
3. Describe the procedure for making a graded nest of a combined piece easier to view.
4. Describe a use for the Scale command.
5. When using the Shrink/Stretch command, what is the effect of entering a negative number? A positive number?
6. Describe the effects of the three options in the Grading box.

Piece Function, Part II Exercises

1. Create an asymmetrical bodice.
   a. Place a bodice front piece in the work area.
   b. Rotate and distribute the waist dart so that 50 percent is in the side seam.
   c. Alter the side seam so that the underarm point is moved up half an inch and inward half an inch. (Select Point>Modify Points>Move Pt Line/Slide.) The point can be moved only in one direction at a time. Move the point up the side seam, remove excess points in the armhole, and smooth the armhole curve. Then move the point along the armhole. In the user input box, select which line the point will slide along and select a value. (Do not forget to decide which end of the line will be used as the base point for the distance to be moved and that a negative sign might be needed.)

d. Mirror the piece along the center front (Piece>Mirror Piece).

e. Draw a line from the bottom of one armhole to the opposite shoulder. Smooth as necessary.

f. Draw a new armhole for the one-shoulder side so that the design is aesthetically pleasing.

g. Split the piece to remove the unwanted shoulder. Split the piece again to create the new armhole. (Piece>Split Piece>Split on Line.) Keep the original pieces to use in matching the back. See Figure 9.9.

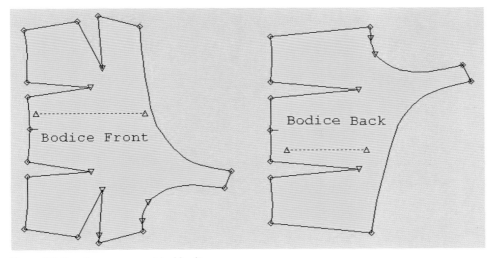

Figure 9.9 Creating an asymmetrical bodice

h. Now create a back bodice piece to match the front. Hints: Move shoulder dart into the neck line and then use the measure function and Mark X Point to match back and front shoulder.

2. Create an attached front facing for a front button blouse with a collar.

a. Add ¾ inch to the front seam line of the bodice to form a button placket. (Line>Create Line>Offset Even. Offset the center front line ¾ inch outside the piece.)

b. Swap internal and external lines. (Line>SwapLine. Remember that the new line is the internal line, even though it is outside the piece.)

c. Create the facing. Create an offset even line 2 inches inside the neckline and another, 2 inches inside the modified center front of the piece. Draw a curved line between the two facing lines (Line>Create line>2 Point-Curve) as shown in Figure 9.10a.

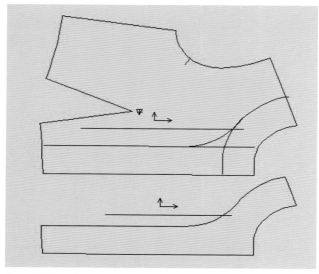

Figure 9.10 a. Creating an attached front facing

d. Separate the facing using the Trace command (Piece> Create Piece>Trace). Follow the instructions in the user input box. Remember to select each line in turn in a clockwise direction.

e. Flip the new facing piece around the center front. (Piece>Modify Piece>Flip Piece. Select Flip About Line in the user input box.) See Figure 9.10 b.

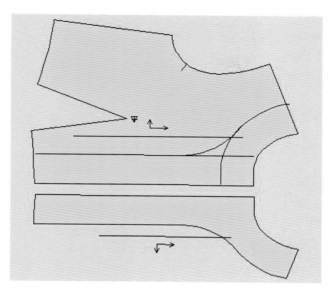

Figure 9.10 b. Creating an attached front facing around the center front

f. Combine the front and the facing. Arrange front and facing so that the center front seam lines are aligned. (Piece> Combine/Merge. In the user input box, select Paste Grading and Keep all Rules.) See Figure 9.10c.

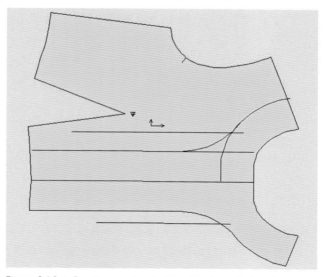

Figure 9.10 c. Creating an attached front facing, aligning the center front seam lines

212

g. Place a notch at each end of the center front of the piece (Notch>Add Notch).

h. Delete unwanted lines (Line>Delete Line). See Figure 9.10 d.

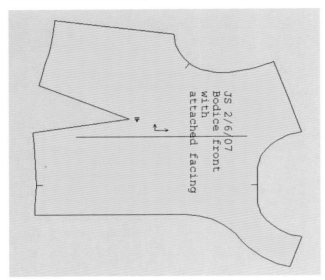

Figure 9.10 d. Creating an attached front facing, adding notches and deleting unwanted lines

i. Annotate the piece. (Piece>Annotate). For this exercise rotate the annotations by 90 degrees and use font size 0.5. See Figure 9.10 d.

j. Add a half-inch seam allowance to the piece.

k. Print piece.

3. Create a waistband.

a. Work with a skirt front and a skirt back.

b. Mirror each piece (Piece>Mirror Piece) so that there is a complete back and a complete front.

c. Select Piece>Create Piece>Binding. In the user input box, enter the width of the waistband in the Binding Width field (usually 2 inches).

d. Select the notch type desired.

e. Starting at the center back, select in turn each line in the waist of the skirt, i.e., the lines between the darts. The lines on either side of the front mirror point have not been merged, so each must be selected. Click OK.

f. Make the waistband one inch longer by creating an offset even line 1 inch from the end of the waist band (Line>Create Line>Offset Even). Swap the internal and perimeter line (Line>Swap Line).

g. Add a notch at the original end point of the waistband.

h. Delete the unnecessary notches on the waistband—too many can be confusing.

i. Add a half-inch seam allowance to the piece.

4. Combine front bodice and skirt pieces to form a sheath dress.

a. Place a matching bodice front and skirt front in the work area.

b. Distribute and Rotate the bodice dart so that 66.6 percent is moved to the side seam. (Piece>Dart>Distribute/Rotate. Use the bust point as the rotation point and the center front seam as the hold line.) See Figure 9.11 a.

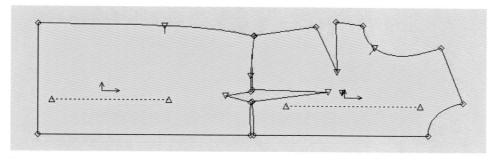

Figure 9.11 a. Combining front bodice and skirt pieces to form a sheath dress.

c. Combine the skirt darts so all of the fullness is in the dart nearest the center front (Piece>Dart>Combine Same Line). See Figure 9.11 a.

d. Using the cursor, place the skirt next to the bodice.

e. On the skirt, draw a vertical line from the skirt waist center front (A) to the dart (B).

f. On the bodice, draw a vertical line from the dart junction with the waistline (C) to the center front (D). (Line>Create

Line>2 Point. From the cursor drop-down menu, select
Vertical.) See Figure 9.11b.

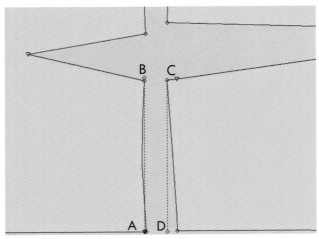

Figure 9.11 b. Adding vertical lines on the skirt and bodice.

g. Swap the internal lines so that they become perimeter lines
(Line>Swap Line).
h. Combine/Merge the bodice and skirt using the lines
between the center fronts and the front darts. See Figure
9.11c.

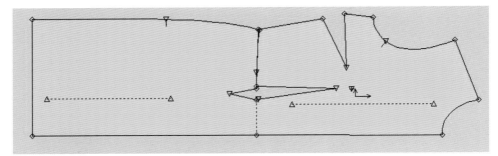

Figure 9.11 c. Combining/merging the front bodice and skirt.

You may find that as the pieces are combined, there are unfilled areas and the image is confusing. See Figure 9.11d.

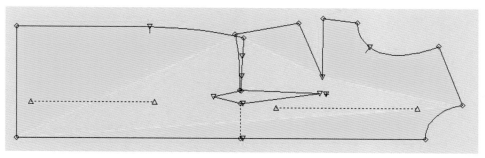

Figure 9.11 d. The combined bodice and skirt with unfilled areas.

As the new piece is completed, the appearance is automatically corrected.

i. Draw a line over the location of the torso dart using Line>Create Line>Digitize. At the end, use the Close Line command from the cursor drop-down menu.

j. At the side of the waistline, draw a short curved line between the bodice and the skirt (Line>Create Line>2 Point Curve). See Figure 9.11e.

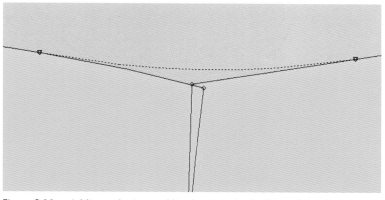

Figure 9.11 e. Adding a short curved line between the bodice and the skirt.

k. Use Line>Replace to make this curved line a perimeter line that joins the side bodice to the side skirt. See Figure 9.11f.

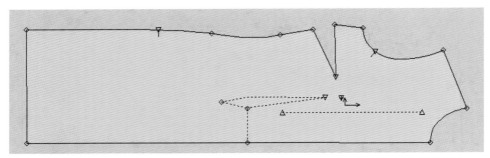

Figure 9.11 f. The completed sheath dress.

l. Delete the skirt grain line.
m. Smooth the side of the piece if needed.

This piece will be graded, but it may be necessary to adjust the location/length of the bodice waistline dart for some sizes.

5. Combine back bodice and skirt pieces to form a sheath dress. Follow a similar procedure as that used to combine the front bodice and skirt.

CHAPTER TEN

Marker Making

Objectives

After studying this chapter, you will be able to

- Check piece categories and assign pieces new categories.

- Create a model.

- Complete the various editors and windows required to make a marker or order a plot.

- Make a marker.

- Understand the Marker Making functions, Toolbar, and Toolbox options.

- Plot a marker.

Introduction

A **marker** is a pattern layout that is placed over fabric to guide a cutter. It is now possible to produce a computerized marker that controls an automatic cutter. Before creating and plotting a marker, it is necessary to create a model. A **model** is a list of pieces that make a complete garment or item. It is also necessary to determine which pieces are to be plotted, what sizes are to be plotted, and how many of each piece and size are to be plotted. In addition, various parameter tables must be completed before a marker can be made. The completion of some of these tables was discussed in Chapter 3 as they are necessary for digitizing. The steps to create and plot a marker are summarized in the following list:

1. Check piece categories or assign pieces new categories.
2. Create a model.
3. Fill in the Model Editor.
4. Check or create an Annotation Table.
5. Check or create LayLimits.
6. Check or create an Order Editor.
7. Complete the Order Process window.
8. Make the marker.
9. Plot the marker.

Checking Piece Categories or Assigning Pieces New Categories

To make a marker, each piece must have a different category. If pattern pieces are used directly from the digitizer, they will probably each have a different category. If pieces have been created in Pattern Design, it will be necessary to assign some of them new categories. You can assign a piece a new category as you go along or you can assign new categories after all necessary pieces have been created. The process to change the category of a piece or to assign a piece a category is as follows:

1. From the Gerber LaunchPad, select Pattern Processing, Digitizing, Pattern Design.
2. Select Pattern Design.
3. Place all the pattern pieces required for the model in the work area.

4. Select Edit>Edit Piece Info. The Tracking Information dialog box will appear. See Figure 10.1.

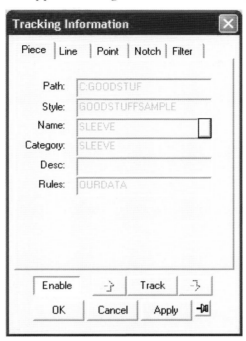

Figure 10.1 Tracking Information dialog box

5. There are two ways to select the piece that will be assigned a category or have its category changed:
   a. Click once on the piece.
   b. Select a piece from the list that can be accessed by clicking on the button to the right of the Name field.
6. Check that the name of the piece and the grade rule table are correct.
7. In the Category field, enter or change the category for that piece, and click on Apply.
8. Repeat numbers 5, 6, and 7 for each of the remaining pieces required for the model.
9. After a category has been assigned or changed, it is necessary to save each individual piece with the new information by selecting File>Save or Save As and following the prompts.

> ## Hint for Success
> When the Tracking Information box is on the screen, it is possible check the name and category of a piece simply by placing the cursor over that piece. If this does not automatically occur, click on the thumbtack symbol at the bottom right of the Piece tab of the Tracking Information dialog box.

Creating a Model

To make a marker, it is necessary to have a model. There are two ways to make a model. A model can be made in Pattern Design or in AccuMark Explorer. After a model has been created (named), it is possible to add newly created pieces to the model as they are being saved by selecting Add Piece to Model/Style in the user input box and following the prompts.

Creating a Model in Pattern Design

To create a model in Pattern Design, follow these steps:

1. From the Gerber LaunchPad, select Pattern Processing, Digitizing, Pattern Design.
2. Select Pattern Design.
3. Place all the pattern pieces required for the model in the work area.
4. Select File>Create/Edit Model>Add Pieces. The Add Pieces dialog box will appear. See Figure 10.2.

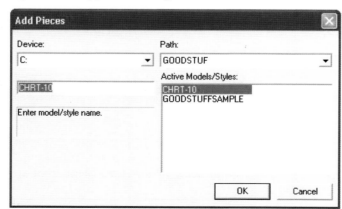

Figure 10.2 Add Pieces dialogue box

5. In the Add Pieces dialog box, enter the name of the new model, and click on OK.
6. Select the pieces to add to the model, and click on OK.
7. A box will appear that shows all of the pieces in the model. Click on OK in the box.

> ## Hint for Success
> The best way to select pieces is to click F2 so all of the pieces in the work area appear on the screen, and then place a marquee box around them.

The model now needs to be edited to define the number of pieces to be cut and the rotation of those pieces. Refer to pages 222–223 for instructions on how to fill in the Model Editor.

Creating a Model in AccuMark

To use this command, follow these steps:
1. From the Gerber LaunchPad, select Marker Creation, Editors.
2. Select the Model Editor icon shown in Figure 10.3.

Figure 10.3 Model Editor icon

3. Check at the top of the window to determine whether you are working with the Metric or Imperial system of measurement. If the measurement system is not the desired one, use File>Open, and then in the Look in: box, select a storage area that is in your desired measurement system. Open a model that is in this system. The information at the top of the page should indicate the change in measurement system. Now open a new model to continue in the correct measurement system.
4. Select File>New.
5. Click in field 1 under Piece Name, and click on the button that appears. The lookup box will appear. Select the folder and the first piece to be added to the model, and click on Open. Repeat the process for the other fields under Piece Name until the model is complete.

6. Select File>Save.
7. Enter a file name for the new model, and click on Save.

Filling in the Model Editor (Creating a Model) Page

If the model was created in AccuMark, continue to fill in the Model Editor. See Figure 10.4. If the model was created in Pattern Design, select Gerber LaunchPad>Marker Creation Editor>Model Editor. Then select File>Open. In Look in, select the correct storage area, then select the name of the model to be used, and click on Open. (Note: Pieces can be added to and removed from a model at any time. To add a piece, see the discussion earlier in this chapter concerning making a model in AccuMark). To remove a piece, place the cursor over the piece, right click, and select Delete Row from the drop-down menu.

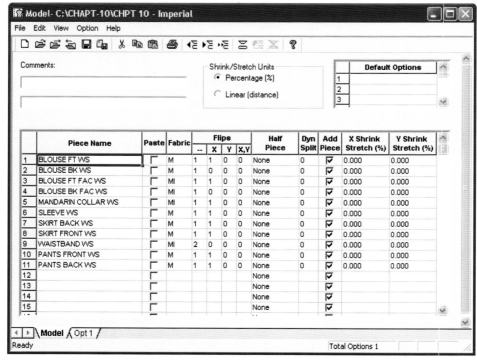

Figure 10.4 Model Editor

To complete filling out the Model Editor, follow these instructions:

1. *Fabric column*: Enter the fabric to be used for each specified piece. By convention, *M* is used for main fabric; *F* is for facing; *MF* indicates that the piece is to be cut from both the main fabric and facing. If this column is empty, then all of the pieces will be cut from the same fabric.

2. *Flips*: The spaces in these columns give instructions for how many pieces to cut and whether mirror images of pieces are to be cut.

   a. In the first column, which is labeled with a dash, enter 1 in every space where there is a pattern piece.

   b. In the X column under Flips,

      i. Enter 0 for any piece that will not need flipping (e.g., a one-piece bodice back).

      ii. Enter 1 for any piece that is to be flipped across the x-axis, such as a sleeve or pants piece. (This means that one regular piece and one flipped piece will be cut, i.e., a right and left piece.)

   c. The Y column under Flips is used to flip pattern pieces across the y-axis. This is generally not done, so 0s often appear in this column.

   d. The X,Y column under Flips is used to flip Pattern Pieces across both the x- and y-axes . This also is generally not done, so 0s often appear in this column as well.

3. *Half Piece*: Generally None is selected for this column. The column is used when fabric is spread double (either tubular or folded fabric), and a piece is shared between two bundles. For example, when fabric is double, two waistbands will be cut out when only one is needed. In this case either Any Dir or Same Dir should be selected.

4. *DYN Split*: This column is used when a large pattern piece has been split to fit in a marker. If a piece has not been split, 0 should be placed in this column.

5. *Add Piece*: If this column is checked, additional pieces or bundles may be added during marker making.

6. Select File>Save or Save As.

Creating and Checking an Annotation Editor

An annotation table needs to be established before ordering a piece or marker plot. The Annotation Editor specifies which information will be plotted on the marker. Please refer to Chapter 2, page 38 for instructions on how to use the Annotation Editor. (To access the editor, select Gerber LaunchPad>Marker Creation, Editors>Annotation> File>Open.) You may use an annotation table from the Gerber training data, one provided by an instructor, or one created using the instructions in Chapter 2.

LayLimit Editor

Lay limits determine how pieces can be manipulated in a marker. The LayLimit Editor determines

1. how the fabric is laid out (for example, as single ply or one of a variety of different ways of folding).
2. whether all of the bundles in a marker are laid out in the same direction. **Bundles** are the parts of a garment ready for sewing. Bundles are usually grouped by size.
3. whether pieces may be flipped (i.e., rotated 90 degrees or 180 degrees. This is not usually done, particularly when a fabric pattern is directional).

It is recommended that students create lay limits for a single-ply fabric with all of the bundles facing the same direction and that only flipping and 180 degree rotating of pieces be permitted. It is suggested that tilting and degrees of rotation are not permitted (though these criteria can be overridden in the marker). Please note that these lay limits are suggested for use with this book. For other purposes, lay limits can be created that allow additional flexibility. A company may have several lay limits with different criteria that can be applied to different fabrics, styles, and price lines.

To access the LayLimit Editor, select Gerber LaunchPad>Marker Creation, Editors>LayLimit Editor icon. See Figure 10.5.

Figure 10.5 LayLimit Editor icon

Completing a LayLimit Editor

Here are explanations about and instructions for completing a LayLimit Editor.

Fabric Spread

The drop-down menu for Fabric Spread gives four options for how the fabric may be spread for cutting: Single Ply, Face to Face, Book Fold, and Tubular. It is easiest to make markers for single-ply fabric.

Bundling

Bundling is the process of sorting out the cut pieces and organizing them so that they are ready for assembly.

The LayLimit Editor has three options for Bundling: All Bundle Same Dir, All Bundle Alt Dir, and Same Size-Same Dir. By alternating piece orientation, it may be possible to lay out pattern pieces more economically. However, if a fabric has an obvious directional pattern or nap, all of the pieces in a bundle should be oriented in the same direction on the marker. Figure 10.6 shows part of a marker with pieces laid out for alternate size bundling.

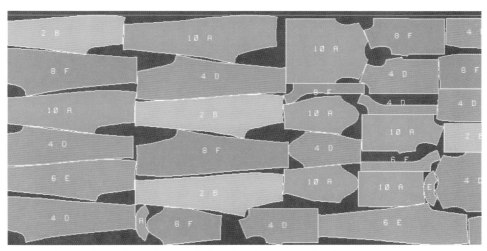

Figure 10.6 Part of a marker with pieces laid out for alternate size bundling.

Category

Piece categories were established when creating the model. For piece categories that require different options than the default setting, enter the names of the categories in the spaces provided.

Piece Options

The default setting will be applied to all of the piece categories not specified in the category list. The Piece Options menu defines the flexibility that the marker maker has when manipulating pattern pieces in a marker. For example, it may allow the marker maker to flip some pieces to conserve fabric. It can also be used to allow for slight off-grain rotation of pieces for more efficient marker making. Clicking on the down arrow in the Piece Options field produces the list of piece options. See Figure 10.7.

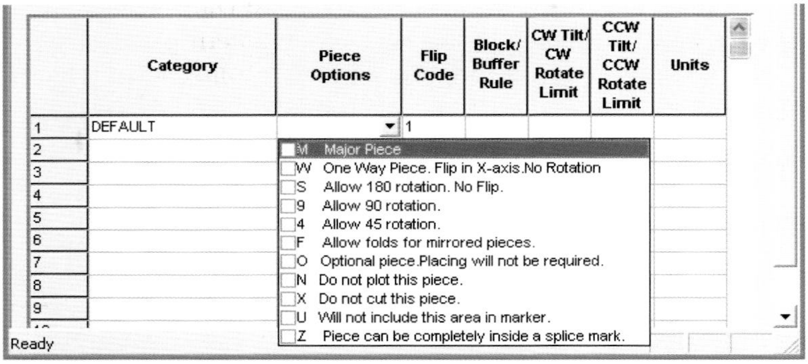

	Category	Piece Options	Flip Code	Block/ Buffer Rule	CW Tilt/ CW Rotate Limit	CCW Tilt/ CCW Rotate Limit	Units	
1	DEFAULT	▼	1					
2		☐M Major Piece						
3		☐W One Way Piece. Flip in X-axis.No Rotation						
4		☐S Allow 180 rotation. No Flip.						
5		☐9 Allow 90 rotation.						
6		☐4 Allow 45 rotation.						
7		☐F Allow folds for mirrored pieces.						
8		☐O Optional piece.Placing will not be required.						
9		☐N Do not plot this piece.						
		☐X Do not cut this piece.						
Ready		☐U Will not include this area in marker.						
		☐Z Piece can be completely inside a splice mark.						

Figure 10.7 LayLimit Editor, Piece Options drop-down menu

Select the desired option(s) by checking in each appropriate box. If no piece option is selected, a piece may still be flipped and rotated 180 degrees during marker making.

Flip Code

Click in a Flip Code field, and then click on the down arrow that appears. This will produce a drop-down menu. See Figure 10.8.

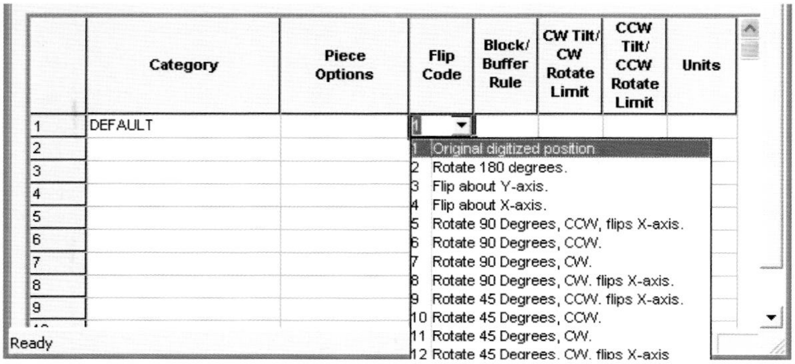

	Category	Piece Options	Flip Code	Block/ Buffer Rule	CW Tilt/ CW Rotate Limit	CCW Tilt/ CCW Rotate Limit	Units	
1	DEFAULT		1 ▼					
2			1 Original digitized position.					
3			2 Rotate 180 degrees.					
4			3 Flip about Y-axis.					
5			4 Flip about X-axis.					
6			5 Rotate 90 Degrees, CCW, flips X-axis.					
7			6 Rotate 90 Degrees, CCW.					
8			7 Rotate 90 Degrees, CW.					
9			8 Rotate 90 Degrees, CW. flips X-axis.					
			9 Rotate 45 Degrees, CCW. flips X-axis.					
Ready			10 Rotate 45 Degrees, CCW.					
			11 Rotate 45 Degrees, CW.					
			12 Rotate 45 Degrees. CW. flips X-axis					

Figure 10.8 LayLimit Editor, Flip Code drop-down menu

Flip codes are used to automatically reorient a piece when it is ordered in a marker. This option is used when it is easier to change the orientation in marker making than it is in digitizing or pattern-making (for example, turning pieces to bias or cross-grain patterns). Figure 10.9 includes diagrams of the Flip Codes.

Flip Codes

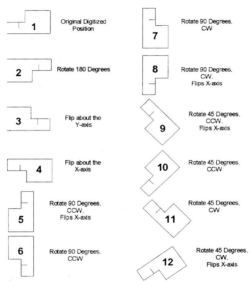

1	Original Digitized Position
2	Rotate 180 Degrees
3	Flip about the Y-axis
4	Flip about the X-axis
5	Rotate 90 Degrees. CCW. Flips X-axis
6	Rotate 90 Degrees. CCW
7	Rotate 90 Degrees. CW
8	Rotate 90 Degrees. CW. Flips X-axis
9	Rotate 45 Degrees. CCW. Flips X-axis
10	Rotate 45 Degrees. CCW
11	Rotate 45 Degrees. CW
12	Rotate 45 Degrees. CW. Flips X-axis

Figure 10.9 Flip codes

Block/Buffer Rule

Block/Buffer Rules are used to create the extra space around pieces that is needed when automatic cutters are used. These rules, created in the Block/Buffer editor, are not covered in this book.

CW Tilt/CW Rotate Limit and CCW Tilt/CCW Rotate Limit

The information in these two fields determines how far a piece may be tilted or rotated in the clockwise (CW) or counterclockwise (CCW) direction.

Units

This is a field with a drop-down menu. It is used to determine whether the tilt/rotation is measured in inches or degrees.

Order Editor

The Order Editor page creates an order for a marker. The purpose of this editor is to name the marker and define which LayLimit, Annotation Table, and Notch Table are to be used. It is used to define the width of the fabric to be used, the different sizes to be on the marker, and the quantity of each size.

Filling in the Order Editor

In order to complete this editor, follow these steps:
1. Select Gerber LaunchPad>Marker Creation, Editors>Order Editor icon. See Figure 10.10.

Figure 10.10 Order Editor icon

2. Fill in the Order tab. See Figure 10.11.

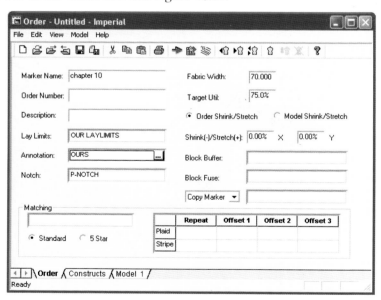

Figure 10.11 Order tab of Order Editor

a. In the Marker Name field, enter a name for the marker.
b. In the Fabric Width field, enter the cutable width of the fabric. This is usually about two inches less than the actual width of the fabric.

c. The Target Util field may be ignored for our purposes. It sets the goal for fabric utilization in the marker. Usually a marker maker aims for a fabric utilization of 75 percent or greater.

d. The Shrink (–)/Stretch (+) field is used to counter the effect of a fabric shrinking or stretching after cutting. Filling in these fields will shrink or stretch the pieces used by the percentage indicated in the field. Generally for student work nothing should be entered in these fields.

e. The Matching Standards is beyond the scope of this book.

f. In the Lay Limits field, right click on the right edge of the field to access the lookup box. Ensure that you are in the correct storage area. Select the appropriate lay limit table, and click on Open.

g. In the Annotation field, right click on the right edge of the field to access the lookup box. Ensure that you are in the correct storage area. Select the appropriate Annotation Table, and click on Open.

h. In the Notch field, P-Notch is the default and will appear automatically when the Order Editor is opened.

i. All of the other fields should be ignored for our purposes.

3. The Constructs tab, concerns areas in a marker that are not to be used, such as areas of flawed fabric. Discussion of constructs is beyond the scope of this book.

4. Fill in the Model 1 tab. See Figures 10.11 and 10.12.

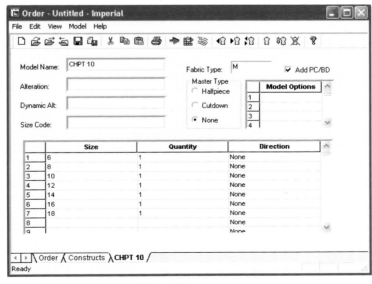

Figure 10.12 Model 1 tab of Order Editor

Select the Model 1 tab in Order Editor.

a. In the Model Name field, right click on the right edge of the field to access the lookup box. Ensure that you are in the correct storage area. Select the appropriate Model and click on Open.

b. In the Fabric Type field, enter the abbreviation for fabric type to be used for this marker (e.g., *M* for main fabric, *I* for interfacing, and *L* for lining).

c. Ignore the following fields: Alteration, Dynamic Alt, Size Code, Master Type, Model Options, and Add PC/BD. These are related to alterations and not covered in this book.

d. In the Size, Quantity, and Direction fields, enter the desired information:

i. *Size*: Specify the sizes desired, one size per row.

ii. *Quantity*: Enter the number of each size desired (these numbers are in proportion to the actual number required. For example, if a manufacturer plans to make 10,000 size 2 garments, 20,000 size 4 garments, and 30,000 size 6 garments, then the marker will have pattern pieces for one size 2, two size 4, and three size 6).

iii. *Direction*: Specify the direction the size will be laid out on the marker. If None is selected, the information on the lay limit table will be applied.

5. Save the order by selecting File>Save.

Order Process

Processing the order is a very important stage that the novice often forgets. To complete this stage, follow these instructions:

1. Select Gerber LaunchPad>Marker Creation, Editors>Order Process icon. See Figure 10.13.

Figure 10.13 Order Process icon

2. Click at the right side of the Order Name field to open the lookup field in which order names are listed.

3. Select the name of the order to be processed, and click on Open. See Figure 10.14.

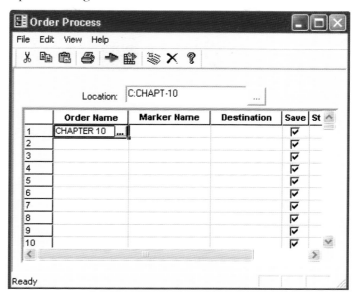

Figure 10.14 Order Process window

4. Select File, and select Process All.

Making the Marker

To practice the use of the various marker-making functions, it is suggested that you use a sample marker, your own marker, one provided by an instructor, or one found in the Gerber training data.

To access the Marker Making screen, follow these steps:

1. On the Gerber LaunchPad>Marker Creation, Editors.
2. Double click on the Marker Making icon, shown in Figure 10.15.

Figure 10.15 Marker Making icon

The Marker Making window will then appear. See Figure 10.16.

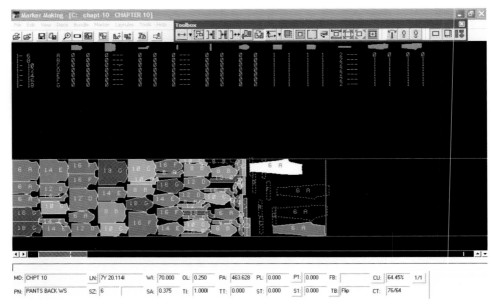

Figure 10.16 Marker Making window with incomplete marker

Components of the Marker Making Screen

The following components may appear in different areas depending on how the screen is set up:

1. *Marker Information Box*: Located at the bottom of the screen, this box provides information about the marker, lay rules, pieces, and the piece that is highlighted on the screen. See Figure 10.17.

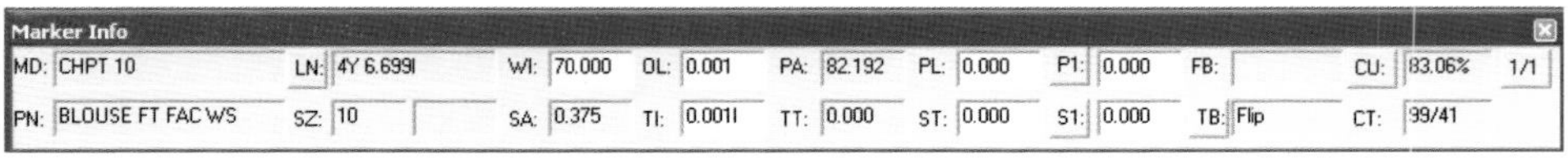

Figure 10.17 Marker Information box

Table 10.1 summarizes the information displayed in each field. The information in the white fields can be changed by right clicking in the field and filling in the popup box. For example, the width of the fabric, the overlap amount, or tilt increments can be changed. To overlap or tilt a piece, it may be necessary to override lay limit rules.

Table 10.1 Marker Information Box Summary

MD	Displays the model name
PN	Displays the name of the piece highlighted in the marker
LN	Displays the length of the marker in yards and inches or meters and centimeters (depending on the user environment table used)
SZ	Displays the size of the highlighted piece
WI	Displays the width of the fabric being used for the marker. The width of the fabric can be changed: Click in the field, enter a new width, and click on OK.
SA	Displays the seam allowance for split pieces as defined in the user environment table used. This is not the same as the perimeter seam allowance on pieces.
OL	Displays the overlap amount when pieces overlap. It can be changed: Click in the field, enter a new amount, and click on OK.
TL	Displays the tilt increments used when pieces are tilted. It can be changed: Click in the field, enter a new amount, and click on OK.
PA	Displays the area of the highlighted piece
TT	Displays the tilt amount of the highlighted piece
PL	Displays the plaid repeat amount
ST	Displays the stripe repeat amount
P1	Toggles between P1, P2, and P3. In the Order Editor, each number is assigned a value for offsetting plaids.
S1	Toggles between S1, S2, and S3. In the Order Editor, each number is assigned a value for offsetting plaids.
FB	Displays the active function box command
TB	Displays the active toolbox function
CU	Current Utilization: The area of placed pieces as a percentage of the total marker area
CT	Displays the number of pieces unplaced/placed
1/1	Displays the icon page number. Other pages of pieces are seen by clicking this button.

2. *Prompt Bar*: Prompts for functions that do not occur automatically will appear here. This bar is located above the Marker Information Box. See Figure 10.16.

3. *Marking Area*: The outline of the area in which the pieces will be placed in the marker. See Figure 10.16.

4. *Menu Bar*: Drop-down menus can be accessed by clicking on functions in the Menu Bar. See Figure 10.18.

Figure 10.18 Marker Making Menu Bar

5. *Toolbar*: This contains icons that are shortcuts to items in the Menu Bar. See Figure 10.19.

Figure 10.19 Marker Making Toolbar

6. *Marker Making Toolbox*: This has icons for additional functions, such as overlapping pieces and sliding groups of pieces into place. See Figure 10.20.

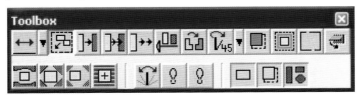

Figure 10.20 Marker Making Toolbox

This may not automatically appear on the screen. Accessing the Marker Making Toolbox and the functions of the icons will be discussed later in this chapter.

Hint for Success

When the Marker Making window opens, sometimes the Marker Making Toolbox is located over the menu bar. Right click on the blue bar and drag the Marker Making Toolbox out of the way.

Displaying Pieces for a Marker

To display pieces to be placed in a marker, follow these steps:
1. Select File>Open.
2. A window will open:
   a. In the Look in field, select the appropriate storage area.
   b. Highlight the marker to be opened, and click on Open.
3. The icon menu will appear. This contains an icon for each piece to go into the marker. Each piece is listed by size, flips are noted where needed, and the quantity of each size is listed. See Figure 10.21.

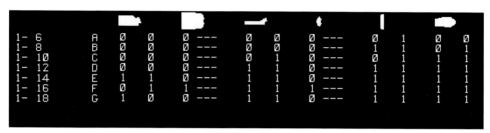

Figure 10.21 Marker Making icon menu

Placing Pieces in the Marker

Pieces can be placed individually or as a group. Pieces requiring matching, such as plaids, must be placed individually. However, this is beyond the scope of this book. When pieces are correctly placed, they are filled with color. If a piece has been taken out of the icon bar but has not been placed, it will appear empty with a dotted perimeter line. To place a piece in a marker, follow these steps:
1. *Individual placement*: There are two ways of moving a piece into the marker:
   a. Sliding the piece from the icon bar
      i. Click on the quantity number in the icon menu below a thumbnail image of the piece you wish to place.
      ii. Hold the left mouse button down, and slide the cursor into the marker-making area, then release the button.
      iii. The filled piece will appear in the marker at the nearest available place to where the cursor was released. This may not make an efficient marker, and the piece may need to be moved using the process described in Step b.
   b. Dragging from the icon bar
      i. Click on the quantity number underneath a thumbnail image in the icon menu.

236

    ii. Release the mouse button. Move the cursor and piece into the approximate position in the marker-making area and click on the mouse to release the piece. An unfilled piece will appear in the marker at the nearest available place to where the cursor was released.

    iii. The unfilled piece is slid into place by clicking on it, holding the mouse button down, and moving the cursor in the direction the piece needs to move. When the button is released, the piece will move in that direction and be placed (become filled) if there is sufficient space.

2. *Group placement*: This makes it possible to place all of the pieces or a selected group of pieces automatically at the same time. To do so, follow these instructions:

    a. Create a marquee box around the pieces. This is a right click and drag box (as opposed to the boxes used in Pattern Design).

    b. The pieces will appear as a "splotch."

    c. To place the pieces, click once on the "splotch," and with the mouse button still down, move the cursor until it is in the marker. A line will appear as the cursor is moved.

    d. Release the mouse button in the marker, and the pieces will automatically be placed. This placement of pieces may not be the most efficient use of the fabric. The patternmaker may wish to change the location of some pieces to improve efficiency.

Hint for Success

To make a tight (efficient) marker, it is necessary to move pieces. This is done by moving the pieces (click, move, click) into approximately the correct location and then sliding them into place by clicking on the piece, and with the mouse button still held down, drawing a line to the desired location for the piece. Note: Pieces cannot be slid past other pieces; they must be moved first.

Saving a Marker

To save a marker, follow these steps:

1. Select File>Save As.
2. If all pieces have not been placed, a message will appear asking, "Are you sure you want to store?" Incomplete markers can be

stored and completed at a later time. If Yes is selected or all of
the pieces have been placed, the Save As dialog box will appear.

3. Select the appropriate storage area for saving, create or select
an appropriate file name for the marker, and click on Save.

Marker Making Functions

Use of the File menu, toolbar, and toolbox gives the marker maker
control in marker making and the ability to use fabric efficiently by
flipping, turning, tilting, overlapping, moving, and separating pieces.
Selected functions will be discussed.

File Function

The File functions allow the marker maker to Open markers, Save
and Save As, and Send markers to a printer or plotter. These commands work in the same manner as similar commands in Microsoft
Windows software applications.

Edit Function

There are four commands in the Edit function: Overlap Amount, Tilt
Amount, Settings, and Undo (move/flip/place). See Figure 10.22.

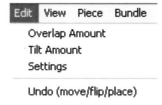

Figure 10.22 Edit function menu

Overlap Amount

Selecting the Overlap Amount command opens a dialog box that asks
for the amount of overlap that may be allowed. Usually, to allow two
pieces to overlap, it is necessary to override LayLimits and to individually place pieces. The override command is discussed later in this
chapter.

Tilt Amount

Selecting the Tilt Amount command opens a dialog box that asks
for the amount of tilt that may be allowed. Usually, to create a tilt, it
is necessary to override LayLimits and to place pieces individually.

Settings

Selecting the Settings command opens a Settings dialog box. See Figure 10.23.

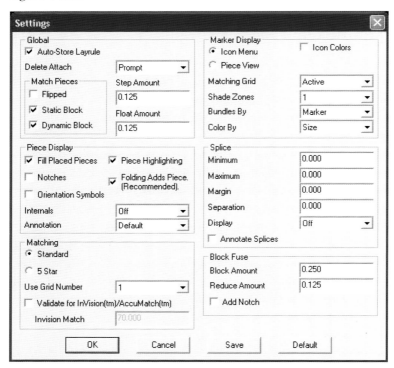

Figure 10.23 Settings window

Generally, the default settings for this box are appropriate for most projects. The dialog box can be used to define step and float amounts. Step and float amounts are the distances that separate pattern pieces when using the Step and Float commands found in the Marker Making toolbox. More information on the use of step and float is found in Table 10.5 on page 246.

Also, the Settings dialog box can be used to determine if notches and orientation symbols are to be shown on the marker. See Table 10.5.

Undo (move/flip/place)

Selecting the Undo (move/flip/place) command undoes previous move/flip/place commands. However, it does not return a piece to the icon menu.

View Function

The View function allows the marker maker to shrink and enlarge the marker-making area. It also provides access to the Toolbox, the Marker Information box, and additional data about the marker. See Figure 10.24.

Figure 10.24 View function drop-down menu

The commands in the View function are summarized in Table 10.2.

Piece Function

Selected commands in the Piece function will be presented: Add Piece, Delete Piece, Return, Unplace, Marry. Figure 10.25 shows the drop-down menu for the Piece function.

Figure 10.25 Piece function drop-down menu

Table 10.2 View Menu Commands

Command	Summary
Next Icon Page	This command is used to access the next page of icons when there are too many icons to fit on the screen.
Zoom	This command is used to enlarge a portion of the work area. Select the command, and click and drag to form a marquee box around the area to be enlarged.
Full Length	Full Length can only be used when Zoom is not in use. Selecting this command shows the entire length of the marker on the screen.
Big Scale	This command is used to return a marker to its original scale. It is also used to enlarge a marker. As opposed to Zoom, this command does not enlarge a specific area of the marker.
Refresh Display	Refresh Display is used to clean the screen and remove ghost particles (leftover bits of erased images).
Toolbox	This command is used to open or close the Marker Making Toolbox.
Marker Information	This command is used to open or close the Marker Information box.
Marker Properties	Selecting this command produces a box with information about size and quantity of the pieces to be placed on the marker.
Zoom Window	This command opens a separate window in the marking area to provide two different views of the marker. This allows accurate placement of pieces while still maintaining a view of the entire marker. In the small window, there are three icons (Zoom, Full Length, and Big Scale) that can adjust the scale of the marker in the window. The window is closed by selecting Zoom Window from the View menu.
Preferences	This provides access to the User Environment Table (UserEnv).

Add Piece

The Add Piece command is used to add extra, duplicate pieces to a marker. Only copies of pieces that are already in the marker can be

added. Pieces can only be added if the Model Editor and the Order Editor are set to Add Pieces. To add a piece:
1. Select Piece>Add piece.
2. Click on the piece to add. It may be in the marker-making area or the menu area.
3. Select OK.

Delete Piece

The Delete Piece command is used to remove a piece or pieces from a marker. Only pieces that were added using the Add Piece command can be deleted.

Return

The Return command is used to return pieces from the work area to the icon bar. There are three options within this command: All, Unplaced, and Bundle. If Bundle is selected, it is necessary to click on a piece from the bundle to return the entire bundle to the icon bar.

Unplace

The Unplace command is used to unplace pieces. Pieces that have been placed in a marker (and been filled with color) will be moved to the side of the marker and appear as unfilled with a dotted outline. It is possible to unplace all of the pieces or small pieces that were not identified as Major Pieces in the LayLimits. Unplaced pieces are moved from the marker-making area and located around it. They are not returned to the icon bar.

Marry

The Marry command is used to form a grouping of pieces that can be moved as a unit. Within this command, there are four options: Create, Modify, Delete, and Delete All.

To create a group, select Create, click on each piece that will be included in the group, and click on OK in the dialog box. There is no indication that the group has been formed, but when one piece in the group is manipulated, all of the other pieces in the group are manipulated in the same manner.

To separate a married group, select Piece>Marry>Delete, and then click on one of the pieces, and click on OK.

Bundle Function

The commands within the Bundle function are used to modify bundles. See Figure 10.26.

Figure 10.26 Bundle function drop-down menu

Select commands will be discussed: Add, Add New Size, Delete, Return, Unplace, Flip, and Reset Orientation.

Add

The Add command is used if it is necessary to insert more versions of a size that is already in the marker. For instance, if a manufacturer has an increased demand for size 16 and needs to make proportionately more products in this size. To use this command, select Add, and then select a piece in the bundle to be added, and click on OK.

Add New Size

The Add New Size command is used to insert a size that is not already in the marker. When the command is selected, a drop-down menu will appear asking if you want to store the marker. If No is selected, all of the placed pieces will be returned to the icon bar when a new size is added. When Yes is selected the marker is saved in its incomplete form. After selecting Yes or No, an Add Size window appears. Click on the model, enter the new size to be added, and click on OK.

Delete

The Delete command is used to remove added bundles. After selecting Delete, click on a piece in the bundle to be deleted. Click on OK to close the command.

Return

The Return command is used to return all of the pieces in a bundle (usually all of the pieces of one size) to the icon bar. Select one piece from the bundle to return.

Unplace

The Unplace command will move all pieces in a bundle (usually all pieces of one size) out of the marker. Select one piece from the bundle to be unplaced.

Flip

The Flip command is used to flip all of the pieces in a bundle 180 degrees across the x-axis. Select one piece in the bundle to flip.

Reset Orientation

The Reset Orientation command is used to return all of the pieces in a bundle to their original orientation (removing any and all flips and tilts). After selecting the command, click on one piece in the bundle.

Marker Function

The Marker function is used to alter a marker. See Figure 10.27.

Figure 10.27 Marker function drop-down menu

The command Return All Pieces removes the pieces from the marker and returns them to the icon menu.

Marker Making Toolbar

The Marker Making Toolbar contains shortcuts to some commands. To customize this toolbar, double click in the empty space of the toolbar. The Customize Toolbar dialog box will appear. Icons can be selected by clicking on them and then selecting Add. To use the default toolbar, click on Reset in the Customize Toolbar dialog box.

See Figure 10.19. Table 10.3 lists the default Marker Making Toolbar icons and their uses. Placing the cursor over each icon produces a popup box with the use of the icon.

Marker Making Toolbox

The Marker Making Toolbox provides additional commands for manipulating pieces being placed in the marker. See Figure 10.20. The toolbox is a floating bar that can be placed anywhere on the screen by right clicking on the top of the bar, dragging it into place, and then releasing the mouse button. If the toolbox is not visible on the screen, it can be accessed by selecting View>Toolbox. The toolbox commands are applied using the right button on the mouse.

The Marker Making Toolbox has two sections: Modifiers and Functions.

1. *Toolbox Modifiers*: Selection of these icons determines which toolbox functions can be applied. If a modifier is active, the icon button will appear depressed. The modifier icons are situated at the right side of the toolbox. Table 10.4 provides a summary of the role of each of the modifier icons.

Hint for Success

To use a Marker Making Toolbox function, it is usually necessary to select an override icon and an icon to determine whether placed pieces, unplaced pieces, or icons may be modified. Table 10.4 shows which icons should be depressed to override the LayLimits.

2. *Toolbox Functions*: The toolbox gives the marker maker a great deal of flexibility in creating a marker. For example, use of the toolbox functions allows accurate placement of pieces in specific locations; pieces to be slid into place according to area, length, or height; groups of pieces to be moved together; and butting, overlapping, flipping, rotating, or tilting. Table 10.5 provides a summary of the Marker Making Toolbox functions.

Hint for Success

Make sure you save your marker before exiting the marker making screen.

Table 10.3 Marker Making Toolbar

	Open		Big Scale
	Open Next		Create Marry
	Save		Add Piece
	Save As		Add Bundles
	Zoom		Copy Marker
	Full Length		Return Unplaced Pieces

Table 10.4 Summary of the Uses of the Toolbox Modifier Icons

If the function is active, the icon button will appear depressed.

	Free Rotation: Used to rotate a piece while sliding it into place so that the piece will fit into the space allowed. The amount of rotation allowed is set by the LayLimits unless they are overridden.
	Global Override: Used to override the settings selected in the LayLimits. It remains on until it is turned off.
	Toolbox Override: Used to override the settings selected in the LayLimits. It turns off automatically after a piece is placed in the marker.
	Placed: A toolbox modifier. When selected, placed pieces may be selected and modified using Marker Making Toolbox commands.
	Unplaced: A toolbox modifier. When selected, unplaced pieces may be selected and modified using Marker Making Toolbox commands.
	Icons: A toolbox modifier. When selected, pieces from the icon menu may be selected and modified using Marker Making Toolbox commands.

Table 10.5 Summary of Marker Making Toolbox Functions

Icon	Purpose	Instructions for Use
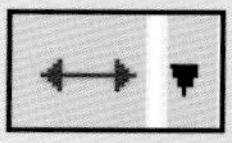  	*Autoslide*: Used to place pieces automatically according to area, length, or height. The arrow on the right produces a dialog box for selecting which criteria are to be used. The icon changes according to how pieces will be placed.	
	*Group Slide*: Used to select a group of pieces and slide them into place together.	1. Select a toolbox modifier icon to determine whether placed or unplaced pieces will be grouped. 2. Select Group Slide. 3. Create a box (click the right mouse button, drag, and release the button) around the pieces to be grouped together. 4. Use the left mouse button to drag the group of pieces into place.
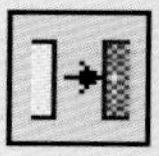	*Butt*: Used to move a piece into the marker in the direction indicated so that it touches another piece.	1. Select Butt. 2. Use the right mouse button to select the piece to move. 3. Use the left mouse button to drag a line in the direction of placement. 4. Release the left mouse button.
	*Overlap*: Used to overlap pieces by up to an amount determined by using Edit/Overlap or the OL box in the Marker Info Bar.	1. Select Overlap. 2. Use the right mouse button to select the piece to overlap. 3. Use the left mouse button to drag a line in the direction of overlap. 4. Release the left mouse button. 5. See Figure 10.28. 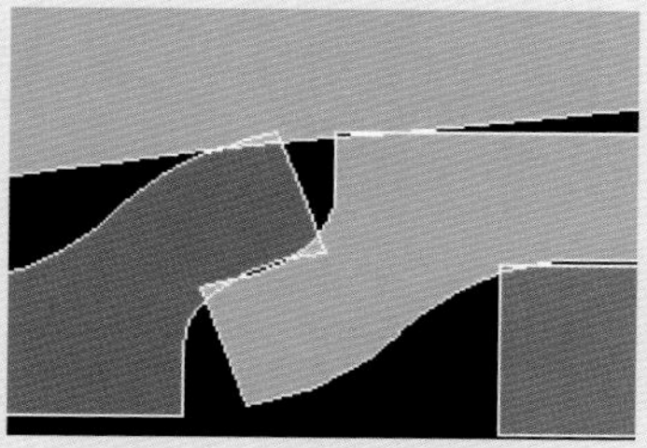

Figure 10.28 Overlapping pieces

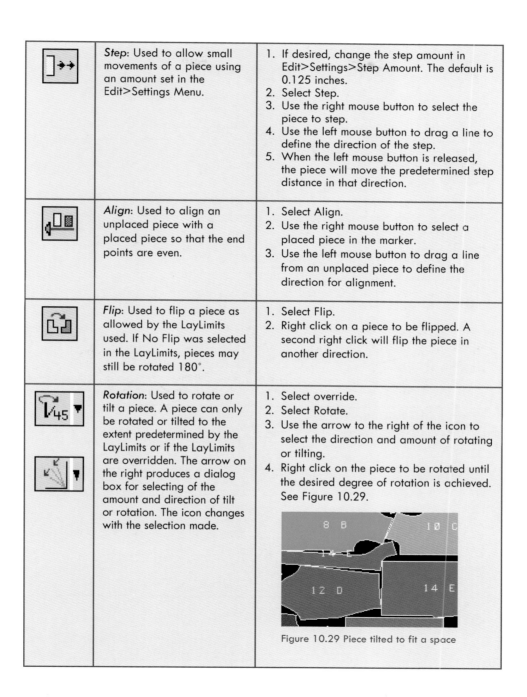	*Step*: Used to allow small movements of a piece using an amount set in the Edit>Settings Menu.	1. If desired, change the step amount in Edit>Settings>Step Amount. The default is 0.125 inches. 2. Select Step. 3. Use the right mouse button to select the piece to step. 4. Use the left mouse button to drag a line to define the direction of the step. 5. When the left mouse button is released, the piece will move the predetermined step distance in that direction.
	Align: Used to align an unplaced piece with a placed piece so that the end points are even.	1. Select Align. 2. Use the right mouse button to select a placed piece in the marker. 3. Use the left mouse button to drag a line from an unplaced piece to define the direction for alignment.
	Flip: Used to flip a piece as allowed by the LayLimits used. If No Flip was selected in the LayLimits, pieces may still be rotated 180°.	1. Select Flip. 2. Right click on a piece to be flipped. A second right click will flip the piece in another direction.
	Rotation: Used to rotate or tilt a piece. A piece can only be rotated or tilted to the extent predetermined by the LayLimits or if the LayLimits are overridden. The arrow on the right produces a dialog box for selecting of the amount and direction of tilt or rotation. The icon changes with the selection made.	1. Select override. 2. Select Rotate. 3. Use the arrow to the right of the icon to select the direction and amount of rotating or tilting. 4. Right click on the piece to be rotated until the desired degree of rotation is achieved. See Figure 10.29. Figure 10.29 Piece tilted to fit a space

Table 10.5 Summary of Marker Making Toolbox Functions (*cont.*)

	Place: Used to place pieces at a chosen location, rather than sliding pieces into place.	1. Select Place. 2. Position a piece in the desired location by clicking on it, dragging it, and releasing it in the desired location. 3. Place the cursor over the piece, and right click to place the piece.
	Block/Buffer: Used to add or remove blocking or buffering. Only needed when automatic cutters are to be used.	
	Split: Used to split a piece in a marker along a previously determined line (an internal line labeled P).	
	Fold: Used to close or open a mirrored piece.	
	Center: Used to place a piece in the center of an empty area.	1. Select Center. 2. Position the piece in an empty area, and then right click. (A piece can not be centered if there are not placed pieces or a marker edge on three sides of it.)
	Fit Piece: Used to place a piece in a tight area where it may be difficult to slide a piece into place.	1. Select Fit Piece. 2. Position the piece in the empty area by clicking and dragging, and right click.
	Float Piece: Used to move a piece away from other pieces by the amount specified in the Edit> Settings window. Float command can only be used once per piece, and may move a piece in the X or Y direction.	1. If desired, change the step amount in Edit>Settings>Float Amount. The default is 0.125 inches. 2. Select Float Piece. 3. Right click on a placed piece to float it.
	Matching: An advanced function used for matching pieces on fabrics with stripes, plaids, or other patterns.	

Plotting

To plot a marker, it is necessary to fill in the Marker Plot (MarkPlot) box. To do this, follow these steps:

1. Access the Marker Plot (MarkPlot) box. It may be accessed in two different ways:

   a. From the Marker Making screen, select File>Send To Plotter. When accessed this way, the name of the marker will automatically appear in the Marker Name field.

   b. From the Gerber LaunchPad, select Plotting and Cutting>Marker Plot. See Figure 10.30.

Figure 10.30 Marker Plot icon

   When accessed this way, click in the Marker Name field to access the Lookup Marker Name window. Check that you are in the correct storage area. Highlight the name of the desired marker, and click on Open.

2. Fill in the fields of the MarkPlot window (see Figure 10.31):

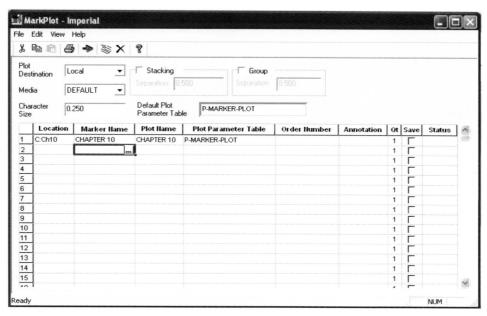

Figure 10.31 MarkPlot window

a. From the Plot Destination menu, select Local.
b. Check Save to save the plot file.
c. Check that the plotter has been turned on.
d. Select File>Process All.

Summary

A marker is a pattern layout that is placed over fabric to guide a cutter. Before creating and plotting a marker, it is necessary to create a model or a list of pieces that make a complete garment or item and to determine which pieces are to be plotted, what sizes are to be plotted, and how many of each piece and size are to be plotted. It is also necessary to complete various editor windows and parameter tables.

The seven steps to complete before making a marker are:

1. Check piece categories or assign new categories to pieces (each piece in a marker must have a different category).
2. Create a model (a model may be made in Pattern Design or in AccuMark).
3. Fill in the Model Editor.
4. Check or create an Annotation Table.
5. Check or create LayLimits.
6. Check or create an Order Editor.
7. Process the order.

To make a marker, each piece must have a different category. No two pieces in a marker may have the same category.

The marker-making window is found by going to the Gerber LaunchPad and selecting Marker Creation, Editors. Select the Marker Making icon to make the Marker Making window appear. Select File>Open to display pieces to be placed in a marker. Pieces can be placed individually or as a group. Using the File menu, Marker Making Toolbar, and Marker Making Toolbox gives the marker maker control in marker making and the ability to use fabric efficiently by flipping, turning, tilting, overlapping, moving, and separating pieces. It is necessary to complete the MarkPlot box to plot the marker.

Key Terms

bundling   marker
bundles   model
ghost particles

Review Questions

1. What is a marker?
2. Why is a model important when making a marker?
3. What is the purpose of an annotation table?
4. What is the purpose of LayLimits?
5. Why is it important to create a tight marker?
6. How is a tight marker created?

Marker Making Exercises

1. Practice moving a piece in a marker.
   a. From the Gerber Launch Pad, select AccuMark Utilities>AccuMark Explorer. Select a folder that contains a marker. To open the Marker Making screen, double click on the name of the marker.
   b. Return all of the pieces to the icon bar using Piece>Return>All.
   c. Place the pieces in the marker.
   d. Add a new size or another bundle of the same size.
   e. Change the direction of one of the sizes. (Select Bundle>Flip, and then choose one piece of the size to be flipped.)
   f. Make the marker tight so that the pieces fit closely together and use as little space as possible.
   g. Work with the View function to the see the marker full length and at a big scale and to zoom in on sections of the marker. (To zoom, you must select the Zoom command and then make a click-drag-click marquee box around the area to be enlarged.)
   h. Zoom so that your entire marker is visible on the screen but still fairly large.
   i. Print a hard copy.

2. Tilt and overlap pieces. Continue using the marker from the previous exercise.
   a. Tilt one piece slightly so that it makes a tighter marker. (Override>Free rotate>right click on the piece selected to rotate.)
   b. Move one piece so that it slightly overlaps another piece. (Select the Overlap icon, select the piece to move with the right mouse button, and then use the left mouse button to move the piece to the desired overlapping location.)
   c. Zoom so the tilt and overlap areas are on the screen.
   d. Print a hard copy.
3. Create a marker using a model of your own. Follow through the entire process as described in this chapter.

CHAPTER ELEVEN

WebPDM, Part I

Objectives

After reading this chapter, you will be able to

- Discuss the use of WebPDM in the fashion industry.
- Log into WebPDM and change your password.
- Create and save folders.
- Open an existing folder.
- Place an image in a Folder Summary.
- Edit images in Folder Summaries.

Introduction

Product Development Management (PDM) software is used by apparel companies worldwide to manage style information efficiently and to track the stages of the design and manufacturing process. WebPDM provides the additional benefit of 100 percent up-to-date information to company employees in a variety of different locations and to suppliers and vendors. It shortens the development cycle and reduces development costs. According to Gerber Technology, there are more than 22,000 users worldwide.

Gerber Technology WebPDM software has 40 user-defined general-purpose forms that can be used to enter sketches, full-color drawings, garment measurement specifications, and tables that define the specifications, information about fabrics and notions, cost specifications, construction details, care instructions, and any other information that may be required. All pages for a specific product are linked under a style description header. Because the pages are accessed online through an intranet, an extranet, or a secure internet site, communication time is reduced, accuracy and efficiency are improved, and data replication is eliminated. Collaboration and standardization between the three components of a fashion-related company (design, production, and sales) are possible. Instant communication can be extended to suppliers and buyers for integrated implementation.

User Groups and a system of permissions and approvals provide specific individuals with different levels of access to read and/or change various pages in the software. For example, a technical designer creates the pages for a garment, the supervisor can modify the pages and give final approval for the pages, and the manufacturer can only view the pages and does not have permission to make changes. WebPDM has the capability to include voice messages, full-color drawings, sketches, and videos.

In addition, the system provides automatic tracking in History Notes that include modifications made to a folder and the date, time, and author of the changes. It is possible to add information to the history record as changes occur. Thus, it would be possible for an employee to state in the history that the changes were authorized by a supervisor. It is possible for managers and executives to monitor the design process during all stages of development. For instance, an administrator (supervisor or instructor) can access a folder and read all of the history notes to determine when the folder was last opened, when changes were made, and who made those changes. WebPDM also incorporates email so information can be sent automatically to those who need to know about last-minute changes.

Academic institutions may have a limited number of WebPDM pages available, but usually, they have enough for student work. Access to pages and administration of those pages is organized when the software is initially installed. Before students can enter the system, an administrator (usually the instructor of the course) enters each student's name and password into a User Group. Students have the opportunity to change their passwords.

It is recommended that students have computer images available, either on the hard drive or a removable storage medium, for importing into folders. These images can be computer-generated flat sketches, images from a digital camera, or scanned images. **Flat sketches**, or **working sketches**, are important components of a completed folder. They are proportioned drawings of garments that show the exact details of trimmings and seam lines. See Figure 11.1 for an example of a flat sketch.

Figure 11.1 A flat sketch

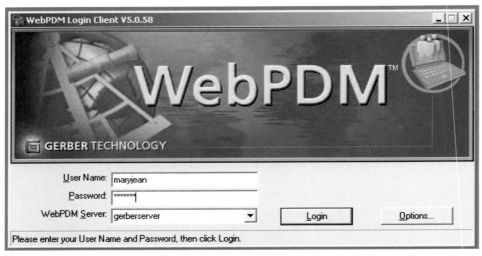

Figure 11.2 WebPDM Login

Logging In

The Login process for WebPDM is as follows:
1. Go to WebPDM Login. See Figure 11.2.
2. In the WebPDM server field, type in the appropriate information as provided by your instructor.
3. Type in your user name (the name you were given by the server administrator).
4. Type in your password as established by the server administrator.
5. Click on Login.
6. The WebPDM menu bar will open. See Figure 11.3.

Figure 11.3 WebPDM menu bar

Changing a Password

1. Select Administration on the menu bar.
2. A drop-down menu will appear. Only User Administration will be accessible. Select User Administration.

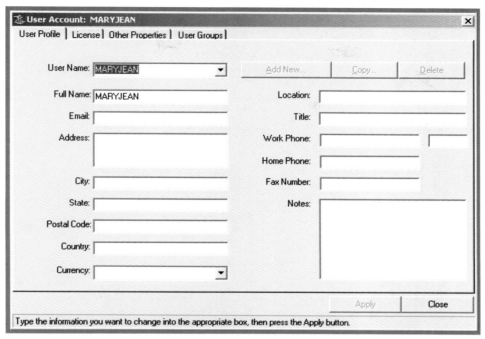

Figure 11.4 User Account dialog box

3. Your User Account dialog box will appear. See Figure 11.4.
4. Select Other Properties. Type in the new password and confirm the new password.
5. Click Apply. If the Apply box remains gray, the information typed in the New password and Confirm password boxes is not the same. It is necessary to repeat the process.
6. You will be asked if you want save the new password, click on Yes. An Add History Note page will appear. Select OK.
7. Close the User Account dialog box.

It is also possible for an administrator (instructor) to change a user (student) password. Thus, the administrator (instructor or supervisor) always has access to all work. In the industry, a supervisor can change a password to lock dismissed employees out of the system.

Creating a New Folder

1. On the menu bar, select File, and a drop-down menu will appear. See Figure 11.5.

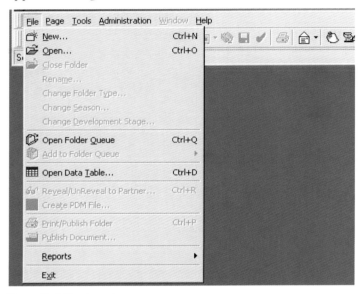

Figure 11.5 File drop-down menu

2. Select New. The Create New Folder Wizard will open. See Figure 11.6.

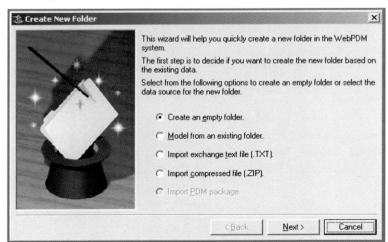

Figure 11.6 Create New Folder Wizard

3. Select Create an empty folder.
4. Click on Next.
5. Fill in page 2 of the Wizard. See Figure 11.7.

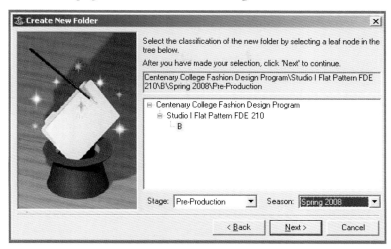

Figure 11.7 Page 2 of the Create New Folder Wizard

    a. Select your classification. For students, this will probably be your class name and section. Check with your instructor.
    b. In the Stage field, select Pre-Production.
    c. In the Season field, select the appropriate season.
6. Click on Next.
7. Fill in page 3 of the Wizard. See Figure 11.8.

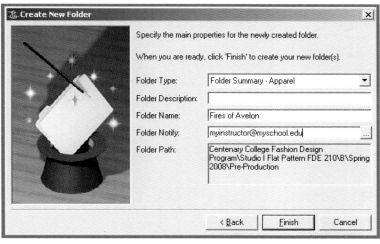

Figure 11.8 Page 3 of the Create New Folder Wizard

> a. Folder type should be Folder Summary—Apparel. This may be different for each organization.
>
> b. Folder description may remain blank.
>
> c. Folder name: This field must be filled. It is suggested that students use their initials or the name of their design.
>
> d. Folder notification: If an email address is typed in this field, an email will be sent to that address when changes are made in the folder. This is very useful in a design house. Students may be required to email the course instructor.
>
> e. Folder path is a recap of the previous pages.

8. Select Finish. This opens the Folder Summary.

The Folder Summary

When a folder is created, several fields in the Folder Summary fill in automatically. See Figure 11.9.

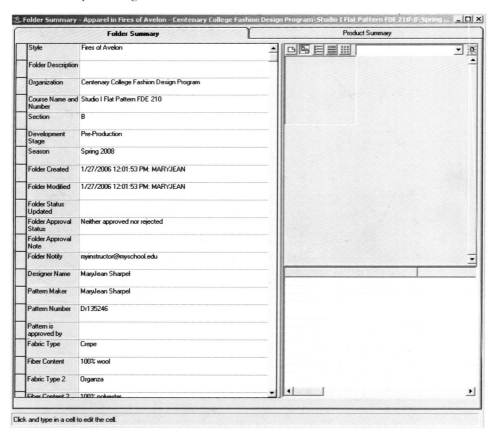

Figure 11.9 Several fields filled in automatically in the Folder Summary.

Fields that were entered as the page was created cannot be edited; some other fields can be filled in by clicking in the field.

Fields that should be filled in include:

Designer name
Patternmaker
Pattern number
Fabric type
Fabric content
Fabric type 2
Fabric content 2
Size range
Sample size
Project due date
Special instructions

Additional fields may have been added by the administrator, such as Instructor's Name and Date Submitted to Instructor.

Approval fields such as fabric approval and pattern approval have toggle buttons. Due date fields have a drop-down calendar.

Saving a Folder Summary

The Summary Folder is saved by use of the WebPDM menu bar. If this is not visible, restore the window—make the page smaller by use of the middle button at the upper right of the screen.

1. Select Page on the menu.
2. Select Save in the drop-down menu.
3. Select OK in the Add History Note window.

Hints for Success

To change the information on a saved Folder page, it is necessary to use the Edit command. The Edit command is found by selecting Page from the WebPDM menu bar.

Opening an Existing Folder

1. Go to File in the PDM menu bar, and click Open. The Open an Existing Folder window will appear. See Figure 11.10.

2. At the top of the lower display area are five buttons that determine the format of the display. The Display option buttons are described in Table 11.1.

3. There are four ways to access a folder. The two ways presented are Folder and Organization and Date Modified.

   a. Folder and Organization:
      i. In the Search drop-down box, select Folders.
      ii. Select the Folder & Organization tab.
      iii. In Found In, highlight Entire Organization (or your class number).
      iv. Highlight Pre-Production, Approved, and Inactive Styles as needed.
      v. Highlight seasons as needed. To select all seasons, click on the first season, holding the shift key, and click on the last season. All seasons selected will be highlighted blue.
      vi. If the folder has an image, go to the Search field and select Images in Folders. If the folder has no image, select Folder.
      vii. Click on Find Now.

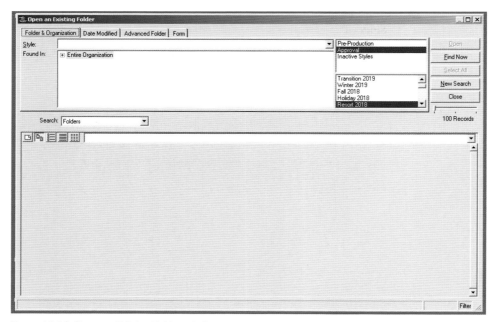

Figure 11.10 Open an Existing Folder window

Table 11.1 Display Option Buttons for Opening an Existing Folder

	Shows last image accessed
	Shows all available images as thumbnail views with the image title and brief description
	Shows very small images accompanied by folder information
	Shows text only
	Shows names only

viii. The images or titles of all available folders will appear in the lower half of the screen. Select the folder to open by clicking on the folder title or image.

ix. Click on Open.

b. Date Modified:

i. Select the Date Modified tab.

ii. In the Search field, select either Folders or Images in Folders.

iii. Selection choices are:

- All Folders/Images.
- Find all folders/images created or modified between specified dates or during the previous specified months or days.

iv. Click on Find Now.

v. The images or titles of all available folders will appear in the lower half of the screen. Select the folder to open by clicking on the folder title or image.

vi. Click on Open.

To Place an Image in a Folder Summary

There are four ways to add a document (image) to a Folder Summary: import, link, copy, or create.

1. *Import document from a file*: This may be used to import a picture or document from Photoshop, Illustrator, or Excel, or a jpeg from a digital camera or scanner.
2. *Link to existing document*: This can be used to bring in an image that already exists in WebPDM. An image brought in this way will be dynamically linked to images in other folders; if you change the image in one folder, it will be changed in all folders.
3. *Copy from exiting document*: This is also used to import an image that already exists in WebPDM, but the image is not linked to the original; so if it is changed, it will not change other versions of the image in the system.
4. *Create a new document*: This launches you into another program and should not be used as it takes up a license space and may prevent other students from using Web PDM.

Importing a Document from a File

The desired image should be available on the computer or a removable storage device.

1. Right click in the space to receive the image. See Figure 11.11.

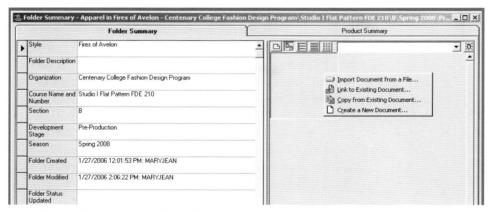

Figure 11.11 Adding a document (image) to a Folder Summary

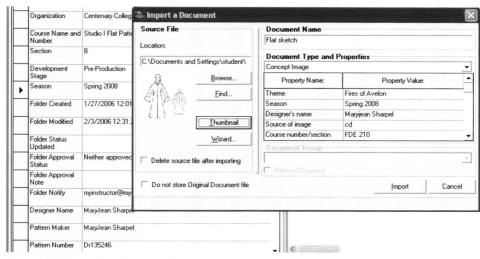

Figure 11.12 Importing a Document dialog box

2. Click on Import Document from a File. The Import a Document dialog box will open. See Figure 11.12.
3. Find and select a picture by using either Browse or Find as you would to find any computer file in any Microsoft program.
4. To preview the picture before importing it, click on thumbnail.
5. On the right side of the Import a Document window, you may determine the information that will be linked to the picture. The fields available will vary from company to company. There is a drop-down menu to indicate the document type (Concept Image, Technical Sketch, Fabric, and so on). In addition to the document type name, information that may be linked to the document includes image name, theme, season, designer name, source of image, and more.
6. Select Import.
7. Save the folder Summary Page by selecting Save in the Page drop-down menu on the WebPDM menu bar.
8. To continue working on this page (such as adding another picture), it is necessary to go to WebPDM menu bar>Page>Edit.

266

Linking to an Existing Document/ Copying from Existing Document

> ### Hint for Success
>
> It is highly recommended that images and documents in student work are not linked to other student folders. This will avoid the possibility that student work may be modified by other students by mistake.

The processes of Linking to an Existing Document and Copying from Existing Document are discussed together because the processes for both are similar.

1. Right click in the space to receive the image.
2. Select either Link to Existing Document or Copy From Existing Document. This opens the Select an Existing Image window that is similar to the Open an Existing Folder window as seen Figure 11.10.
3. To show all the images in folders, proceed in the same way as for Opening an Existing folder.
4. Click on the image to be imported or copied and click Select.
5. The Copy an Existing Document window will appear. This is similar to the Importing a Document window as shown in Figure 11.12. Fill in as appropriate. Remember that any changes in information on a linked image will change that information in all places that the image is used.
6. Select Import/Copy.
7. Save Folder Summary Page (WebPDM menu bar>Page>Save).
8. In order to continue working on this page (such as adding another picture) it is necessary to go to WebPDM menu bar>Page>Edit.

Hint for Success

Often the WebPDM menu bar is hidden behind the current page. This page can be restored to see the WebPDM menu bar. It is important to remember to manipulate the sizes of the components of a page to see all of the information (text and/or images).

Editing Images

Access the image edit menu by right clicking in the picture on the Folder Summary Page. See Figure 11.13.

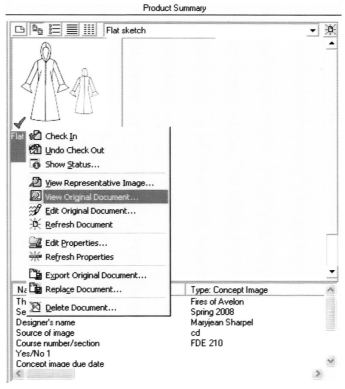

Figure 11.13 Image edit menu

Table 11.2 summarizes the functions of each icon.

Table 11.2 Image Edit Menu Icons

Icon	Icon title	Description
	Check In	If there is no check in the lower left-hand corner of the image, the image will be printed when the folder is printed.
	Check Out	If there is a check in the lower left-hand corner of the image, it will be excluded from the printed version of the folder. The original image cannot be edited, except by the person who checked it out. No one except the person (including administrators) who has checked an image out can check it in. • A green check on the screen means that it can be checked in by the current user. • A red check means that it cannot be checked in by the current user.
	Show Status	Selecting this will provide information (Status, Usage, Group, and Properties) about the image and indicate whether it is checked out, and if so, by whom and when.
	View Representative Image	This shows a larger image that can be left open while working on other pages.
	View Original Document	This launches the original document.
	Edit Original Document	This will go to the software system in which the original image was created and launch a PDM version of the original. Editing will change the image in this folder and in linked versions of the image.
	Refresh Document	The image is pulled from the original source and redrawn.
	Edit Properties	A fill-in box appears allowing for modification or entry of information to be attached to the image.
	Refresh Properties	The properties are pulled from the WebPDM database and redisplayed.

	Export Original Document	This allows the original document to be sent to another file (outside the PDM system).
	Replace Document	This replaces the document and all linked documents. It allows a document to be replaced by a file created outside the system.
	Break Link	It breaks the link between the document in the folder and copies of the document in other folders.
	Delete Document	This removes a document from the folder. If the image is not in any other folders, it will be removed from WebPDM as well. After a document has been removed from WebPDM, it will still appear in the database until WebPDM is closed.

Summary

WebPDM software shortens the development cycle and reduces the development costs of a garment. There are 40 user-defined forms that can be used to enter sketches, full-color drawings, measurement specifications, information about fabrics and notions, cost specifications, construction details, and other information. Instant communication between all collaborating parties is possible. Information can be shared easily through a system of user groups, permissions, and automatic tracking. Folders can be created, saved, and modified. Images such as flat sketches can be imported into a WebPDM folder summary.

Key Terms

flat sketches
working sketches

Review Questions

1. How many user-defined general purpose forms are included in WebPDM?

270

2. How are pages in WebPDM accessed?
3. What is the purpose of the history notes?
4. What are flat or working sketches?
5. List two ways to access a folder.
6. List four ways to add a document/image to a Folder Summary.

WebPDM, Part I Exercises

1. Creating a Folder Summary page.
   a. Work through the process described in the text and create a folder. Add at least one image with attached information to your folder.
   b. Save the Folder Summary page.
2. Editing a Folder
   a. Open the folder created in Exercise 1.
   b. Change the information attached to the image. (Do not forget that after a page has been saved, it is necessary to go to WebPDM menu bar>Page>Edit.)
   c. Save the folder again.

CHAPTER TWELVE

WebPDM, Part II

Objectives

After reading this chapter, you will be able to

- Add, open, and delete pages.

- Complete the AML Measurement Specification Worksheet and AML Multi-Sample Evaluation Worksheet.

- Fill in the Color Component, Construction Details, and Line Assortment pages.

- Fill in the Dimension Data Table and complete Design and Cost Specifications Pages.

- Print contents of a folder.

Introduction

In this chapter you will learn how to add pages to your folder. These pages may include an **AML** (Advanced Measurement Library) Measurement Specification Worksheet, an AML Multi-Sample Evaluation Worksheet, Color Component, Construction Details, Line Assortment, and a Cost Sheet. In an academic setting, the following additional forms may be available: Instructor Comments and a Student/Instructor Collaboration Form. The selection of pages is determined by the administrator when the program is set up. General information about adding and opening pages will be presented first. Then a summary of selected pages will be provided.

Folder Pages

The pages in a folder can be accessed by many people simultaneously, but edited by only one person at a time. When an existing page is opened, it is in Save mode. To modify the page, it is necessary to go into Edit mode. (To do so, double click on the page or go to WebPDM menu>Page>Edit.)

Adding New Pages

You cannot add a new page until you have saved the page you are working on.

The general process for adding a page is:
1. Go to the WebPDM menu.
2. Select Page>Add. This will open the Add a Page wizard as shown in Figure 12.1.

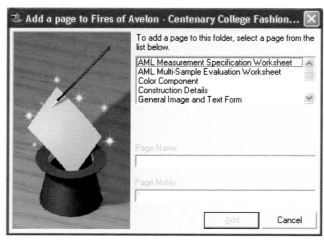

Figure 12.1 Add a page wizard

3. Select the page to add and follow the prompts.
4. After a new page has been added, it is saved by selecting WebPDM menu>Page>Save.

Opening Existing Pages

From the WebPDM menu, select Page>Open Page. A list of existing pages will appear; select the desired page to open.

Deleting Pages

It is possible to delete pages.

Go to WebPDM menu>Page>Delete. A list of existing pages will appear. Select the pages to delete, and click on the Delete button.

Completing Pages in a Folder

Instructions are given for completing the following pages in a folder: AML Measurement Specification Worksheet, AML Multi-Sample Evaluation Worksheet, Color Component, Construction Details, and Line Assortment.

AML Measurement Specification Worksheet

The AML Measurement Specification Worksheet must be added before the AML Multi-Sample Evaluation Worksheet because information from the Specification Worksheet is transferred in to the Multi-Sample Evaluation Worksheet. To open a Measurement Specifications Worksheet, it is necessary to fill in a series of wizard pages, select the company whose grade rules you want to use, the size classification, the size range and specific sizes, sample size, and the product type. The possible selections can vary from company to company. There are five tabs in the AML Measurement Specification Worksheet: Header, Worksheet, Imperial POMs, Metric POMs, and Images.

Header Tab

The Header tab is shown in Figure 12.2. It provides an overall summary of the information in the folder.

Worksheet Tab

The Measurement Specifications Worksheet opens on the page for adding garment specifications. It may show a list of **POMs** (points of measure), sizes, and other information. See Figure 12.3.

For some size classifications and product types, the page may open with no default POMs. See Figure 12.4.

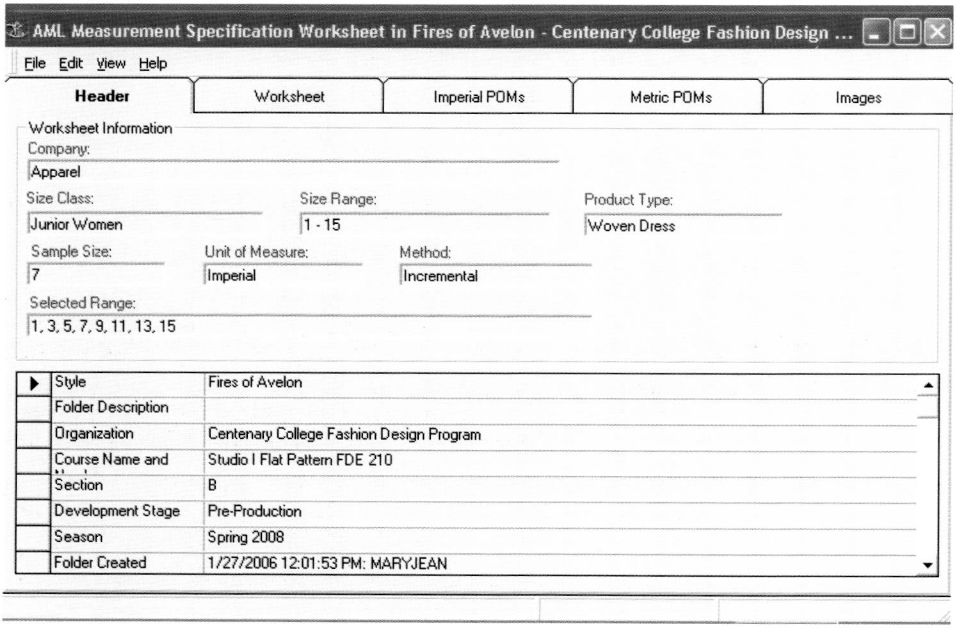

Figure 12.2 Measurement Specification Worksheet Header tab

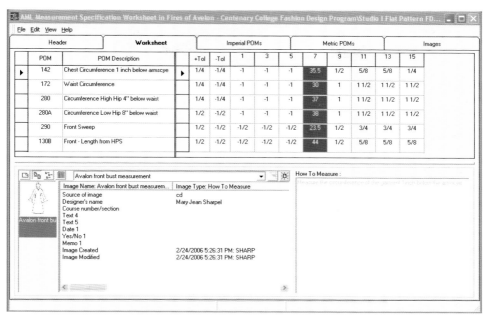

Figure 12.3 AML Measurement Specification Worksheet with POMs

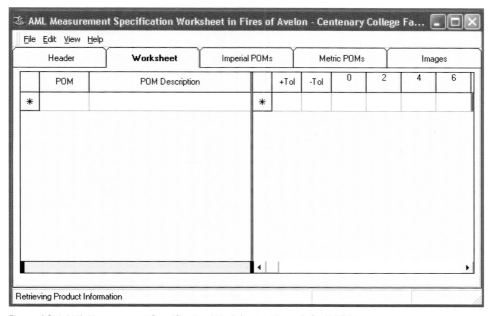

Figure 12.4 AML Measurement Specification Worksheet with no default POMs

In the Gerber system, each POM is described and given a unique reference number. Figure 12.5 shows a flat sketch labeled with WebPDM POM reference numbers.

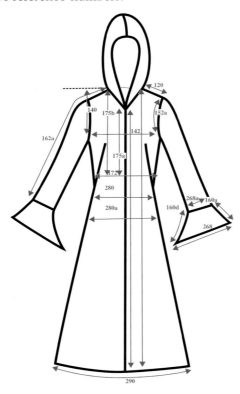

Figure 12.5 Flat sketch with selected numbers that WebPDM uses to reference different POMs

Hint for Success

Reminder: Do not forget that you must be in Edit mode before information can be added to a page. Edit mode is accessed by either going to WebPDM menu>Page>Edit or by double clicking in a field and waiting for the page to enter Edit mode.

New POMs can be added in two ways:

1. In an empty POM description field, type in a new description.

2. Place the cursor in an empty POM or POM description field. Select Add New POM either from the right button drop-down menu or from the worksheet File drop-down menu. A list of POM descriptions will appear. Make a selection, and click on OK.

It is also possible to copy POMs from an existing worksheet. Highlight a line by clicking in the far left column and follow standard copy/paste procedures. Lines can only be pasted into a worksheet in the same size class.

Next to each POM are columns for plus and minus tolerance and incremental changes between sizes at this measurement point. For more information on tolerances and grade-size changes, see the sidebar entitled, "Measuring Garment Specifications." When measurement POM descriptions are selected from the Gerber database, tolerances and grade differences are entered automatically. These may be changed if they are not appropriate. If POM descriptions are typed in, a technician must also add appropriate numbers for tolerance and grade-size difference.

It is possible to add an image of each POM and measurement instructions. The image is added in the appropriate space at the bottom left part of the worksheet. The process for adding the image is identical to the way an image is added to the Summary page. The text is added at the bottom right of the screen. The image and measurement instruction for a POM will only be seen when that POM is highlighted. See Figure 12.3.

Hint for Success

Beware: The tolerances and grade size differences that appear automatically may not be appropriate for all uses. The technical designer may need to change these numbers.

Measuring Garment Specifications

Specifications, or specs, are the finished dimensions of each size of a garment. They are developed by manufacturers for each garment style and displayed in garment specification tables. They are usually accompanied by flat sketches and guidelines for measurement locations. Specification tables have two major functions: to create grade rules and to maintain quality control when assessing whether finished garments have the correct dimensions. When a specification table is used for quality control, it will indicate the acceptable tolerance—the amount of variation from the standard dimensions that a company will accept. Tolerance will be different for different points of measure; for instance, a dress may be acceptable if the chest circumference is up to half an inch greater or smaller than the specification, whereas the length may be acceptable if it is three-quarters of an inch different from the specification.

In the past, a designer or manufacturing company would supply the grader with specifications for a particular garment, and the grader would create a set of grading rules and make patterns for each size of the garment. Now, many manufacturing companies have an established set of grading rules that are used during pattern grading and for calculating the dimensions of garments.

When creating and using a specification table, it is necessary that an adequate number of measurements are used to clearly define the garment and that the location of each dimension to be measured is precisely designated. It is essential that all parties involved in taking measurements fully understand the specification table.

The locations of measurements are called points of measure, often abbreviated to POMs. Some measurements may be taken as a circumference and others as a width. It is customary, but not always the case, that the circumference is used when measuring the bust, waist, and hips and that width is used when measuring legs, arms, and neck. Measurement points are defined by reference to a known point. For example, it may be determined that the bust measurement is taken one inch below the armseye. When length measurements are taken, it is necessary to define each end of a measurement, such as high point shoulder, armseye, or center back neckline.

In the past, most companies had a booklet that contained a list of measurements and diagrams and instructions explaining exactly where and how measurements should be taken. The booklet was used by patternmakers, graders, production personnel, and technical designers involved in quality control. Now many companies store this information in Gerber Web PDM, where it can be accessed by all who need it.

The Gerber Specifications Worksheet is preset with many possible POMs. However, it may still be necessary to add points of measure for details such as hoods, fancy cuffs, belts, or asymmetrical lines. Gerber gives each POM an identifying number. The system uses a convention whereby most length measurements start with 1 and most width measurements start with 2. Each company may create its own system for identifying points of measure.

Imperial and Metric POM Tabs

The Imperial POMs and Metric POMs tabs open windows that show the measurements adjusted for each size using the size differences that were indicated on the worksheet. See Figure 12.6. Information cannot be added directly to this page, but must be added using the worksheet.

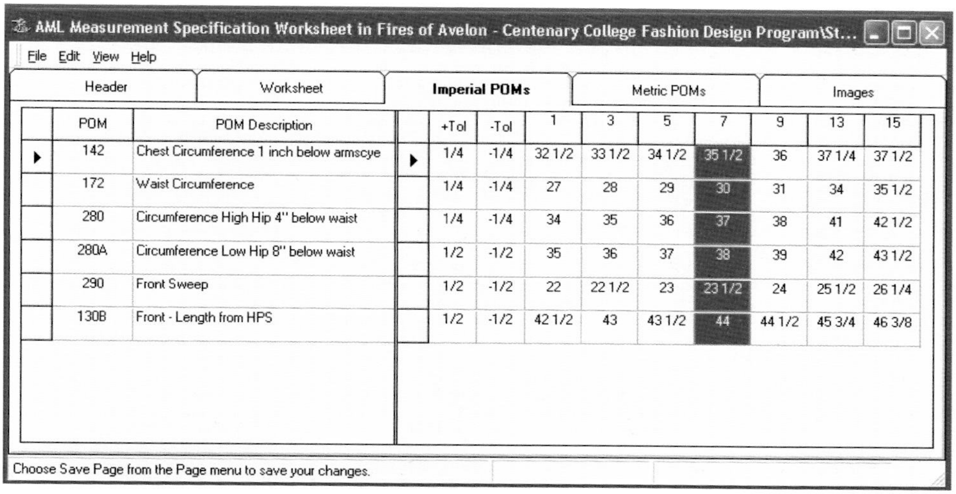

Figure 12.6 Imperial POM tab of AML Measurement Specification Worksheet

Hint for Success
Remember to save your page before closing.

AML Multi-Sample Evaluation Worksheet

The AML Multi-Sample Evaluation Worksheet is used to evaluate the specifications of a finished garment. It can be used to determine if the garments coming from a factory meet the garment specification tolerance standards. To add this worksheet, go to Page>Add. The Add a Page wizard will appear. Select AML Multi-Sample Evaluation Worksheet. Work through the wizard selecting the size to be sampled and the number of samples to be evaluated. Each worksheet has a site for adding identification information about the sample to be evaluated. The evaluator fills in the actual sample garment measurements in the appropriate fields. Scrolling across the screen will show spaces for the number of samples selected to be evaluated. The computer calculates the difference between the actual and the manufacturer's specified measurements for each sample evaluated (or for each evaluator). If the sample measurement is outside the tolerance standards, the field will be highlighted in red. See Figure 12.7.

Within this worksheet, there is a Sample Image/Comments tab that opens a worksheet used to insert a picture of a sample and comments. This worksheet can be used to communicate problems to the production facility or vendor.

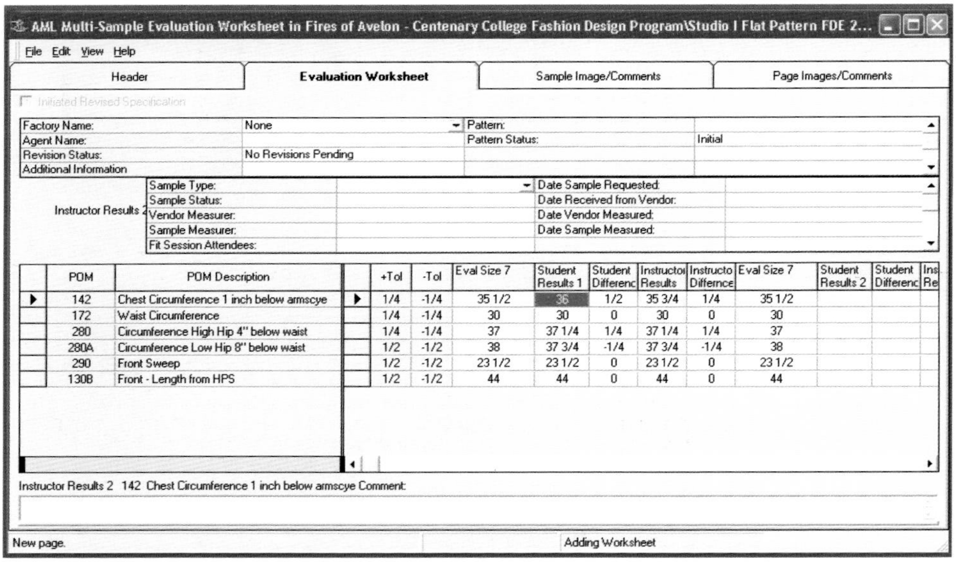

Figure 12.7 AML Multi-Sample Evaluation Worksheet

Color Component

A style may be made in a variety of different colors, known as colorways. The Color Component page is used to provide information about the color for each component for each colorway. For example, a white shirt may have white buttons, and a blue shirt may have blue buttons. Images can be added to the page. Figure 12.8 shows the Color Component page. To open the color component page, select Page>Add and in the wizards, highlight Color Component and click on Add.

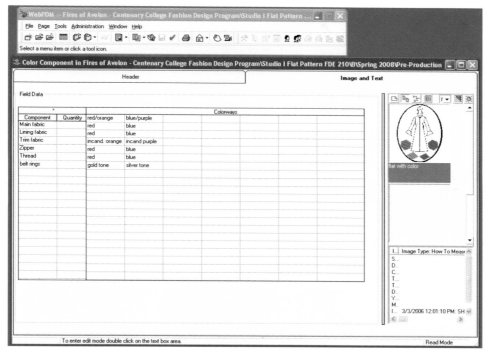

Figure 12.8 Color Component page

Construction Details

The Construction Details page is used by a designer to inform a manufacturer about how a garment should be constructed. This page is added in the same way as the color component page. Generally, a company will have an established database of instructions. Appropriate instructions can be selected and attached to the folder

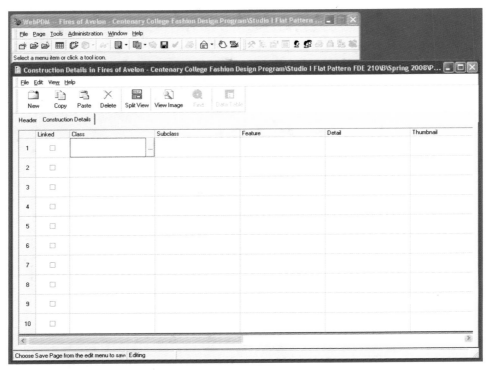

Figure 12.9 Construction Details page

for each style. Construction details include information about attaching labels (such as size, care, and fiber content). Figure 12.9 shows the Construction Details page. Most versions of PDM have some data supplied by Gerber Technology. To add data to the Class, Subclass, and Feature fields, left click in the right corner of the field, and select the most appropriate item from the drop-down menu. Each field must be filled in sequentially from left to right. See Figure 12.10.

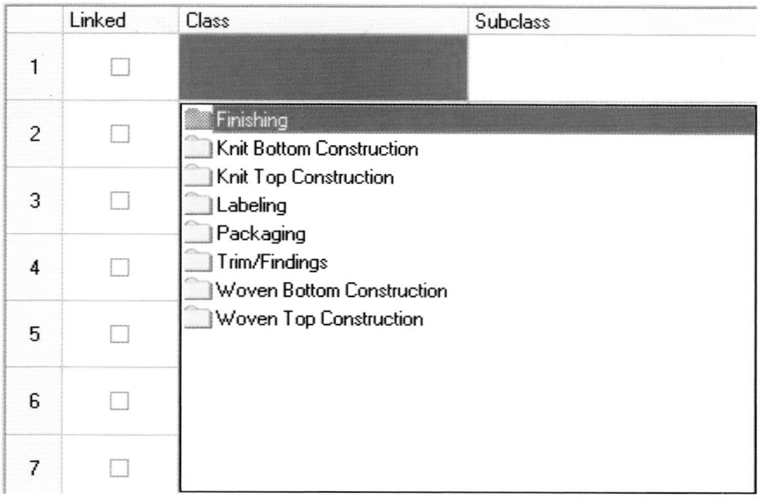

	Linked	Class	Subclass
1	☐		
2	☐	Finishing	
		Knit Bottom Construction	
3	☐	Knit Top Construction	
		Labeling	
		Packaging	
4	☐	Trim/Findings	
		Woven Bottom Construction	
5	☐	Woven Top Construction	
6	☐		
7	☐		

Figure 12.10 Construction Details; Class field drop-down menu

Information can be typed in the Details field except when the Class is linked.

Images can be added in the Thumbnail field by right clicking and following the instructions for insertion. The process is similar to the process for adding other images in PDM. If there is a check in the Linked box, the item is linked to the database and images cannot be added. Uncheck the Link box to add images. After an image has been added, select anywhere in the row and click on View Image to see a thumbnail.

In the Class, Subclass, and Feature fields information can be selected from the drop-down menus. New information cannot be directly typed into these fields. To add information that is not in the drop-

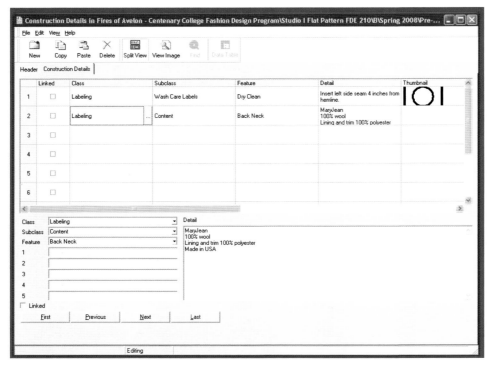

Figure 12.11 Construction Details with Split View

down menu select Split View. See Figure 12.11. Highlight a row by clicking on the row number, then type the information to be added in the appropriate box in the lower half of the screen. The information will appear automatically in the corresponding field of the selected row. Information in these field can only be edited by using the lower section of the split view. Information can be added to the Detail field directly or in the lower half of the split screen. It may also be edited in each location. The field in the upper half of the split screen show a maximum of three lines of content. Additional information can be found by scrolling down or by using the bottom half of the split screen.

Line Assortment

The Line Assortment page can be used to group together related garments that make up a line or collection. A completed line can be presented as a whole. Information related to each garment can also be included on the page. The information automatically entered in the page when a folder is opened is dependent on the attributes preselected by the form administrator. Such information can include price, color choice, fabric, and season. Other fields for attributes can be entered on the page, and information can be typed in. To access and use the Line Assortment page, follow these steps:

1. Go to Page>Add>Line Assortment>Add. The Basic Line Assortment page (See Figure 12.12.) and the Available Attributes window will open.

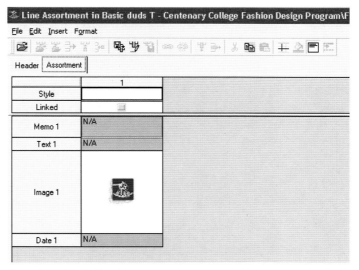

Figure 12.12 Basic Line Assortment page

2. This window shows all the available attributes (those preselected by the form administrator). For a very basic line assortment, there may be no attributes. Double click on an attribute that you wish to include in your Line Assortment.

When new styles are added, the information for these attributes will be automatically added. See Figure 12.13.

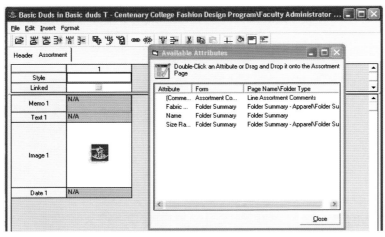

Figure 12.13 Available Attributes selection box within Line Assortment

3. To add new attributes, select Insert>Insert Attribute. The Available Attributes selection box will open. Double click on Assortment Comments, and in the appropriate space, enter the label for a new attribute. (The information for this new attribute will not automatically appear, but must be typed in when a new style is added.) Click on OK. See Figure 12.14.

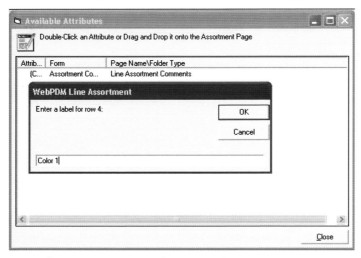

Figure 12.14 Line Assortment: Adding new attributes

Additional new attribute fields can be added in the same way.

4. To enter a style in Line Assortment, double click in the first image field. From the drop-down menu, select Insert Existing Folder. Select the folder to be inserted. Information from the folder that matches the preselected attributes of the Line Assortment page will be entered automatically. Other information can be added by double clicking in a field and typing in the data. It is possible to change information that has been automatically entered, but this will also edit the original folder. To do so, double click in the desired field and type in the new information.

5. Additional styles can be added in the same way. See Figure 12.15.

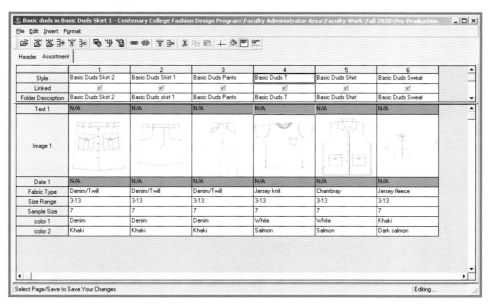

Figure 12.15 Line Assortment with styles added

To delete styles from an assortment, select the style by left clicking in the Style column. Go to Edit>Remove column. Select Yes in the dialog box.

Design and Cost Specification

Creating a cost sheet can be a complicated process. In the clothing industry, PDM is used to keep records of vendors, suppliers, contactors, agents, contracts, and factory costs and how each of these relates to the cost of the finished product. The cost of materials, manufacturing processes, contract work, and overheads are entered on separate data tables in the PDM system and then combined to determine the total cost of garment production. Many data tables that affect Design and Cost Specifications are available.

Data Tables

Companies will complete tables as appropriate to their needs. The available tables include:

> Season Data Table
> Contacts Data Table
> Dimension Data Table
> SubCategories Data Table
> Item Property Data Table
> Contract Data Table
> Factory Rates Data Table
> Operation Properties Data Table
> Currencies Data Table

For student use, it may not be necessary to fill in all of these data tables.

For the purposes of this book, students need to complete a Dimension Data Table to create a simple Design and Cost Specifications Worksheet for a finished garment. To access the Data Tables, follow these steps:

1. Select File in the WebPDM menu bar.
2. Select Open Data Table. See Figure 12.16.

Figure 12.16 Open Data Table

Dimension Data Table

In PDM, a **dimension** is defined as a variable (such as color or size) that affects the cost of a garment or raw material. For student work, only the color dimension will be used and students will add their own color(s). The process of filling in the Dimension Data Table is as follows:

1. In the WebPDM menu bar, go to File>Open Data Table>Dimension Data Table.
2. Students may add a Dimension Type or use a Dimension Type previously entered, such as color. To add a new Dimension Type,
   a. Click on the arrow next to New and select Dimension Type.
   b. A dialog box will appear. Type a brief description of the new dimension type (up to 15 letters) in the Short Description field. More details can be added in the Long Description field.
   c. Select OK to save the information. It will appear on the left of the screen under Dimension Type.
3. To add Dimension Details to a Dimension Type:
   a. Highlight the desired Dimension Type, click on the arrow next to New, and select Dimension Detail.
   b. Complete the short and long description boxes. It is suggested that students add their own color choices, or, if their color selection is in the database, they do not need to add a Dimension Detail.
   c. Click the arrow in the Dimension Type field, and select the appropriate Dimension Type for this detail (Color).
   d. Click on the arrow in the Ownership field, and select the part of the organization that will be using the new Dimension Detail. (For student use, it is recommended that all students have access to all of the information.)
   e. Click on the arrow in the Classification field, and select the best descriptor for the Dimension Detail (Color).
   f. Select the Color Season tab to identify the season. It is suggested that students select All Seasons.
   g. Click on OK to save the data and close the box. The new Dimension Details will appear in the right section of the screen when the appropriate Dimension Type is selected on the left of the screen.

Completing the Design and Cost Specification Page

1. Open the folder for your garment, and select Page>Add.
2. Select Design and Cost Specification>Add. To begin setting up the new page, select Next.
3. A dialog box will appear. In the Dimension 1 field, select Color. All other fields may be left empty. (Information about creating Categories, SubCategories, and Types is included in the chapter exercises on page 295.) See Figure 12.17.

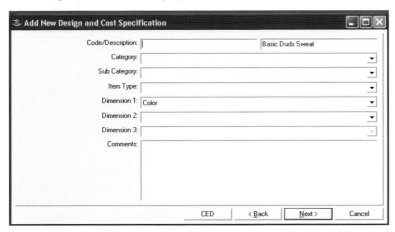

Figure 12.17 Add New Design and Cost Specification: Dialog box 1

4. Select Next. A new dialog box will appear. This box is used to select the color dimensions of the garment. See Figure 12.18.

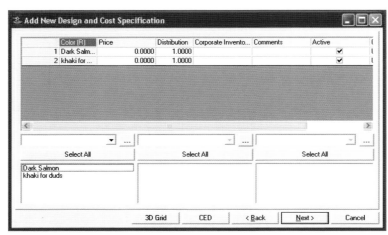

Figure 12.18 Add New Design and Cost Specification: Dialog box 2

Colors can be selected in one of two ways.

a. Double click on the arrow in the field above Select All in the first box. Click on the desired color. This color will appear in the Color field in the top area of the dialog box.

b. To select more than one color, click on Select All in the first box. A list of all available colors will appear below Select All and also in the Color field in the top area of the dialog box.

c. Remove unwanted colors by highlighting and pressing Delete on the keyboard.

5. Click on Next. Choose Do Not Select First Component. Click on Next. Click on Finish.

6. The Product Summary tab of the Design and Cost Specification page will open.

7. Select the Product Details tab. See Figure 12.19.

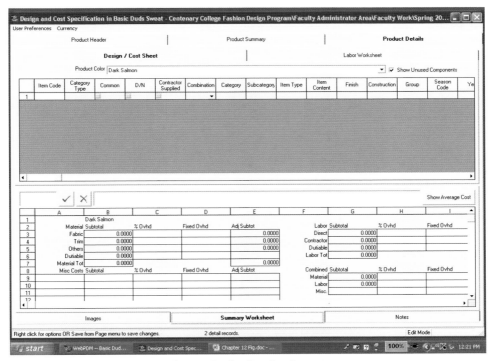

Figure 12.19 Design and Cost Specification: Product Details tab

Fill in the Fixed Ovhd fields for fabric and labor. Total material cost, labor cost, and accrued subtotal will be calculated automatically and appear in the appropriate boxes.

8. Select Page in the WebPDM menu bar>Save.

Hint for Success

Remember: The WebPDM menu bar may be hidden behind the current page. To see it, you may have to move the page or make it smaller by clicking on the restore button (the middle button at the top right of the page).

Print/Publish Folder

PDM does not print in the same format as it appears on the screen. Before starting, check that your printer is on and connected to the computer.

1. Select File>Print/Publish folder. The Print/Publish dialog box will appear.
2. Put a check in the box next to Printing. In the Print Group Field, select "Your Organization" Complete Style Package.
3. Check the pages you wish to print. See Figure 12.20.

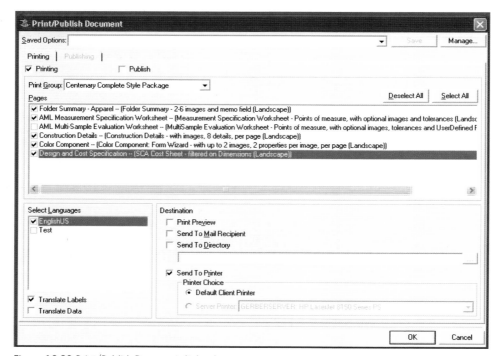

Figure 12.20 Print/Publish Document dialog box

4. In the Select Languages field, select EnglishUS.
5. Place a check next to Translate Labels.
6. Check Send To Printer. Do not select any other destinations. Select OK. A series of Report Option dialog boxes (one for each page to be printed) will appear. Leave all options on these pages on default. Select OK for each page.

Summary

Important components of PDM are the AML Measurement Specification Worksheet, AML Multi-Sample Evaluation Worksheet, Color Component, Construction Details, Line Assortment, and Design and Cost Specification page. The Multi-Sample Evaluation Worksheet is used for garment specifications and has columns for plus and minus tolerance and incremental changes between sizes at each measurement point. The Sample Image/Comments tab can be used to communicate problems to the production facility or vendor. The Construction Details page is used by a designer to inform a manufacturer about how a garment should be constructed. Construction details include information about attaching labels (such as size, care, and fiber content). The Line Assortment page can be used to group together related garments that make up a line or collection. A Dimension Data Table is completed before a Design and Cost Specification page is completed.

Key Terms

AML	specs
colorway	specifications
dimension	tolerance
POM	

Review Questions

1. Why is the AML Measurement Specification Worksheet added before the Multi-Sample Evaluation worksheet?
2. Why may it be necessary to change the tolerances and grade size differences on the Worksheet tab of the AML Measurement Specification Worksheet?
3. What is the purpose of the AML Multi-Sample Evaluation Worksheet?

294

4. What is the purpose of the Sample Image/Comments tab in the AML Multi-Sample Evaluation Worksheet?
5. What information is included on the Construction Details page?
6. How is a Line Assortment page used?

WebPDM, Part II Exercises

1. Adding and filling in pages.
   a. Open the folder created in Chapter 11.
   b. Add the following pages to your folder: AML Measurement Specification Worksheet, AML Multi-Sample Evaluation Worksheet, Construction Details, and Design and Cost Specification. Fill in a Dimension Data table if this is needed to open a Design and Cost Specification page. (It may be possible to use Color Dimension Details entered by previous students or faculty members.)
   c. Print copies of your folder for your portfolio.
2. Practice using Data Tables.
   Practice filling in Data Tables that an employee in the apparel industry may need to complete.

Contacts Data Table

This data table contains information about all of the agents, vendors, mills, factories, and others associated with a company. It is completed as follows:

   a. Go to File>Open Data Table>Contacts Data Table. On the left of the screen is a default list (nondeletable) of the following Contact groups: Agent, Factory, Mill, Third Party, and Vendor.
   b. To add a new contact to one of the Contact groups, highlight the group. Click the arrow next to New, and select Contact Data.
   c. A dialog box will appear. Type a brief description of the new contact (up to 15 letters) in the Short Description field. Type in the full name of the contact in the Long Description field.
   d. Click on the arrow in the Ownership field, and select which part of the organization will be using the new contact.

    e. Select the Address tab, and type in the address, phone number, and additional details of the new contact.

    f. Click on OK to save the data and close the box. The new Contact information will appear in the right section of the screen when the appropriate Contact Group is selected on the left of the screen.

SubCategories Data Table

The outline of this table once created for a company or academic situation will only rarely need to be changed. Each company will have a different structure appropriate to its needs. The table is used to organize and categorize raw materials and finished products and to act as a search mechanism for locating items in the PDM system. There are three levels of organization: Category, SubCategory, and Type. When initially opened, the SubCategories Data Table has two main categories, Item Category and Operational Category. It is suggested that the Item Category should be split into several categories. The software provides categories for Finished Products (P), Fiber (F), Trim (T), and Other (O). It is further suggested that for student use the Finished Product Category should be split into subcategories such as Pants, Shirts, Skirts, Dresses, and Evening Wear. The process of filling in the SubCategories Data table is as follows:

    a. Go to File>Open Data Table>SubCategories Data Table.

    b. In most situations, new categories will not need to be added. A company or institution will have all the categories needed already available.

    c. It may also be unnecessary for students to add new SubCategories. To add a new SubCategory to a Category, highlight the Category on the left side of the screen. Click on the arrow next to New, and select SubCategory. A drop-down menu will appear. Confirm that the Category and Category Type are correct. If they are not, change them by using the arrow in the appropriate field. In the Category Type field, select the appropriate abbreviation. Fill in the Short Description and the Long Description fields with the title of the SubCategory, such as Woven Shirt or Dress. Select OK to save and exit.

d. To add a Type to a SubCategory, highlight the SubCategory on the left side of the screen. Click on the arrow next to New, and select Type. A drop-down menu will appear. Confirm that the Category, SubCategory, and Category Type fields contain the correct information. Fill in the Short Description and the Long Description fields with the title of the Type. Click on OK.

e. For Raw Materials, the process for adding Categories, SubCategories, and Types is similar to that for adding Finished Product information. Categories may include groups such as Labels, Fabrics, Trim, and Packaging.

Item Property Data Table

The Item Property Data Table is used to add information about item properties. It is usually used to describe information about raw materials.

a. Go to File>Open Data Table>Item Property Data Table.

b. In the left side of the field, highlight a Type (the Item for which data is being added), and click on New.

c. A dialog box will appear. The Item Code field can be left blank. In the Description field, enter a description of the item. Confirm that the Category, SubCategory, and Item Type fields are correct.

d. In the Dimension 1 Type field, make a selection from the drop-down menu.

e. Select the Additional Properties tab. In the UOM (units of measure) field, select the units of measure for the given item.

f. In the Owner field, select which part of the organization will use this item. Leave all other fields blank.

g. Select the Item Details tab. A dialog box will open. In the Color area, click on Select All. A list of the colors that were entered in the Color Dimension of the Dimension Data Table will be displayed. Select the desired colors by removing those not wanted. See Figure 12.21. To remove a color, highlight the color in the area below Select All, and press Delete on the keyboard.

h. Additional fields can be filled in. Most fields are completed by double clicking in the field and filling in the appropriate

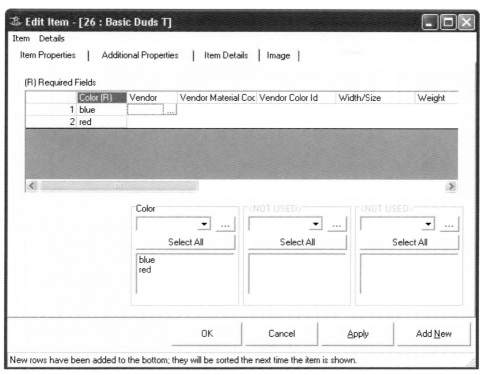

Figure 12.21 Item Property Data Table: Details tab

information. To select a vendor, click on the right edge of the Vendor field to open a dialog box. Select Find Now. Highlight the appropriate vendor. Select OK. The name of the vendor will appear in the appropriate box.

i. Select OK to save and close.
j. To edit an Item Property, double click on the name of the item on the right side of the screen.

Glossary

AM An abbreviation that indicates that this command is specific to AccuMark.

AML Acronym for Advanced Measurement Library.

annotations Notes that will be plotted on the pattern pieces.

attribute A special characteristic applied to a point, used to ensure precision and control grading.

block The same as a sloper. The term block is commonly used outside the United States. See also *sloper*.

break points The sizes at which the grade rules change. They are usually sizes 10 and 16 in Missy sizes.

bundles The parts of a garment ready for sewing. Bundles are usually grouped by size.

bundling The process of sorting cut pieces and organizing them so that they are ready for assembly. Bundles are the parts of a garment ready for sewing. Bundling is usually done by size.

cardinal points The points on the perimeter of the pattern where dimensional changes occur during grading.

Cartesian graph A graph that has two axes that cross at a right angle and divide an area into four equal quadrants.

CCW Acronym for counterclockwise rotation.

colorway A variety of different colors.

copying Data is copied from a storage area to another area or to a removable storage medium. The original data remains in the original storage area.

CW Acronym for clockwise rotation.

dart apex The tip of the dart.

dead zone The outer three inches of the digitizing table that are insensitive to the cursor signals.

default An option or setting that is assigned automatically unless an alternative is specified.

deleting The act of removing a data file.

digitizer A device used to enter information into a software system. It consists of a digitizing table, a digitizing cursor, and a digitizing menu.

digitizing The process of tracing a sloper/pattern piece into the computer and entering information about that sloper/pattern piece.

digitizing cursor The means to enter information into the computer. It is used to trace the outline of the sloper and input information that is included on a pattern piece. It is also used on the digitizing table menu to give the computer information about the stages of the digitizing process. It has two parts: the crosshairs and the buttons.

digitizing menu Sensitized diagram similar to a keyboard where specific instructions can be given to the computer.

digitizing table A large work area that can be adjusted by height and angle. It is connected by cable to the computer and to the digitizing cursor. It holds the piece to be digitized and receives the digitizing signal from the digitizing cursor.

dimension A variable, such as color or size, that affects the cost of a garment or raw material.

dragging Data can be copied from one area to another by using the "click and drag" method.

drop-down menu List of commands that appears when activated.

exporting Data is copied from the hard drive to a removable storage medium as a zip file that can only be unzipped using Gerber software.

flat sketches Proportioned drawings of garments that show the exact details of trimmings and seam lines. Flat sketches may include notes about garment construction details.

function keys Shortcuts for certain functions. The function keys are located above the numbers on a standard keyboard.

function menu bar Organizes the features used in patternmaking. It is located at the top of the screen.

GO Acronym for grain orientation.

ghost particles Leftover bits of erased images.

grade rule The amount of increase or decrease in size at each cardinal point. There will be different grade rules for different points.

grade rule table Where all of the grading measurements are stored. A rule defines how far a cardinal point will move right or left and up or down on the Cartesian graph to change the dimensions of the pattern for the next size.

grading The process of changing the size of a sample pattern: scaling it up and down to create a range of sizes.

hardware Basic computer equipment that includes keyboard, mouse, printer, plotter, and digitizer.

hold line The line that will not move when a dart is rotated. Usually the center front or the center back will be the hold line, but other lines may also be selected for design purposes.

icon bar Displays the pieces selected for use. The icon bar may be located at the top or bottom of the screen.

importing Copying data in a zip file format from a removable storage medium to the Gerber System.

information bar It contains the following information: model or style name, name of currently selected piece, current pieces button, size of the current piece, cut or sew, unit of measurement chosen. It is usually located below the scroll bar at the bottom of the screen but can be placed at the top of the screen.

intermediate point Digitized point between graded points, especially on curves; grade rules can be applied to intermediate points.

look-up field Allows the user to select from a preestablished list, such as a list of pattern pieces.

marker A pattern layout that is placed over fabric to guide a cutter. In the industry, it is now possible to produce a computerized marker that controls an automatic cutter.

master pattern Style pattern with added fashion details and trued seams. It is usually made only in the sample size.

model A garment or item or all the pattern pieces required for a particular style.

nested Different sizes of a pattern piece stacked on top of one another so that the incremental differences can be seen.

notch A slash or V-shaped cut on a piece perimeter used to match garment sections during construction of the garment.

parameter A property that defines a system and determines or limits its performance. Parameters can be thought of as sets of rules that can be changed.

perimeter The outer edge of a sloper or pattern piece.

piece This term is used in Gerber Pattern Design to refer to a sloper that is being modified to make a pattern.

piece verification The process of checking the accuracy of the digitizing process.

plotter Draws full-size or scaled pattern pieces and markers.

point A defining mark on a pattern or sloper.

POM Acronym for Point of Measure.

production pattern The final perfect pattern. It is in all sizes that are to be made, and each piece has the appropriate seam allowance. To reduce cost, production patterns are often simplified versions of a master pattern.

prompt An instruction that assists the user to complete a task; it is also used for input of specific measurements and other options required by the current function.

reduction factor Determines the number of points to be reduced. If the factor is too high, many points will be removed and the shape of the sloper may be drastically changed.

reference point Point to which a notch is attached. It may be the actual point, a different notch, a line, or an intersection of lines. When a reference point is modified, the notch is also modified.

renaming Changing the name of a data file.

sample pattern Style pattern developed from a basic block or sloper.

saving AccuMark tables are saved to a folder by using the Save or Save As command in the File drop-down menu. This data can then be exported.

silhouette table Alternative to the digitizing table; this table is more technologically advanced than the digitizing table.

sloper A pattern piece needed for a fitted garment with the minimum of ease and no style lines or seam allowances. The darts are shortened to the appropriate distance from the pivot points, but the pivot points are marked. They are used as the basis of flat pattern design or computer-aided design. See also *block*.

Smooth Factor Determines the rate of smoothing in lines. The higher the number, the more quickly smoothing occurs, but lines may change shape more than intended when the number is too high.

smoothing point Point inserted by the computer to create curved or smooth lines as they would appear when plotted; this point cannot be graded.

specs See *specifications*.

specifications The finished dimensions of each size of a garment.

storage area Folder of related work such as pattern pieces and a marker for a particular style.

thumbtacks Used to define the beginning and end of a distance.

toggle buttons Allow the user to select options from a list or to turn commands/options/ functions on and off.

tolerance The amount of variation from the standard dimensions that a company will accept.

toolbar The toolbar can be located at the sides, top, or bottom of the screen depending on personal preference. It can be customized to hold the functions/commands that are used frequently, such as zoom in, zoom out, undo, and redo.

user input box The user input box is usually located on the right side of the screen, but it may be moved to the left. It contains the current function name and provides user prompts.

work area The drafting of patterns is done in this area.

working sketches See *flat sketches*.

Appendix 1
Fraction to Decimal Conversion Table

¹⁄₁ = 1	¹⁄₂ = 0.5	¹⁄₄ = 0.25	¹⁄₈ = 0.125	¹⁄₁₆ = 0.063
		³⁄₄ = 0.75	³⁄₈ = 0.375	³⁄₁₆ = 0.188
			⁵⁄₈ = 0.625	⁵⁄₁₆ = 0.313
			⁷⁄₈ = 0.875	⁷⁄₁₆ = 0.438
				⁹⁄₁₆ = 0.563
				¹¹⁄₁₆ = 0.688
				¹³⁄₁₆ = 0.813
				¹⁵⁄₁₆ = 0.938

Appendix 2
Grade Rule Table: OURDATA

Rule Number	1		2		3		4		5	
Size Breaks	x	y	x	y	x	y	x	y	x	y
2 – 10	0	0	0	0.125	0	0.250	0.125	0.250	0.125	0.125
10 – 16	0	0	0	0.125	0	0.375	0.125	0.375	0.125	0.188
16 – 22	0	0	0	0.125	0	0.500	0.125	0.500	0.125	0.250

Rule Number	6		7		8		9		10	
Size Breaks	x	y	x	y	x	y	x	y	x	y
2 – 10	0.250	0.125	0.250	0.063	0.250	0	0.250	0.094	0	−0.125
10 – 16	0.250	0.188	0.313	0.063	0.250	0	0.313	0.125	0	−0.188
16 – 22	0.250	0.250	0.313	0.125	0.250	0	0.313	0.188	0	−0.313

Rule Number	11		12		13		14		15	
Size Breaks	x	y	x	y	x	y	x	y	x	y
2 – 10	−0.063	−0.063	−0.063	0.063	0	0.125	0	0.063	0.125	0
10 – 16	−0.063	−0.063	−0.063	0.063	0	0.188	0	0.063	0.125	0
16 – 22	−0.063	−0.063	−0.063	0.063	0	0.313	0	0.125	0.125	0

Rule Number	16		17		18		19		20	
Size Breaks	x	y	x	y	x	y	x	y	x	y
2 – 10	0	−0.063	−0.375	0	−0.375	0.250	−0.250	0.250	0	0.188
10 – 16	0	−0.063	−0.375	0	−0.375	0.375	−0.250	0.375	0	0.250
16 – 22	0	−0.125	−0.375	0	−0.375	0.500	−0.250	0.500	0	0.313

Rule Number	21		22		23		24		25	
Size Breaks	x	y	x	y	x	y	x	y	x	y
2 – 10	−0.250	−0.188	−0.250	0.125	−0.25	0	−0.25	−0.063	−0.375	0
10 – 16	−0.250	−0.250	−0.250	0.125	−0.25	0	−0.25	−0.094	−0.375	0
16 – 22	−0.250	−0.313	−0.250	0.125	−0.25	0	−0.25	−0.125	−0.375	0

Rule Number	26		27	
Size Breaks	x	y	x	y
2 – 10	−0.375	0.125	−0.25	−0.125
10 – 16	−0.375	0.125	−0.25	−0.188
16 – 22	−0.375	0.125	−0.25	−0.25

Index